Riddles + intention

solution vs re...

riddles — operate to make mundane significant
— make something certain   auratic

THE FEELING OF READING

— meaningful / symbolic
— s

— objective element — intention that addresses a mystery
                      mystery intention

insoluble

all objects but always disrespectful
intent to puzzle is created in language

all objects & events ~~share~~ share in mystery
— word + thing
— precede object   dependent
Language — unless mysterious
Logos - logic   riddle has   looks for solution
                       language has   to mean
                       meanings

Word — not only solution but also intention

unless mysterious   productive distinction

riddle   — circular
words   that which
               turns   — solution is absolute

Language intention to ←→ solution
        hide

The Feeling of Reading

AFFECTIVE EXPERIENCE

&

VICTORIAN LITERATURE

Rachel Ablow

EDITOR

THE UNIVERSITY OF MICHIGAN PRESS · ANN ARBOR

Copyright © by the University of Michigan 2010
All rights reserved
Published in the United States of America by
The University of Michigan Press
Manufactured in the United States of America
⊛ Printed on acid-free paper

2013   2012   2011   2010   4   3   2   1

A CIP catalog record for this book is available from the British Library.

Library of Congress Cataloging-in-Publication Data

The feeling of reading : affective experience and Victorian literature
    / Rachel Ablow, editor.
        p.   cm.
    Includes index.
    ISBN 978-0-472-07107-4 (cloth : acid-free paper) — ISBN 978-0-
472-05107-6 (pbk. : acid-free paper)
        1. English literature—19th century—History and criticism.
    2. Books and reading.   I. Ablow, Rachel.
    PR463.F43   2011
    820.9'008—dc22   2010007944

Acknowledgments

I wish to thank the contributors for their enthusiasm for the project and their good humor throughout the process; it has been a pleasure and a privilege to work with them. I also wish to thank David Kurnick for his invaluable assistance in the early stages of this project. I am grateful to the two anonymous readers for the University of Michigan Press for the extraordinary thoughtfulness of their reports: as one contributor commented, "It is so wonderful to be really *read*." Jonathan Freedman and Daniel Hack both provided crucial advice at critical moments in the process. Without Ruth Mack's encouragement and support this project might never have been completed. Alison MacKeen, now at Yale University Press, deserves thanks for her early support for the project. Thomas Dwyer and Alexa Ducsay, at the University of Michigan Press, have been wonderful to work with throughout.

Contents

Introduction

THE FEELING OF READING

RACHEL ABLOW

> *With Bewick on my knee, I was then happy: happy at least in*
> *my way. I feared nothing but interruption, and that came too*
> *soon.*
> — Charlotte Brontë, *Jane Eyre* (1847)[1]

Why is Jane Eyre happy? The answer might seem obvious: she is happy because, like us her readers, she is lost in a book. She is thus happy because, as
Georges Poulet puts it, she is "thinking the thoughts of another": her psychic
landscape has been taken over by a text to which she willingly surrenders—a
state of affairs that in the last few decades has come to seem at least as dangerous as it is pleasurable.[2] At least since Michel Foucault's influence began to
be felt in literary studies in the 1970s, and D. A. Miller's impact on Victorian
studies began to be registered in the 1980s, readerly absorption has tended to
be regarded as an insidious means by which we are interpellated into a social
order. The project of literature, Miller writes, "relentlessly and often literally
brought home as much in the novel's characteristic forms and conditions of
reception as in its themes, is to confirm the novel-reader in his identity as 'liberal subject.'"[3] At precisely the moments when we feel ourselves to be most
free from social determinations—as, for example, when we are happily lost in
a book—we are supposedly most thoroughly overwritten by ideology.

Despite Miller's and his inheritors' dire predictions, however, Jane isn't simply a passive audience. "Shrined in double retirement" in the window seat, hidden from her malicious cousins who threaten to interrupt her, she is less absorbed in the text before her than actively inventing her own narratives on the basis of the materials and psychic space it provides.[4]

> The letterpress [of Bewick's *History of British Birds*] I cared little for, gen-
> erally speaking; and yet there were certain introductory pages that, child
> as I was, I could not pass quite as a blank. They were those which treat of
> the haunts of sea-fowl; of "the solitary rocks and promontories" by them
> only inhabited; of the coast of Norway, studded with isles from its south-
> ern extremity, the Lindeness, or Naze, to the North Cape. . . . Of these
> death-write realms I formed an idea of my own: shadowy, like all the half-
> comprehended notions that float dim through children's brains, but
> strangely impressive.[5]

Jane barely registers the text in front of her, instead deriving her happiness from her ability to make up her own stories on the basis of what she half-reads and only dimly understands. Further, rather than a problem to be rectified, this antisocial, inaccurate, and pleasurable reading is offered in the text almost as a badge of honor: an indication that Jane is interesting and imaginative, and hence someone with whom we might want to identify both ourselves and our reading practices.

The essays collected in *The Feeling of Reading* suggest that Jane's experi-ence in this scene might ultimately be paradigmatic—or at least symptom-atic—of Victorian reading much more generally. Together, these essays demonstrate that in the mid- to late nineteenth century, reading was com-monly regarded as at least as valuable as an affective experience as it was as a way to convey information or increase understanding. They underscore the intended activity of the reader and the extent to which she or he was expected and encouraged to participate in the production of the text. And they illumi-nate the ways in which text and world were commonly conceived as produc-tively opposed to one another rather than as cognitively or experientially linked. By virtue of a renewed attention to feeling rather than knowing, a very different world of reading comes to light—one in which the intended reader's reactions to the text may be "micromanage[d]," as Garrett Stewart has ar-gued, but in which that micromanagement involves autonomy as well as de-termination, escape from as well as assimilation to the world outside the text.[6]

Ten years ago Eve Kosofsky Sedgwick offered a challenge to historicist critics whose "scholarship rel[ies] on the prestige of a single, overarching narrative: exposing and problematizing hidden violences in the genealogy of the modern liberal subject."[7] Taking Miller's *The Novel and the Police* (1988) as a way to demonstrate the problems posed by New Historicism, Sedgwick claims that his argument is problematic, first for logical reasons, because (as she admits that Miller would concede) it is "entirely circular: everything can be understood as an aspect of the carceral, therefore the carceral is everywhere."[8] Second, his argument poses political problems, since having "an unmystified, angry view of large and genuinely systemic oppressions does not *intrinsically* or *necessarily* enjoin on that person any specific train of epistemological or narrative consequences."[9] And finally, it offers aesthetic difficulties, for the insights yielded by his "strong theory" are ultimately less pleasurable than those generated by his local insights.[10] In place of the paranoia of New Historicism, therefore, Sedgwick offers something she calls "reparative" reading: "The desire of a reparative impulse," she explains, "is additive and accretive. Its fear, a realistic one, is that the culture surrounding it is inadequate or inimical to its nurture; it wants to assemble and confer plenitude on an object that will then have resources to offer to an inchoate self."[11] In urging critics to embrace a critical practice that offers "plenitude" to its object, and "resources" to its practitioner, Sedgwick provides a necessary corrective to the suspicion that characterizes many Foucauldian readings. At the same time, however, "reparative reading" threatens to reproduce at least some of the limitations of what she calls "paranoid reading" insofar as both approaches threaten to establish the critic's conclusions prior to her engagement with the text. Reparative reading may be opposed to paranoia in its effects, in other words, yet it too assumes a fundamentally ethical or expressive stance toward its object.

Over the past few years, many scholars of reading—several of whom are represented in this collection—have been formulating an approach to Victorian reading that is neither paranoid nor reparative but instead attuned to a different model of historical specificity: interested in what nineteenth-century readers and writers *thought* they were doing. Rather than asking how we "do" read, or in how we "should" read—the two options Sedgwick offers[12]—these critics have asked, how we are *expected* to read, a question that leads to some interestingly unpredictable answers. How did nineteenth-century readers and writers think about the experience of reading? What did they regard as its pleasures and dangers? And what does that tell us about the texts themselves? Answering questions like these requires that we remain attentive to the contradictions, exclusions, and blindnesses those projects sometimes involved. But on a fundamental level, this project requires a willingness to accommodate ambivalence, ambiguity, and perhaps most important, surprise.

The critics represented here embrace a wide spectrum of approaches to reading. What they share, however, is a rejection of either strict historicism or dogmatic formalism. Instead of choosing a single camp, these critics put these two ways of defining the object of study into productive dialogue, asking both how we can reconstruct the alien historical circumstances of Victorian reading *and* how those distant reading experiences are restaged in attentive acts of reading in the present.[13] Together, the essays in this collection demonstrate how often an attention to the historical specificity of Victorian reading practices returns us to the issues of physical and emotional feeling. The last few years have seen an explosion of interest in reading and feeling, and the Victorian period has held a privileged position in both.

The nineteenth century saw a massive growth in literacy in Britain, so that by the end of the century the majority of adults were, for the first time, also readers. This development coincided with the vast dissemination of texts that solidified the set of affective expectations we still routinely bring to the experience of reading. Examining Victorians' interest in reading as a site of bodily response and affective experimentation, the contributors to this collection argue that Victorians did not just interpret but also "felt" the texts they consumed. Further, they argue that those feelings direct our attention in directions impossible to predict on the basis of either paranoid or reparative reading alone: toward a renewed interest in what reading can achieve that no other kind of experience can, and hence, too, toward the pleasure to be derived from the disconnection—as well as the connection—between world and text.

The collection opens with Nicholas Dames's argument for the revisionary effects of attending seriously to Victorian novel theory and criticism—forms of writing that still tend too often to be ignored or dismissed. In "On Not Close Reading: The Prolonged Excerpt as Victorian Critical Protocol," Dames reevaluates the common nineteenth-century critical practices of excerpting (printing long passages of the text under review) and paraphrase (plot summary offered in lieu of evaluation). For recent critics, these practices have often seemed like lazy substitutes for "close reading," the practice of finding minute but representative bits of text upon which to practice the skills of rhetorical analysis. According to Dames, such accounts misunderstand the function of these forms of citation. Turning to a variety of Victorian critics and theorists—R. H. Hutton, Geraldine Jewsbury, G. H. Lewes, Margaret Oliphant, and others—he argues that both excerpt and paraphrase exist as ways of producing for the reader, in miniature, the affective processes involved in the temporal workings of long narratives. Rather than offering the "see, it works this way" epistemology of close reading, excerpt and paraphrase function in Victorian reviewing and novel theory as "see, it feels this way." Dames thus offers a new account of what Victorian critics considered significant about the texts they reviewed: feeling rather than thinking; temporality rather than isolated, individual moments. He also begins to suggest some of the limitations of our own criticism that, because of its embeddedness in epistemological concerns, refuses to excerpt or paraphrase as one way in which it refuses to *feel*.

Dames's interest in the text as a technology for the production of feeling is counterbalanced by Kate Flint's, Leah Price's, and John Plotz's concerns with how texts served in the nineteenth century as a form of insulation *against* feeling. Kate Flint's "Traveling Readers" reveals how readers used texts as a way to effectively block out the world outside the text. While we are all familiar with novel-reading as itself a form of imaginative transport, Flint examines the relatively ignored question of what happens when reading takes place elsewhere. Focusing on reading that occurs when one is away from "home," and when the books themselves are neither set in, nor overtly relate to, the place in which one is consuming them, Flint argues that Victorian travelers commonly identified taking refuge in a book as an act of self-defense, a way to numb oneself against the foreignness that lies outside of the text. At the same time, Flint also demonstrates how understandings or experiences of texts change according to the location at which they are consumed. Her essay thus examines how well-traveled texts, written in English, were encountered and read by those who were themselves at a distance from the place in which these books were located. Ultimately, then, Flint warns against conflating the material history of the book and the history of subjectivity in reading, dependent though reading necessarily must be on the presence of reading matter in the first place.

Leah Price, too, is concerned with how the text can be used to insulate the reader against the world outside the text. And although in a very different register, she too sees that insulating effect as a way to think about the differences between book history and the history of reading. Her essay, "Reader's

Block: Trollope and the Book as Prop," asks how Victorian culture in general, and the realist novel in particular, defined the relation between the text (a linguistic structure) and the book (a material thing). More specifically, it tries to explain why Victorian writers had such a hard time keeping those two terms in play at once: why when the book-object is represented it's rarely being read, while whenever reading is in fact going on, the material book gets reduced to a metaphor, a distraction, or a joke. Like Flint, then, Price is concerned with excavating usable models for rethinking the relation of literary criticism to book history as well as with remapping the relation between social practices (such as reading) and material culture (including books). Using Trollope's fictional universe as a case study, Price asks what makes the consciousness of the reading character so hard to access, not just for other characters, but for Trollope's own readers? Why does representing the act of reading mean abstracting the visible book? Conversely, why does representing the book (or the newspaper, or the magazine) mean reducing reading itself to an act? Novelists of manners, Price argues, share the challenge facing historians of reading: how to observe an activity against which the social defines itself.

If in Flint's account travelers use books to block out the alienness of new environments, and in the texts Price examines, husbands and wives use newspapers and novels as a way to insulate themselves from the potentially oppressive intimacy of married life, in John Plotz's essay, "Mediated Involvement: John Stuart Mill's Antisocial Sociability," free individuals use texts as a way to preserve all that is valuable about human interaction while staving off the fear that the pressure of other minds might impinge on one's psychic autonomy. John Stuart Mill's foundational *On Liberty* (1851), Plotz argues, transmutes that old demon of free thought, *custom*, into the new demon, *society*, a terrifying force that can either surround one in daily interaction or invade one's mind so surreptitiously and insidiously as to make one serve as one's own worst enemy. In this context, Plotz claims, reading comes to seem like a way to maintain genuine productive communication between uncoerced equals. At the same time, however, Plotz also shows how, in Mill, the experience of reading threatens to become an insidious agent of the social, a way in which the thoughts of others are smuggled into a putatively independent mind.

Like the preceding authors, both Catherine Robson and Herbert F. Tucker are concerned with what the Victorians thought literary texts can do to or for readers that other forms of experience cannot. But unlike the others, they are interested in Victorian ideas about the specificity of poetry in general, and rhythm, in particular. In "Reciting Alice: What Is the Use of a Book without Poems?" Robson asks in what ways the dominant modes and forms of juvenile education in this period might have structured—even while failing to fill—the learner's mind. To explore one aspect of this huge topic, Robson places *Alice's Adventures in Wonderland* in relation to an important contemporary pedagogical practice, the memorization and recitation of poetry by young children. Restoring the history of verse-memorization and recitation Robson claims, allows us to see that the educational practices of the past created vast numbers of properly *prosimetric* minds—consciousnesses that were structured according to the forms of poetry as well as prose. Such forms are both omnipresent and strangely free of content, thus enabling the humorous substitutions of Carroll's text. Substitutions like these, Robson demonstrates, have been a recurring by-product of an educational practice that emphasizes form while leaving content surprisingly underdefined.

While Robson emphasizes the infectiousness of rhythm and rhyme—so readily accessible that years after memorizing them, adults have trouble getting them out of their heads—Herbert Tucker is interested in the sheer exhaustion involved in reading poetry. In "Over Worked, Worked Over: A Poetics of Fatigue," Tucker argues that from the earliest Victorian years, poets renegotiating their contract with a diffuse, even fugitive readership turned traditional versification to purposes that remain palpably legible as, in ergonomic terms, modes of stress management. "Over Worked, Worked Over" examines the long Victorian investment in exhaustion and tracks how this thematic obsession expressed what was at once an aesthetic and an ethical concern for poets who made it a test of the serious artist to tire readers out: to put them through their paces while not quite exhausting their patience. Through a close engagement with some major works of Tennyson—a master at striking this prosodic balance—Tucker demonstrates how Victorian verse practices a calisthenic of focus and relaxation, work and recess. Tucker then moves on to consider some historical analogues of this very Victorian obsession, focusing most closely on Elizabeth Barrett Browning's industrial experiment in the poetics of fatigue, "The Cry of the Children." Demonstrating how the poem cranks out a staccato factory rhythm and then threatens to jolt this mechanical rhythm with a series of interruptions we might think of as work stoppages, Tucker shows how socially resonant the idea of the exhausted reader could become in the hands of a master poet. In their ensemble the examples show that the layered repetition that is prosodic structure offers us vital access to how the Victorian reading of verse *felt*.

The final three essays in the collection shift our attention back to fiction, asking what kinds of literary or psychic effects the Victorians imagined to be unique to fiction or fictionality. In his essay, "The Impersonal Intimacy of *Marius the Epicurean*," Stephen Arata argues that readers reluctant to call Walter Pater's *Marius the Epicurean* (1885) a novel—and there are plenty— generally mistake the nature of the affective response the text demands from its readers. Nearly everyone agrees that Marius's character is presented in a positive light and that his life story possesses an intrinsic interest, yet Pater's narrative techniques seem designed precisely to block all avenues to readerly identification. The foregrounding of the links between sympathy, right feeling, and the moral education of the reader helped make the realist novel the preeminent popular art form of a liberal humanist Victorian culture. Pater, by contrast, embraces an antihumanist aesthetic; in *Marius* he turns away from the representational strategies of the realist novel in order to create instead relations of "impersonal intimacy" between readers and fictional characters. *Marius the Epicurean,* Arata argues, reflects (and enacts) Pater's beliefs concerning the nature of narrative and its role in the formation of readers' subjectivities. Pater rejected models of depth psychology that emerged in the 1860s, which in turn led him to reject the humanist bases of realist fiction. One key effect of his narrative practice in *Marius* is that it works to displace readerly "feeling" in favor of an aesthetic grounded in bodily affect or sensation.

My own essay, "Reading and Re-reading: Wilde, Newman, and the Fiction of Belief," argues that in "The Portrait of Mr. W. H." (1889) and elsewhere, Oscar Wilde argues for the difficulty of holding beliefs *except* as fictions: as ideas that might or might not be true—and, even more important, that might or might not be our own. Further, he implicitly claims to base this argument on an (admittedly idiosyncratic) reading of the work of John Henry Cardinal Newman. Leader of the Oxford movement, famous convert to Catholicism, vociferous antiliberal and author of *An Essay in Aid of a Grammar of Assent* (1870) among many other works, Newman is usually regarded as seeking to defend the utter reliability and knowability of belief. Yet in "The Portrait," Wilde suggests an alternative understanding of Newman: as committed to belief's status as a kind of fiction, insofar as it is vicariated through an aesthetically pleasing and erotically desirable other. Wilde's reading of Newman, I argue, has the potential to provide us with a different way of thinking about the relation between belief and the experience of reading fiction. Rather than providing a way to understand others' beliefs, as some critics have argued, fiction enables its readers to experience what it *feels like* to hold a belief. As a result, it encourages them to take on that belief as if it was their own—a state that ultimately seems indistinguishable from believing it "for real."

In the final essay in the collection, "Reading Feeling and the 'Transferred Life': *The Mill on the Floss*," Garrett Stewart argues that reading and feeling are not meant to be separate things in Eliot's novel. Focusing on the heroine's disappointed lover, Philip Wakem, the "hump-backed" romantic intellectual, Stewart argues that, as with any reader outside the text, Philip's participation in the fantasies and fears of the heroine is inevitably twofold. It begins in passive imagination and then formulates itself to cognition as a kind of sympathetic "belief" (Philip's word) in the Other. Amounting to a disquisition on the fiction of "romantic disillusionment," Stewart claims, Philip's focalizing service in the internalization of Maggie's suffering is crucial for Eliot's rhetorical design. It spotlights the role of temporality and ironic disjunction in the sacrificial subjectivity of Eliot's plotline, where the scapegoated subject becomes objectified in her dashed promise, evacuated of desire before her own eyes. Beyond his role in articulating one horizon of disenchantment's bitter totality in this failed Bildungsroman, Philip's wrenching emphasis on the "gift of transferred life" through feeling defines an affective circuit—opened even (or especially) by his frustrated passion—that does more than embody the cathartic motive for Eliot's overarching plot. It performs for us the ethical imperative to "enact" the other's existence in the very processing of her or his words.

Like the Victorians, we are witnessing a vast shift in popular practices and conceptions of reading. In an age of the Web, text-messaging, Twitter, and Kindle, many have asked how changing protocols of reading will affect our culture more generally. The essays in this collection may not answer this question directly, but they do begin to suggest the nature and the range of practices against which new developments need to be evaluated. They also help clarify how another moment of vast technological change responded to analogous questions. Perhaps most important, they indicate how we might begin to move beyond the rather limited range of terms in which reading is all too often described. In broadening our conceptual vocabulary, the essays in this collection help us begin to reconceive the variety of ways in which texts work. Texts in these essays serve not just as sources of information or even as objects of identification. Instead, they function as barriers, windows, screens; as affective, erotic, and aesthetic objects; and as temporal and rhythmic experiences that may have no real-life substitute or corollary. Reading emerges from these essays as one of the most intriguing and mysterious of practices not just because of its apparent privacy or individuality, but also because of the significance of its consequences, and because those consequences—affective, cognitive, social, and political—can never be fully determined in advance.

NOTES

1. Charlotte Brontë, *Jane Eyre* (1847; London: Penguin, 2006), 11.

2. Georges Poulet, "Phenomenology of Reading," *New Literary History* 1, no. 1 (1969): 55.

3. D. A. Miller, *The Novel and the Police* (Berkeley: University of California Press, 1988), x. Also see Louis Althusser, "Ideology and Ideological State Apparatuses (Notes Towards an Investigation)," in *Essays on Ideology* (London: Verso, 1979), 1–60.

4. Brontë, *Jane Eyre*, 10.

5. Brontë, *Jane Eyre*, 10–11.

6. Garrett Stewart, *Dear Reader: The Conscripted Audience in Nineteenth-Century British Fiction* (Baltimore: Johns Hopkins University Press, 1996), 21. The literature on Victorian reading is far too vast to be summarized here. For overviews, see Leah Price, "Reading: The State of the Discipline," *Book History* 7 (2004): 303–20; and Rachel Ablow, "Victorian Feeling and the Victorian Novel," *Literature Compass* 4, no. 1 (2007): 298–316.

7. Eve Kosofsky Sedgwick, "Paranoid Reading and Reparative Reading; or, You're So Paranoid, You Probably Think This Introduction Is about You," in *Novel Gazing: Queer Readings in Fiction*, ed. Eve Kosofsky Sedgwick (Durham: Duke University Press, 1997), 18.

8. Sedgwick, "Paranoid Reading and Reparative Reading," 14.

9. Sedgwick, "Paranoid Reading and Reparative Reading," 4.

10. "Who reads *The Novel and the Police* to find out whether its main argument is true?" Sedgwick asks. Instead, we read for the "wealth of tonal nuance, attitude, worldly observation, performative paradox, aggression, tenderness, wit, inventive reading *obiter dicta*, and writerly panache" that "shelter in the hypertrophied embrace of the book's overarching strong theory" (Sedgwick, "Paranoid Reading and Reparative Reading," 14).

11. Sedgwick, "Paranoid Reading and Reparative Reading," 27–28.

12. Sedgwick, "Paranoid Reading and Reparative Reading," 2.

13. Thanks to David Kurnick for this formulation.

On Not Close Reading

THE PROLONGED EXCERPT AS
VICTORIAN CRITICAL PROTOCOL

NICHOLAS DAMES

Historians of reading well know the seemingly vast difference between "a reading"—the procedure of set-piece analysis that is often their own most familiar tool—and "reading," that amorphous cultural practice that spreads far beyond any single instance. The desire to excavate a history of reading by performing "a reading," or even studying some past instance of such, appears delusive at best to most contemporary scholars. The history of reading, as if a kind of quantum science, can know movements, trajectories, and forces, but not individual units; as Roger Chartier has claimed, it must "postulate the liberty of a practice that it can only grasp, massively, in its determinations."[1] The singular reading, or reader, in other words, must collapse back into an elusive gerund called "reading" known only by the statistical average of its many different positions. Such a necessity is obviously enabling, since it releases the scholar from responsibility to and for the infinite range of "readings" produced in the past, but it is also disabling: it alienates the literary scholar interested in the history of reading from her subject. What she is trained to produce and teach—the "close reading," the "reading" per se—can never become a tool for arriving at a sense of how readers of the past read. The methodologies of reading history (assessing data, discovering new quantitative models, formulating new approaches) have, it can often seem, little bearing on other professional norms or rationales.

This essay suggests that such an impasse might be avoided, through a specific example and a conceptual argument. The specific example is the practice of lengthy inset quotations in Victorian novel reviewing, from roughly the 1830s to the 1880s. The conceptual argument turns on the term *protocol*, which is intended to function as a bridge between the vast territory of "reading" and the instantiation provided by examples of past "readings." The signature peculiarity of an enormous patch of reviewed text being inserted into a review is something anyone acquainted with Victorian reviewing would know intimately; that peculiarity, however, has never been noted as anything but a sign of lazy hackery or a not particularly exciting example of the *autre temps, autre moeurs* lesson that past writing practices inevitably offer. Considering this characteristic feature of nineteenth-century novel reviewing as a protocol, however—as what I will argue is a procedure broad and yet innocuous enough to be culturally significant—allows us to connect these instances of past "readings" to a sense of Victorian "reading" in a much larger sense. It therefore allows us to use the habitual and still highly developed tool we now call "close reading" to assess the historical oddities of a past reading culture, or, put another way, to use a professional alibi and common practice—the higher literacy that scholars are enjoined to teach and demonstrate—for what we usually call "research."

What is the use of close reading a series of other readings? Potentially tremendous, provided that the kinds of readings we choose to close read are more than merely idiosyncratic and less than zones of cultural contestation. "Close reading" itself, in its recent avatars within the Anglo-American academy, offers excellent contrary examples. Both its culturally and institutionally privileged position in the mid–twentieth century, and what D. A. Miller has called its present "humble, futile, 'minoritized' state," subject of nostalgias and neglect, are simply too visible, even polemical, to be true protocols, which pass largely unacknowledged.[2] Victorian reviews, however, present us with a form of close reading—a strange form in many ways, as I will demonstrate—that is neither valorized nor abjected, but utterly innocuous. Innocuous enough to have gone unremarked by the scholars, and anthologists, who have argued for the interest of the enormous corpus of periodical reviewing in the period.[3] That is the significance of this critical practice for a history of Victorian reading.

Take, for instance, Geraldine Jewsbury's unsigned review of George Eliot's *Adam Bede,* which appeared in a February 1859 issue of the *Athenaeum.* Jewsbury was at that point one of the primary contributors to the *Athenaeum*'s

"New Novels" section, which offered shorter and more frequent reviews than their monthly or quarterly competitors. In many respects the review is ordinary both in its publication context, its place in the reviewer's career (Jewsbury reviewed over a hundred novels a year for the *Athenaeum*), and its place in a reception history of *Adam Bede* (the review was laudatory, to largely the same degree and in the same terms as others).[4] What is compelling about this particular review is its utterly commonplace use of the prolonged excerpt. In order to convey what she calls the "deep impression" the novel has left upon her, Jewsbury offers a 350-word excerpt, a statistically (and visually) significant part of her 1,200-word review. The excerpt is announced, in fact, as the evidence of a *reading*, not merely an assessment: "The duty of a critic is in the present instance almost superseded by the reader. 'Adam Bede' is a book to be accepted, not criticized."[5] At which point a prolonged excerpt—one of Eliot's descriptions of Adam himself—is offered.

Seen by contemporary canons of critical taste, Jewsbury scarcely offers a "reading" at all; the passage is followed by what can only be read as a continuation and amplification of Eliot's description of Adam, as if Jewsbury were not analyzing Eliot but imitating her: "There is, too, the secret of the substantial worth of England, the secret of her strength; it is not the number of men and women with brilliant reputation and lyrically recognized name and fame, that makes the enduring prosperity of a nation, but it lies in the amount of worth that is unrecognized, that remains dumb and unconscious of itself, not clever, but with a certain honest stupidity that understands nothing but doing its best and doing its work without shirking any portion of it."[6] The patently Eliotesque sentiment and syntax constitutes a prolongation of reading, not its antithesis; what it demonstrates is an immersion in the novel complete enough to have rendered critical prose mute. Similarly, the excerpt itself seems to function not as a synecdoche—a part that can express the tendencies of the whole—but as a whole in itself: as a reading experience in miniature. It invites the review's reader to partake in a reading experience with the critic; and in this sense the excerpt is not prolonged so much as minimal—it might be considered as *the smallest viable unit* of the host text that can still express the general tone, or emotional/philosophical contour, of that text. Thus the frequency of apologies for the brevity of these excerpts, which—tempted as we may be to read these as either formulaic or ironic—often express a real willingness to have gone even further, to have shown the reader even more. Walter Bagehot's otherwise very different article "The Novels of George Eliot," an 1860 assessment published in the magisterially toned

National Review, offers an even lengthier excerpt (of close to 700 words) with the embarrassed disclaimer "we can but extract the following passage."[7]

Clearly, then, a different relation of part to whole obtained in Victorian reviewing than in contemporary academic criticism. And just as clearly, that relation expressed significant aspects of the Victorian understanding of novel reading, insofar as these excerpts were meant to serve as invitations to read—as, one might say, occasions for presenting the "readable." Those significant aspects become more apparent the more widespread we understand the phenomenon of the lengthy excerpt to have been. From Jewsbury's short announcement of praise to Bagehot's thirty-page study, the long excerpt may, in fact, have been the single most unifying practice of Victorian reviewing, spanning differences in periodicals, writerly taste, and even writerly politics. It was, in fact, a fundamental example of a "protocol."

By "protocol" I intend specifically to highlight aspects of a writing (and reading) practice that is never explicitly part of a "theory." It might be that our model of what constitutes literary theory is overly restrictive. Many commentators on Victorian reviewing have felt, with Edwin Eigner and George Worth, that literary theory itself barely existed in the nineteenth century in Britain: "It is necessary frequently to read between the lines," they write, "to find English theory almost reluctantly put forth in arguments whose avowed purpose was to protect the English novel from theoretical foreigners and their misguided native disciples."[8] This, I would argue, limits our sense of theory only to moments of methodological self-reflection. While I have argued elsewhere that Victorian writing on fiction was full of such moments, even if we take Eigner and Worth at their word that few if any such theoretical reflections exist, it might be useful to consider the relation of practices that do not rise to the level of methodological self-awareness—such as the prolonged excerpt, for example—to what we rather narrowly call "theory."[9] The protocol is my term for that set of habitual, deeply characteristic, and unexamined operations that express, while not explicitly formulating, a "theory" of the literary.

In the effort to be particularly clear about the range encapsulated by the protocol, some general premises might be useful.

1. A protocol is an unstated, uncodified aspect of professional or generic *techne;* its procedures are not taught as much as absorbed.

2. The protocol is not, generally, subject to ethical evaluation; it does not express the difference between right and wrong, but rather the difference between doing something appropriately and inappropriately.

3. Similarly, it is not a subject of professional controversy; it is neither innovative nor nostalgic, and certainly never scandalous, at least in its own time.

4. It is, in essence, a tool rather than the object of labor; it is the thing worked with, not on.

5. It is also the confluence of material and nonmaterial factors: both the material constraints of a given practice and the kinds of theoretical presuppositions that fit those material constraints.

To say as much demonstrates, at least initially, how little our studies of Victorian criticism of the novel have focused on its protocols. For good reason, perhaps; it is more immediately fruitful to study the explicit controversies fought out in a given period, such as the well-known Victorian debates over realism and its social purpose, or the scandals of a given practice, such as the tendency toward "puffery" endemic to the often-insular world of Victorian reviewing, where friends, or even the author herself, could review a work.[10] In a different vein, the most careful and precise accounts of Victorian periodical reviewing have concentrated on the difficult task of untangling the multiple material conditions of the review: Laurel Brake has, for instance, provided us with a detailed road map of the overlapping determinants of a journal's house style, a writer's commitments, the general expectations of the form, and what anonymity both enabled and proscribed.[11] But in neither case—the history of explicit arguments or the history of material conditions—does the protocol rise to visibility. It is too embedded, and too innocuous, to do so.

It is therefore a deliberately estranging gesture to study the protocol—to, in other words, study the tool rather than the task; it is a gesture that might seem preciously aestheticizing or naive. My gambit here is that one particular protocol of Victorian reviewing, the prolonged extract, offers a productive kind of estrangement, insofar as it reveals presuppositions about the reading act that are not always openly raised in the work of reviewers. It might even be said that those presuppositions cannot have been openly raised, because they were too fundamental to Victorian thinking about novel-reading to have been fully conscious; they formed, I would argue, an unspoken consensus about novel-reading that made some measure of shared discussion possible.

To say as much is not to deny that, lurking in the archive, there might be a clear statement of why the prolonged excerpt is useful and necessary (the reading of Victorian reviews is a task without discernible end); but I would suggest nonetheless that the protocol's ability to reveal the subconscious elements of a practice is a key reason for its importance.

It is further important that the protocol seem to be merely a result of material factors while not being wholly, or satisfactorily, determined by them. The prolonged excerpt might, for instance, be read as a response to the haste of the usual review's composition, as if they were written by harried Grub Street hacks eager to find quick ways to fill space. The "paid-by-the-word" myth surrounding Victorian periodical writing continues to provide an easy alibi for the practice. But the practice is, quite simply, too constant and too widespread, across too wide a range of review styles, to be merely the crutch of the ingeniously lazy reviewer. Jewsbury's brief *Athenaeum* reviews and Bagehot's leisurely efforts for the *National Review* are sufficiently different in tone and approach to demonstrate the point. Surveying the wide range of reviews of fiction, from the prestigious and well-funded journals (*Blackwood's,* the *Edinburgh Review*) to innovative and spirited monthlies (the *Fortnightly Review, Fraser's Magazine*) to squibs published in cramped-type weeklies and dailies (the *Times,* the *Morning Chronicle*), confirms that all demonstrate a similar dependence on the lengthy extract. The taste was a peculiarly British one; writers who modeled their work on Sainte-Beuve and the *Revue des Deux Mondes* school, such as W. C. Roscoe or R. H. Hutton, generally avoided the extract, which was not a staple of French style. It also had a temporal limit. By the 1880s the long extract had begun to disappear from reviews, a fact that the chronological organization of anthologies such as Olmsted's *A Victorian Art of Fiction* makes readily visible. No critic seems to have mourned or celebrated its passing. The protocol has no excitedly announced birth nor, it seems, any dramatically staged death; it gradually appears and passes away with the pace, and invisibility, of a fad.

What can make a protocol visible? With the example of prolonged excerpting in mind, I might suggest that its ridiculousness—its heretical, or even just risible, appearance considered from contemporary canons of taste—is one of the more useful signs that one is in the presence of a protocol. The Victorian practice of citation can only seem to us as overcitation— as, in fact, an abandonment of critical responsibility. Thus many anthologies of Victorian reviews redact these citations in part or entirely, amply expressing our modern certainty that the most sophisticated criticism stands at a tactful distance from the source text or finds a language in which to re-describe it. D. A. Miller has described this tact as the fear of our "almost in-fantile desire to be *close,* period, as close as one can get, without literal plagia-rism, to merging with the mother-text."[12] In this respect Victorian criticism seems notably unembarrassed, unencumbered by the boundary issues that constitute the neurosis of modern criticism. But the heretical or ridiculous might, of course, signal not a failure but a different set of priorities in play—thus the potential importance of what embarrasses us in the literary practices of the past.

The prolonged excerpt was, in the way of most protocols, a material solu-tion to a felt theoretical desire: to find a way to convey the effect of reading. That it easily ate up space for harried reviewers may have come as a benefit, but it was not, I want to argue, its primary or originary purpose. What is at stake in the excerpt per se—not necessarily in every excerpt's immediate im-pulse, but in *the practice of lengthy excerpting*—is a consideration of what it means to read a novel, what it means to think about reading a novel, and how, therefore, to bridge the gap between a critic's "reading" and the cultural habit of "reading" that it reflects on and yet also mirrors. One excellent example of the excerpt's role in bridging "a reading" and "reading" is also one of the more widely anthologized Victorian reviews: Margaret Oliphant's 1862 piece "Sen-sation Novels," an omnibus piece published in *Blackwood's* that took a sternly, and incisively, negative position on the newly fashionable subgenre. What Oliphant wishes to demonstrate about sensation fiction—both the source of its appeal and, ultimately, the source of the danger it represents to British cul-ture—cannot be conveyed without the prolonged excerpt. Citations of sev-eral hundred words structure the piece, and it is Oliphant's purpose to "read" them.

What Oliphant means by "reading" these excerpts, however, is far from what we might today call "close reading," although it is no less theoretically buttressed. The difference is at first signaled by the length of the citations: whole scenes rather than mere passages. It is further indicated by what fol-lows the citations, for example, on the famous scene from Collins's *The Woman in White* in which Walter Hartright first meets, on a moonlit Hamp-stead Heath, the novel's eponymous specter:

> Few readers will be able to resist the mysterious thrill of this sudden touch. The sensation is distinct and indisputable. The silent woman lays her hand upon our shoulder as well as upon that of Mr Walter Hart-

right—yet nothing can be more simple and clear than the narrative, or more free from exaggeration.[13]

Or this, after over six hundred words cited from the scene when Hartright discovers the relationship between the Woman in White, Anne Catherick, and his love, Laura Fairlie:

> Nothing can be more delicately powerful than this second shock of surprise and alarm. It is a simple physical effect, if one may use such an expression. It is totally independent of character, and involves no particular issue, so far as can be foreseen at this point of the story. . . . The reader's nerves are affected like the hero's. He feels the thrill of the untoward mystery. He, too, is chilled by a confused and unexplainable alarm. Though the author anxiously explains that the elucidation of character has not been in his hands incompatible with the excitement of narrative, these two startling points of this story do not take their power from character, or from passion, or any intellectual or emotional influence. The effect is pure sensation, neither more nor less; and so much reticence, reserve, and delicacy is in the means employed, there is such an entire absence of exaggeration or any meretricious auxiliaries, that the reader feels his own sensibilities flattered by the impression made upon him.[14]

What Oliphant intends to evoke is the sheer feeling of Collins's novel, and while that feeling can be described, it can also, and more profitably perhaps, be *induced* in the reader of the review by the very process of reading, over Oliphant's shoulder as it were, the long citations she has chosen. Oliphant's "reading" of our reading is not a process of uncovering what was not-quite-noticed in the passage, and certainly not a process of demonstrating her ingenuity or subtlety. It is instead an echoing of what we, doubtless, have just felt, as if to say: did you feel that? Did you feel how much you enjoyed it, and how little you thought while feeling it? The passages are, in a sense, self-explanatory, or at least self-evident. The commentary that follows is not explication, nor an admiring or censorious analysis of stylistic or technical quirks. It is instead an admission of the critic's essential oneness with the critic's reader; it exists to affirm that "our" response is the same as the critic's. It says not, Look what I can see, but Look what we both see and feel; it describes agreement rather than ingenuity. Oliphant's acuity as a critic is evinced not by the dexterity of her commentary but in the judiciousness in which she has chosen, and extracted, precisely the passages (and at precisely the length) *that would in a short span produce the very affects that are most relevant to the ex-perience of the work* and that could be felt by both critic and critic's reader. Her acuity is marshaled to describe an emergent subgenre, sensation fiction, whose reading-effects were both particularly salient and worrisome; as a result, the protocol of the long excerpt is more vivid here (and in other reviews of sensation fiction) than in other reviews, although its purpose is the same throughout the corpus of Victorian reviewing.

Oliphant's reading does more, however, than suggest that the office of the critic in the 1860s was very different than the office of the academic critic today. It suggests a fundamental interest in affect, and furthermore, an interest in the temporality of affect: what *kinds* of feelings a novel produces, and *how long* those feelings persist. In regard to Collins, Oliphant suggests that his affects are physiological—or simply physical—and that affects like those are violent, short-lived, and quite possibly addictive, since elsewhere in the review she writes of the "violent stimulant of serial publication."[15] This sensitivity to the quality and intensity of affects produced by fiction, the technical means by which they are produced or balked, and the possible ethical (or social) significance of these affects, is virtually a summary of the qualities most valued in Victorian criticism. It is no surprise that Oliphant's tour de force remains, despite its illiberal attitude toward the reading public, a touchstone of Victorian critical work. But it is worthwhile repeating that all these higher aims—the sensitivity of the critic to technique, morality, and feeling—are enabled by the prolonged excerpt. Only with the assistance of carefully judged scenes, which can be tested upon the reader of the review, can the critic summon into existence those affects that are the object, after all, of their pursuit.

If anything separates the prolonged excerpt from modern norms of close reading, it is its status as self-evident, requiring little or no work from the critic to demonstrate its significance. Rather than comment, the excerpt more usually calls forth apologies for its necessary conclusion, as with the following, from a review of Elizabeth Elton Smith's 1836 *Three Eras of Woman's Life:*

> We had marked down many more passages for quotation, as containing reflections, either striking, new, or newly put, and of substantive interest; but the extreme length to which our observations have extended compels us to stop here, and we reluctantly omit them.[16]

Or this, from G. H. Lewes's important 1859 reassessment of Jane Austen, following an excerpt of over a thousand words from *Emma:*

Our limits force us to break off in the middle of this conversation, but the continuation is equally humorous. Quite as good in another way is Miss Bates with her affectionate twaddle.[17]

When the excerpt is supposed to elicit disapproval rather than pleasure, the critical remark is more usually a claim for its obvious representativeness such as this, from Thomas Cleghorn's 1845 comments on *Martin Chuzzlewit*:

> Our quotations have shown, what might be verified by fifty more, that many parts of this work are composed in the most careless and even slovenly manner; bearing evident marks of having been written, as it were, at a canter, by a man of consummate ability, with great exuberance of spirits, but sometimes affecting an unnatural vivacity that he may hide an occasional flagging.[18]

Regardless, the excerpt requires no serious effort toward critical redescription, aside from perhaps a flourish of the figurative. It is, to coin a term that Victorian reviews seem to need, *autoanalytic*; its very presence obviates commentary. This is equally the case whether the extract demonstrate ineptness or skill, whether it elicit disapproval or a laugh; the form of the extract presupposes a readerly response that is standard and general, one whose deviations from a norm would be insignificant. In this sense, the prolonged extract is an apt tool describing realist fictions, which, as Elizabeth Ermarth has demonstrated, depended on a notion of cultural consensus.[19]

The notion of a standard, general response means that different passages can do the same work. This is of course true of passages from one novel (should the discussion between Mrs. Elton and Emma fail to convince us of Austen's observational humor, Lewes points us to Miss Bates), but equally true of passages from different novels and even different writers. The purpose of the extract is to elicit an affect; if an unrelated passage works as well, why not use it also? So Lewes, in his article on Austen, while remarking on "the effect which her sympathy with ordinary life produces," turns for evidence to a passage of almost four hundred words from George Eliot's *Scenes of Clerical Life*. This is of course an occasion to publicize the work of his partner, but also a claim—not unfamiliar from Victorian reviews—of the essential substitutability of literary passages that produce similar "effects."[20] The exchange of a Regency author for a contemporary is irrelevant as long as the chosen passage amply instantiates the "effect" that Lewes seeks to identify. Unlike some of his sloppier peers, Lewes does not attempt any of his own language to further specify this effect; the passage speaks for him.

Of course, the protocol of the long excerpt does implicitly structure what the critic can find to say about a chosen novel. In general, two kinds of moments are most frequently cited: scenic or character descriptions (i.e., pauses of narrative time); or discursive moments that seem to directly indicate an authorial attitude. The extent to which description is mentioned in Victorian reviews might lead a contemporary scholar to rethink a general neglect of such moments; their weight in reviews of the time is difficult to overestimate. Lewes's largely negative 1850 review of Charlotte Brontë's *Shirley* pauses to cite several moments that demonstrate "the real freshness, vividness, and fidelity, with which most of the characters and scenes are described"; following a passage evoking a storm, Lewes adds a remark that, more directly than usual, speaks to the Victorian critic's interest in "effect": "It gives one a chill to read such a passage!"[21] What these descriptive or discursive moments offer is a relief from context. Context—the state of full possession of what precedes a passage—is the enemy of the long excerpt; it undermines the excerpt's purpose of speaking to the review-reader as directly as it spoke to the novel-reader. While largely solved by turning to nonnarrative moments, this dilemma is nonetheless frequently a subject of the reviewer. Whitwell Elwin's massive 1855 review of Thackeray's *The Newcomes* offers an initial disclaimer.

> The merit of the "Newcomes" cannot be judged by quotations. They are like the stones of the temple, whose beauty is in their proper place, as parts of a design. Characters are built up bit by bit, and many admirable traits depend for their effect upon the knowledge of the antecedents. The passages we give are selected because they can be separated from the context, and not because they are otherwise the best.[22]

This is as clear a statement of a contradiction at the heart of a protocol as one could wish. The review demands extracts; the temporal (and informational) flow of a novel implies a context to every such extract, a context impossible to fully reconstruct: thus the process of reading an extract in a review is not identical to the process of reading the passage in the novel. It might be ventured here that perhaps all protocols are practices whose familiarity masks a methodological crux—or, perhaps, implicitly suggests an alternative to a dominant methodology.

Certainly it was the case that plot was at the center of most mid-Victorian accounts of the novel's generic specificity. As Lewes put it 1865: "The distinctive element in Fiction is that of plot-interest. The rest is vehicle. If critics would carefully specify the qualities which distinguish the work they praise, and not confound plot-interest with other sources of interest, above all not confound together the various kinds of plot-interest, readers would be guided in their choice, and have their taste educated."[23] Confident generalizations like this, however, openly conflicted with the kind of practice Lewes himself employed when writing reviews. The conflict might be better explained as that between two different conceptions of the temporality of the affects of reading. In one—the "official" version, so to speak—"plot-interest" directs affect in a largely accumulative, forward-driven process toward a final discharge. In the other—the unofficial and more demotic version represented by the protocol of the long extract—the affects of novel-reading are *rhythmic:* brief (at least brief enough to be capable of extraction from context) and recurrent (thus ensuring the representability of the extract). Plot, in this version, is less important than the knitting of affective strands into a consistent, or at least unique, pattern.

Put another way: what rests at the heart of the theory of reading offered by the long extract is not an issue of length (the space taken up by, or yielded to, the object of analysis) but an issue of time: the time it takes, while reading, to have a feeling. The unit of feeling implied by Victorian critical protocols is remarkably brief: a passage, a description, an authorial sentiment. These extracts are meant ideally to be monads, single—perhaps even foreshortened— examples of repeated affective prompts. It bears remarking that a central topic within western European psychology in the second half of the nineteenth century was what came to be known as "psychophysics," or the study of the timing of neural operations. Psychophysics eventually sought a minimal unit of consciousness or sensation, something that might be the basis for a system of neural measurement, and it also sought the experimental means by which to isolate previously unimaginably brief sensations.[24] In its own way, Victorian criticism attempted something similar. Through the use of the extract, critics sought to break down (literally, *analyze*) the rhythmic recurrences of novel reading into their smallest constitutive units. The habitual tics of Victorian reviewing that surrounded these extracts—the apologies for having to cut them short, the exclamations of enthusiasm or disapproval, the reluctance to turn back to the passage to break it down further—all stem from this central purpose.

All of which is another way of saying that the long excerpt is not an ex-

ample of the Victorian period's more culturally celebrated manner of citation, the "touchstone." Matthew Arnold's initial description, from "The Study
of Poetry" (1880), proclaims a mode of reference different in procedure and
intent.

> Indeed there can be no more useful help for discovering what poetry be-
> longs to the class of the truly excellent, and can therefore do us most good,
> than to have always in one's mind lines and expressions of the great mas-
> ters, and to apply them as a touchstone to other poetry. Of course we are
> not to require this other poetry to resemble them; it may be very dissimi-
> lar. But if we have any tact we shall find them, when we have lodged them
> well in our minds, infallible touchstones for detecting the presence or ab-
> sence of high poetic quality, and also the degree of this quality, in all other
> poetry which we may place beside them. Short passages, even single lines,
> will serve our turn quite sufficiently.[25]

The touchstone refers to a wholly different mode of reading, one that mines
"short passages, even single lines," in order to produce a set of mnemonic
standards. The prolonged excerpt defeats memorization—not only through
its length, but through its very normality. Adapted to the norms of novel
reading, where memorization is not an issue, the prolonged extract expresses
not the exemplary but the typical—and not a memory of a reading, but an
occasion to immerse oneself again in the rhythms of a reading. The extract is
not to be quoted aloud as evidence of a culturally well-furnished mind, or entered into a commonplace-book as part of an autodidact's education, but instead simply experienced as representative of the text in question.

This Victorian protocol has not disappeared; it has instead gone underground, and can only be used by critics working, for whatever reason—although usually by the grace of extraordinary prestige—outside the norms of
academic practices, even if (or, because) pioneering figures such as Erich
Auerbach or Leo Spitzer made prolonged excerpts a key part of their critical
practices. Two recent examples are instructive, because they show the range
of different tones and tasks for which the long extract can be made useful and
appropriate: Slavoj Zizek's *The Parallax View* (2006) and James Wood's *How
Fiction Works* (2008). Wood's deliberate hearkening back to early-twentieth-
century theories of fiction such as Percy Lubbock's 1921 *The Craft of Fiction* or
E. M. Forster's 1927 *Aspects of the Novel* nonetheless revises his conscious pre-

decessors, because unlike either Lubbock or Forster his work is studded with enthusiastic, and unusually protracted, citations. It was Lubbock who had suggested "reading" was not a sufficient method by which to analyze fiction.

> To grasp the shadowy and fantasmal form of a book, to hold it fast, to turn it over and survey it at leisure—that is the effort of a critic of books, and it is perpetually defeated. Nothing, no power, will keep a book steady and motionless before us, so that we may have time to examine its shape and design. As quickly as we read, it melts and shifts in the memory; even at the moment when the last page is turned, a great part of the book, its finer detail, is already vague and doubtful. . . . The experience of reading it has left something behind, and these relics we call by the book's name; but how can they be considered to give us the material for judging and appraising the book?[26]

Given that we do not (normally) memorize fiction, the act of prolonged citation is for Lubbock a misrepresentation of the process whereby reading passes into an internalized image of the novel. To stay true to this internal image, citation must be replaced by paraphrase, Lubbock's preferred protocol. It had also been the preferred protocol of Lubbock's mentor Henry James, whose reviews are notably and pointedly free of prolonged extracts. The lesson: "reading" is not a route to "analyzing."

Thus while borrowing the nonspecialist's vocabulary and deliberately unsystematic approach of Lubbock and Forster, Wood's is what we might call a neo-Victorian act of criticism: interested in finding and citing the basic monads by which a novel acts upon the reader. As with the Victorian protocol he uses, these monads are often descriptions. And as with his Victorian predecessors, Wood risks the charge of a naive enthusiasm for his chosen passages and authors—although his professional status insulates him from what would otherwise be a lapse of professional decorum. His work threatens to replace epistemology (since James and Lubbock, the reigning problematic of fiction) with affect, which, while at the center of Victorian critical efforts, can now only be embarrassing.

As for Zizek, the prolonged citation and "reading" of the final pages of James's *Wings of the Dove* that he presents as the climax of his genealogy of contemporary "materialism" could not be farther from the usual contexts of Victorian criticism—Zizek's Lacanian vocabulary is perhaps the opposite pole from Wood's generalist tone. But the (to academic eyes) excessive length of his extracts from *Wings* employs a Victorian methodology. Not simply does the unembarrassed admiration with which the extracts begin sound Victorian—"Here are the brilliant last pages of the novel, arguably James's supreme achievement"—but also the extracts' status as what I have called "autoanalytic" samples.[27] Reading James, albeit with Zizek over our shoulder, we are meant to sense exactly what Zizek has already sensed, with only the most minimal of assistance. Extracting becomes an invitation to read, and reading becomes an immediate, if condensed, experience of exactly what the critic has preceded us in experiencing. The "normative" status of reading— the essentially Victorian notion that, with more or less accuracy, different readers have the same affects—can be as useful to a philosophically inclined critic as to a periodical reviewer.

All of which is to suggest that if the protocol of the long extract has meaning beyond the archival or antiquarian—merely a way of understanding a vanished conception of reading—its meaning for us will be in the embarrassment it provokes. Not so much the embarrassment of a transparent affection or distaste for a given text, but the embarrassment provoked by the assumption that to connect "a reading" to "reading" implies some sense of a common range of reading, a response that almost all readers would have. The embarrassment, in other words, of imagining readers as a loose (not at all "close") community— of using the excerpt as a way of *pointing*, both to a reading community and to the text, rather than as the basis of any more virtuosic gesture.

NOTES

1. Richard Chartier, *The Order of Books: Readers, Authors, and Libraries in Europe between the Fourteenth and Eighteenth Centuries,* trans. Lydia Cochrane (Stanford: Stanford University Press, 1992), 23.

2. D. A. Miller, *Jane Austen, or the Secret of Style* (Princeton: Princeton University Press, 2003), 58.

3. See, for instance, the major anthologies of Victorian criticism of the last several decades: Edwin Eigner and George Worth, eds., *Victorian Criticism of the Novel* (Cambridge: Cambridge University Press, 1985); David Skilton, ed., *The Early and Mid-Victorian Novel* (London: Routledge, 1993); Solveig Robinson, ed., *A Serious Occupation: Literary Criticism by Victorian Women Writers* (Peterborough: Broadview, 2003); and John Charles Olmsted's invaluable three-volume collection *A Victorian Art of Fiction: Essays on the Novel in British Periodicals* (New York: Garland, 1979). Two other important surveys of the period's literary theory, primarily based in periodical essays, are similarly silent on the issue of the lengthy excerpt: Richard Stang, *The Theory of the Novel in En-*

gland, 1850–1870 (New York: Columbia University Press, 1959); and Kenneth Graham, *English Criticism of the Novel, 1865–1900* (Oxford: Clarendon Press, 1963).

4. For the figures, and attributions of Jewsbury's anonymous work for the "New Novels" section, see Monica Fryckstedt, *Geraldine Jewsbury's* Athenaeum *Reviews: A Mirror of Mid-Victorian Attitudes to Fiction* (Uppsala: Acta Universitatis Upsaliensis Anglistica Upsaliensia, 1986).

5. "New Novels," *Athenaeum* 1635 (February 26, 1859): 284.

6. "New Novels," *Athenaeum:* 284.

7. William Bagehot, "The Novels of George Eliot," *National Review* 11 (1860): 209.

8. Eigner and Worth, *Victorian Criticism,* 1.

9. For an argument that Victorian reviewers possessed a coherent and widespread theory of fiction, see Nicholas Dames, *The Physiology of the Novel: Reading, Neural Science, and the Form of Victorian Fiction* (Oxford: Oxford University Press, 2007).

10. For examples of puffery and self-reviewing, see John Mullan, *Anonymity: A Secret History of English Literature* (Princeton: Princeton University Press, 2007), 183–216.

11. See particularly Laurel Brake, "Literary Criticism and the Victorian Periodicals," *Yearbook of English Studies* 16 (1986): 92–116.

12. Miller, *Jane Austen,* 58.

13. Margaret Oliphant, "Sensation Novels," *Blackwood's Edinburgh Magazine* 91 n.s. (May 1862): 571.

14. Oliphant, "Sensation Novels," 572.

15. Oliphant, "Sensation Novels," 568.

16. Anon., "The Three Eras of Woman's Life," *Athenaeum* (July 2, 1836): 462.

17. G. H. Lewes, "The Novels of Jane Austen," *Blackwood's Edinburgh Magazine* 86 (July 1859): 112.

18. Thomas Cleghorn, "Writings of Charles Dickens," *North British Review* 3 (May 1845): 74.

19. See Elizabeth Ermarth, *Realism and Consensus: Time, Space, and Narrative* (Princeton: Princeton University Press, 1983).

20. Lewes, "Novels of Jane Austen," 104.

21. G. H. Lewes, "Currer Bell's *Shirley,*" *Edinburgh Review* 91 (January 1850): 161.

22. Whitwell Elwin, "The Newcomes," *Quarterly Review* 97 (September 1855): 351.

23. G. H. Lewes, "Criticism in Relation to Novels," *Fortnightly Review* 3 (December 15, 1865): 354.

24. For an extended discussion of psychophysics in relation to Victorian literary criticism, see Dames, *Physiology of the Novel,* 176–90.

25. Matthew Arnold, "The Study of Poetry," *The Complete Prose Works of Matthew Arnold,* vol. 9, *English Literature and Irish Politics,* ed. R. H. Super (Ann Arbor: University of Michigan Press, 1973), 168–69.

26. Percy Lubbock, *The Craft of Fiction* (New York: Viking, 1957), 1.

27. Slavoj Zizek, *The Parallax View* (Cambridge: MIT Press, 2006), 133.

Traveling Readers

KATE FLINT

We are no longer there: this is what real reading is.
—Hélène Cixous,
Three Steps on the Ladder of Writing[1]

Reading has the power to transport one. Its capacity for dislocation is double: it can annihilate or transform our habitual "I" or "we," allowing us temporarily to feel as though we are someone else, and it can reposition us spatially or temporally, allowing us to occupy an imaginary, noncircumstantial relationship to "here" and "now." To read, in other words, is to travel, as Tom Pinch realizes in *Martin Chuzzlewit* (1843–44) when he looks in at the booksellers' windows in Salisbury, containing

> the spick-and-span new works from London, with the title-pages, and sometimes even the first page of the first chapter, laid wide open: tempting unwary men to begin to read the book, and then, in the impossibility of turning over, to rush blindly in, and buy it! Here too were the dainty frontispiece and trim vignette, pointing like handposts on the outposts of great cities to the rich stock of incident beyond.[2]

This display of books is figured as an incitement to imaginative voyaging. The reader as traveler: such an image may conjure up escapism pure and simple, in the sense that the mind is sent off on vacation. And I want here to put forward the further claim that the image of the traveling reader connotes not just mental mobility, but agency as well—something more than unreflective tourism. It assumes survival skills, such as the ability to comprehend conventions (plots, techniques of characterization, stock types) and the competence to negotiate challenges (disrupted expectations, the presence of the unsaid or the unsayable, disguises, suggestive images, shifts of perspective and of narrative voice)—all the while participating in the salient conditions of traveling: provisionality and process. In more literal terms, reading invites one to experience, in one's mind's eye, encounters with landscapes and with peoples that one will never meet in reality (as well as allowing the examination of one's own society with the defamiliarizing eye of a visitor). The more static, the more homebound the reader, the greater the probable gulf between page and experience, and the greater the possibility for mental expansion. "Remember," exhorts one of the very many advice texts devoted to the activity of reading that were aimed at the domesticated mid-Victorian woman,

> that, by the means of books, you may become great travellers; and forgetting scrubbing-brush and needle for a time, you may sail across oceans, and learn how God has fitted distant nations to live where He has placed them, and to enjoy the very different scenes and life of either burning Africa or icy Greenland.[3]

These textual explorations, pilgrimages, and nomadic wanderings draw on and incite the state of mind invoked by Friedrich Nietzsche in *Ecce Homo:* "When I picture a perfect reader, I always picture a monster of courage and curiosity, also something supple, cunning, cautious, a born adventurer and discoverer."[4]

The version of reading that I have just been outlining is a very familiar one. It is predicated on the idea that the reader is already "at home," sitting in well-known surroundings from which she or he can be temporarily displaced through textual consumption. But what if the reader is already in motion? What does it mean to read when one is *away* from home? At its most basic, reading may be less a means of engaging with elsewhere than of filling the time, rather than the space, involved in traveling. The narrator of Herman Melville's *White-Jacket* (1850) opens chapter 41 by asserting, "Nowhere does time pass more heavily than with most man-of-war's men on board their craft in harbour. One of my principal antidotes against *ennui* in Rio was reading."[5] Adopting a resistant attitude toward one's surroundings through taking

refuge in a book may be an act of self-defense on the part of the less inquisi-
tive or the apprehensive traveler, numbing her- or himself against the foreignness that lies beyond the text—a blatant refusal of the potential for transformation offered by travel, as witnessed by John Ruskin when he
encountered two American girls on a train from Venice to Verona, who pulled
down the blinds the minute that they entered their railway carriage, as if deliberately shutting out the stunning scenery outside, and sprawled among its
cushions.

> They had French novels, lemons, and lumps of sugar to beguile their state
> with; the novels hanging together by the ends of string that had once
> stitched them, or adhering at the corners in densely bruised dog's ears, out
> of which the girls, wetting their fingers, occasionally extracted a gluey
> leaf.[6]

The domestic version of these vacationing girls, as careless of the landscape as
they are of books themselves, is the commuting reader, supplying her- or
himself from station bookstalls, emporia of cheap novels. The American
Agnes Repplier noted, in 1893, how "the clerks and artisans, shopgirls, dress-
makers, and milliners, who pour into London every morning, have, each and
every one, a choice specimen of penny fiction with which to beguile the short
journey."[7] Journeys themselves may, of course, provide haphazard, serendip-
itous, and unreliable encounters with reading material. To sneak a look at
one's neighbor's supply of fiction may be a means of embarking on one's own
imaginative mental excursions, but this runs the risk of being a partial and
frustrating experience, as transient and segmented as a short journey itself.
Elizabeth Gaskell, writing to her daughters, owned up to just such textual in-
quisitiveness.

> in the 'bus I sate next to somebody . . . he read "Little-Dorrit" & I read it
> over his shoulder. Oh *Polly*! he was such a slow reader, *you*'ll sympathize,
> Meta won't, my impatience at his *never* getting to the bottom of the page so
> we only got to the end of the page. *We* only read the first two chapters, so I
> never found out who "Little Dorrit" is, only the story opens in a prison at
> Marseilles, a Swiss & an Italian prisoner getting their dinners. 2nd chap.
> English characters introduced in quarantine at Marseilles[,] heroine's
> name Pet Meagles, had a little twin sister, the remembrance of whom is al-
> ways pricking her relations up to virtue, & who, I suspect, is "little Dorrit."[8]

But rather than dwell on the physical and material challenges of reading on the road, I want to turn my attention to what happens when the circumstantial positioning of a traveling or displaced reader—including her or his access to books—actively intersects with the mental voyaging that is invited by her reading material. I will primarily be concerned with fiction, since to read a novel was, in the nineteenth century, to undertake a particular kind of immersive traveling down lengthy routes. As John Plotz has recently noted in his book *Portable Property*, a novel is, too, a particular form of cultural export, "a curious combination of its material and textual properties, readily assimilable neither to the world nor to the sublime realm of poetic experience"—and its prose, too, often depicts material objects that mimic the properties of the book itself, enhancing one's perception of "the disjunction that arises between the broadly shared, interchangeable, impersonal meaning and the poignantly personal aspect."[9]

Plotz's primary concern is with the way in which cultural value circulates—from the heart of the empire out to the colonies. But I am interested in a process that pretty much short-circuits this circulation: what, I want to ask, if the reader's mental voyage is not outward, engaging with new circumstances—not toward the strange, as it might be if one were reading "at home," but toward the familiar—back toward "home" itself? Under such circumstances, what happens to the sense of identity, both personal and national, that a reader already possesses? Does such reading tend to work to disrupt this sense, or to confirm and consolidate it? And how might a reader export her habitual mind-set when it comes to reading about the locations to which she travels, even though her attitudes toward the places themselves may be more thoughtful and critical—criticizing even the stance of native readers toward their own domestic reading?

I will return to the question of escapism in relation to both reading and travel, and the place that reading can play not in changing and expanding the mind, but in providing a kind of stabilizing confirmation of the known when one has been physically transported from the familiar. What interests me more generally is an issue that is frequently passed over in the study of reading practices: the production of meaning that results from reading particular texts in specific places, where location intersects both with the subjectivity of the individual reader and with the text itself. What difference, in other words, might it make *where* one reads a book? And, in relation to this, can one retain the possibility that the imagination is in some ways transnational, and "the home of nonstandard space and time," as Wai Chee Dimock calls it, while at the same time giving due weight to the specifics of reading's contexts?[10] Do

some subgenres travel better—or worse—than others?[11] As increasing attention is paid to the distribution and development of print culture, the "geography of the book,"[12] as we come to have a far more precise idea about what
novels may have been relatively readily available and to whom, and where and
how readers might have obtained them, what may be the relationship between this empirical knowledge and our hypotheses concerning a book's potential signification?[13] In other words, I set out to consider what kind of con-
vergences it may be possible to construct among three elements—the
physical mobility of texts themselves, the known and imagined responses of
the reader who is her- or himself displaced and/or in transit, and the useful,
but complex, metaphor of reading as a form of traveling.

"An act of reading," as Stephen Mailloux has succinctly put it, "is precisely the
historical intersection of the different cultural rhetorics for reading such texts
within the social practices of particular historical communities"[14]—or, to put
it more bluntly, if a text travels, one might well expect it to be read differently
in different places. Reading a novel in situ, in the actual location of its imagined action, once one has traveled away from the familiar, may bring to life
otherwise intractable pages, as Mark Twain's housekeeper, Katy Leary, discovered. In the writer's household, Mrs Clemens kept Miss Leary under close
scrutiny, supervising and discussing her reading with her. Shocked after she
found the housekeeper immersed in a "bad" French novel that she had found
in the billiard room ("Yes, I took in every word, and it explained everything
very plain"), Mrs Clemens recommended a different mode of Francophone
encounter: *A Tale of Two Cities*. But, said Leary,

> I really couldn't worry through the book. It wasn't until we went to France
> and seen the Tuileries and the Bastille and the things that was in that book
> that I wished I could have read it. Then I said: "Oh, wouldn't I like to have
> the *Tale of Two Cities* now! *Now* I could understand it." So we got it again.
> Mrs Clemens' sister, Mrs Crane, got it. She wanted to read it, too. She
> wasn't any better than I was, because she could never read it in America,
> either; but she read it there, and I read it as soon as she was through with
> it. Why, I was just crazy about it then. Yes, it makes quite a difference after
> you have seen the places and know about the people.[15]

On the other hand, reading when one is traveling may return one to where
one has come from. Emily Eden wrote in her arch, ironic way from India on
August 22, 1838:

We had an arrival two days ago of a box of new books; that is, new to us. You may remember them in the early part of the reign of Victoria the First, but the pleasure of seeing them is very great. I have read all our old ones (and we have a great collection) at least three times over, even including the twenty-one volumes of St. Simon, which I read once on board ship and now again here, and it certainly is a wonderfully amusing book. I must have begun it again if the box had not appeared. To think of our only having received in this legal, direct manner, the eighteenth number of Pickwick! We finished it six months ago, because it is printed and reprinted at Calcutta from overland copies. Mais, je vous demande un peu—what should we have done, if we had waited for the lawful supply, to know Pickwick's end?[16]

Eden was accompanying her brother George, who had become governor-general of India in 1835. Her letters home, while displaying a combination of curiosity, amusement, and frustration at the people, the ceremonies, and the landscapes she encounters, are also full of tropes that play on the differences between mental and physical distance. But it would seem that Eden wants fiction to be a distraction from her current dusty and sometimes dangerous surroundings, a means of reassuring herself that there is a pleasant stability awaiting her when she returns. "'Boz' is the only real reading in the amusing line—don't you think so?" she asks, contrasting him favorably with Catherine Gore.[17] Yet whereas *Pickwick* may have provided this amusement, *Nicholas Nickleby* evidently did not. "Does not that book drive you demented?" she asks her sister. She recalls, from some years previously, a trial concerning an atrociously run Yorkshire school, speculates that this incident inspired Dickens's writing, and concludes, "I wish he would not take to writing horrors, he realises them so painfully."[18] This does not appear to be the England she wishes to think of as "home."

Caren Kaplan, investigating the scope and limitations of the metaphor of "travel" when it comes to intercultural relations, reminds one of the burden of the Euro-American historical context that lies behind the term. "That is, 'travel,' as it is used in Euro-American criticism, cannot escape the historical legacies of capitalist development and accumulation, of imperialist expansion, and of inequities of numerous kinds."[19] In her letters home, Eden often displays the capacity to challenge the cruder manifestations of the colonizing mind-set and even demonstrates that she is able to distance herself from "home" through imaginative gestures, speculating how, in a future century, an Indian ruler might visit the ruins of London in much the same manner as Macaulay's New Zealander. For her, the political shape of the world is not irrevocably fixed. Moreover, outside England, with its increasingly prescriptive notions about woman's role, her class position combined with the fact of her transplantation from her native land to grant her a discursive confidence that might have been less readily available to her, as a woman, were she to have remained at home. In turn, of course, the shifts of location that she had experienced and that had allowed her these flexible perspectives were a by-product of her social and economic privilege.[20] Nonetheless, the sense of "home" that she wants her private reading to supply is a reassuring one: she does not need her country of origin to be turned into a location riddled with new causes for anxiety.

The pleasure taken by Emily Eden in Dickens's fiction was clearly culturally specific to her relationship to her native country, and as both Meenakshi Mukherjee and Priya Joshi have shown, the novels that were read and emulated with the greatest enthusiasm by native-born Indians by no means overlapped with the favored reading of the ruling colonial English.[21] For once fiction travels to new readerships and engages with other cultural traditions, its significance, its cultural capital, and its capacity to provoke different forms of desire and nostalgia are, clearly enough, frequently transformed. And yet some authors, for a range of reasons, experienced less troubled global diffusion than others. Take the probably best known British fictional export of the nineteenth century. George Gardner, in *Travels in the Interior of Brazil* (1846), recalls his trip to Diamantina, in Minas Gerais, a mining town situated in high, barren hills.

> In one of the houses where I occasionally visited, I met with Portuguese translations of Sir Walter Scott's "Ivanhoe," and "Guy Mannering." They had been sent from Rio de Janeiro to one of the daughters of the family by whom they had been read with the greatest admiration; she had received an excellent education, and composed verses fluently. I was rather surprised when informed that neither a bookseller's shop, nor a library, existed in the city.[22]

The reading material, however, was not a matter for surprise. If one British author might be relied upon to turn up within the Americas, South and North, in and out of travel writing, in and out of fiction, it was Walter Scott. "The victories of Napoleon were not so wide, nor his monuments so likely to endure," wrote W. B. O. Peabody in the *North American Review* of this cultural colonization.[23] Bento, narrator of Machado de Assis's *Dom Casmurro* (1899), which opens in Rio around 1857, tells how José Dias, honorary member of his family, "having just been reading to my mother, and Cousin Justina, had his head full of Walter Scott."[24] To take another fictional example, this time from the Northern Hemisphere, in *The Virginian* (1902), Owen Wister's ranching romance set in Wyoming, Molly Clark, the new schoolteacher at an isolated schoolhouse, writes back home for books, including "a number of novels by Scott, Thackeray, George Eliot, Hawthorne, and lesser writers."[25] This is no nostalgic return to the security of texts familiar from her native Vermont, however, but a wholesale exportation of culture in the interests of wooing the handsome, but uncultivated ranch hand, who in turn is described as admiring not just the ideals of chivalry celebrated by *Woodstock,* but Scott's portrayal of Queen Elizabeth, finding an affinity with someone else prepared to invest every quality they possess in the opportunities that present themselves.

Susan Stanford Friedman has asked pertinent questions about the international reception of Virginia Woolf.

> In what way has she taken root and grown in different national soils? Should her English point of origin constitute a privileged site for reading? Or, leaving British soil, does Woolf lose her right to be read in her own national context? Is there a global Woolf, a transnational phenomenon or set of meanings?[26]

Is there, then, a global Scott? Certain general factors in Scott's reception seem to cut across specific reading communities. Carlyle's review of J. G. Lockhart's *Life of Sir Walter Scott,* a piece that became the reference point for many later critics, commended his "general *healthiness* of mind";[27] he was praised for the democratic spirit underpinning his interest in all types of people and for his capacity to combine entertainment with more serious passages of philosophizing—in other words, for the way in which he countered the most commonly voiced objections to the genre of the novel as lightweight, distracting, or corrupting. More than this, Scott was, in Christopher Harvie's words, "the acknowledged precursor of those reconstructors of historic identity who were to dominate European nationalism in the nineteenth century."[28] Certainly, his themes fitted these struggles when they took place in a displaced context (a displacement, on this occasion, not just geographical but temporal). Yet it does not seem that one can rely on political identification to supply the reasons for the enthusiasm with which Scott was read. B. J. Tysdahl considers this issue in relation to Norway. Although the political and cultural relations between Norway and Denmark provided an extremely close parallel to Scottish/English history—a northern country intertwined with a more prosperous one to the south, according to his extensive examination of library records—historical awareness seems to have played no part in the choice of Scott's novels by nineteenth-century borrowers: rather, they looked to his plots for entertainment and escapism, in a way that should make one cautious about making ready generalizations about the complexity and depth of identification that takes place when reading about unfamiliar territory.[29]

Escapism, once again, lies at the heart of the responses to Scott provided by that exemplary literary tourist, Harriet Beecher Stowe. In *Sunny Memories of Foreign Lands* (1854), she compulsively (and probably with a view to her own readership) authorizes and authenticates her responses to the northern British locations she visits by noting their fictional resonances: "Carlisle is the scene of the denouement of Guy Mannering"; "the cars stopped at Lockerby, where the real Old Mortality is buried"; "it is in this cathedral [Glasgow] that part of the scene of Rob Roy is laid."[30] But one thing disappoints her (in addition to Abbotsford itself), and that is the lack of response she finds to their famous author among the Scottish people. In making her Abolitionist speeches, she can invoke the name of Bannockburn and bring down the house, but a mention of Scott falls into near silence. She surmises that this is because "Scott belonged to a past, and not to the coming age. He beautified and adorned that which is waxing old and passing away," and the feudalism that provides the basis of many of his plots is something ordinary people would be glad to see the back of. Yet for an American reader, "our sympathies are so unchecked by any experience of inconvenience or injustice in its consequences,—that we are at full liberty to appreciate the picturesque of it."[31]

Stowe's response—especially that word *picturesque*—is particularly illuminating, since she can hardly be said to be someone innocent of issues concerning human rights. At the time of her travels, she was engaged on what was essentially a politically motivated consciousness-raising tour, building on the support for abolition that *Uncle Tom's Cabin* had stimulated. But it is as though her political self had gone on vacation when it came to reading Scott. As her example illustrates, to read novels in conjunction with travel as a leisure pursuit may amount to more or less the same thing as staying at home and reading a text that has been transplanted from its original context. Or perhaps, rather, it is best seen as a doubled act of escapism, since its initial pleasures are consolidated by the further imaginative release of envisaging one's location as being temporally and socially otherwise than it is.

But what of books that are read away from "home" and yet are emphatically not a source of escape, even if they bring certain forms of pleasure and, indeed, of recognition and identification with them? The Yorkshirewoman Mary Taylor, friend of Charlotte Brontë, traveled to New Zealand in 1845, where she lived for eighteen years, keeping a draper's shop in Wellington before returning, eventually, to England. In August 1850, she had a peculiarly *unheimlich* reading experience: if an exceptional experience, as well, it is nonetheless one that throws into sharp relief how reading about the distant yet highly familiar can both annihilate space and time *and* sharply accentuate them. This experience was a literalization of Plotz's point that the Victorian novel could be highly successful in "producing a public form of portable privacy. It postulates ties activated precisely because they are *my* ties of affection and no others."[32] "After waiting about six months," Mary Taylor wrote back to Charlotte, "we have just got Shirley. It was landed from Constantinople one Monday afternoon just in the thick of our preparations for a 'small party' for the next day." She and her cousin Ellen stopped rearranging their room and opened the box, falling hungrily on the letters from home that, among other delights (including stay-laces and garters), it contained. The novel itself had to wait until after the festivities.

> On Wednesday I began Shirley and continued in a curious confusion of mind till now principally abt the handsome foreigner who was nursed in our house when I was a little girl.—By the way you've put him in the servant's bedroom. You make us all talk much as I think we shd. have done if we'd ventured to speak at all—What a little lump of perfection you've made me! There is a strange feeling in reading it of hearing us all talking. I have not seen the matted hall and painted parlour windows so plain these 5 years.[33]

In describing the home of the Yorke family in her novel, Charlotte Brontë drew directly on Mary Taylor's former surroundings, siblings, and self. The young Mary appears as Rose, who at one point shares her impressions of Ann Radcliffe's *The Italian* with Caroline Helstone. The gothic romance, she says, feeds her longings to travel, and she expansively gestures to the breadth of her hunger for experience:

"The whole world is not very large compared with creation: I must see the outside of our own round planet at least."

"How much of its outside?"

"First this hemisphere where we live; then the other. I am resolved that my life shall be a life: not a black trance like the toad's, buried in marble; nor a long, slow death like yours in Briarfield Rectory."[34]

And now, the adult embodiment of this young wanderlust is reading a version of her juvenile self, which is both like and not like herself; a character in fiction, and one with an existence in the known, material world. This Yorkshire home, however, can now exist for Taylor only in memory, and through the words of others.

So what—this is the question that perplexes Mary Taylor—is reality, and what exists in her imagination? The point that recurs, in her letters back to her childhood friend in Yorkshire, is that distance makes it almost impossible for her to tell. The distinction between real space and the events that take place within it, and discursive space, has been collapsed by geographical circumstance. A couple of years earlier, Taylor writes that she has received and read *Jane Eyre*. "It seemed to me incredible that you had actually written a book. Such events did not happen while I was in England. I begin to believe in your existence much as I do in Mr Rochester's. In a believing mood I don't doubt either of them."[35] Her correspondence is suffused with a sense of doubleness, a sense of inhabiting two spaces simultaneously: "One world containing books England and all the people with whom I can exchange an idea; the other all that I actually see and hear and speak to."[36] On another occasion, she tells Charlotte that the "best part of my life is the excitement of arrivals from England. Reading all the news, written and printed, is like leading another life quite separate from this one."[37] She was delighted when her cousin came out to join her, since, as she wrote to Ellen Nussey, this freed her up to talk about issues on which she had previously been silent: "Some of them had got to look so strange I used to think sometimes I had dreamt them. Charlotte's books were of this kind. Politics were another thing where I had all the interest to myself."[38]

Wellington was not, in fact, utterly without intellectual stimulus at this time, although Taylor speaks only glancingly and disparagingly of the circulating library and of the inauguration of a mechanics' institute that held weekly lectures. These were, apparently, on nonliterary subjects, such as phrenology, astronomy, and terrestial magnetism. The *Wellington Indepen-*

dent regularly carried advertisements announcing the arrival of new books: for example, on July 31, 1850, the merchant William Lyon informed readers that he had just received, from the *Constantinople,* Thackeray's *Pendinnis* [*sic*], eighteen volumes from Murray's Home and Colonial Library, cheap editions of Dickens's novels, forty-five volumes of the Family Library, and eighteen volumes of Burn's Fireside Library (the next boats in, he advertised on August 10, would deliver a cheap edition of Scott). The merchandise included popular scientific works as well.[39] The contents of this shipment alert one, again, to the production of books for a specifically overseas market, retailing far more cheaply than within England: Tauchnitz's "Continental" editions, John Murray's "Colonial and Home Library," Bentley's "Empire Library," Macmillan's "Colonial Library Series," Heinemann's "Colonial Library of Popular Fiction," and so on, their numbers increasing in the latter decades of the century.

But it would seem that Taylor's recurrent emphasis on the gap between the world of the sender and that of the receiver—an emphasis that called attention to her cultural isolation—was a way for Taylor to establish her own location through tropes of distance. After she finishes *Jane Eyre,* she wants to communicate with Charlotte: "I went to the top of Mt. Victoria and looked for a ship to carry a letter to you. There was a little thing with one mast, and also H. M. S. Fly, and nothing else."[40] And yet reading (both novel and letters) confuses this sense of remoteness: it calls into question the stability not just of a binary model that would posit a distinction between real and imaginary, but between home and away.

The doubleness experienced by Mary Taylor was not, however, limited to the epistemological vertigo concerning the difficulty of adjudicating between the real and the fictitious when both are encountered through the medium of the written word. The fact that she experiences her friend's (and others') novels as means of accessing both the world of the imagination and the realm of ideas coexists with her perception of them as material goods, as commodities. When she visited Bethune and Hunter's warehouse, in April 1850, to purchase washing blue and saltpeter, tea and pickles, there, on top of the clerk's desk, "was a circular from Smith and Elder, containing notices of the most important new works. The first and longest was given to *Shirley* a book I had seen mentioned in the Manchester Examiner as written by Currer Bell. I blushed all over."[41] Blushed at what? At the intrusion of the personal, the imaginative world of her combined past and present, into the everyday, disrupting normally safe lines of demarcation? At the thought that she was privy to the secret of "Currer Bell's" true identity? Whatever the reason, her first responses to Charlotte Brontë concerning the work—or at least, what she had seen of it to date—were telling. Although she employed the directness of the personal voice and the license of friendship, her comments relate not to companionship or distance, but to the world of work: her particular habitus when she meets with the material reality of Brontë's novel.

> I have seen some extracts from Shirley in which you talk of women working. And this first duty, this great necessity you seem to think that *some* women may indulge in—if they give up marriage and don't make themselves too disagreeable to the other sex. You are a coward and a traitor. A woman who works is by that alone better than one who does not and a woman who does not happen to be rich and who *still* earns no money and does not wish to do so, is guilty of a great fault—almost a crime—A dereliction of duty which leads rapidly and almost certainly to all manner of degradation.[42]

Mary Taylor's is an active response, in part in keeping with the relative polemics of the text she is encountering, but above all seeing her reaction to her reading material as a means of reestablishing a dialogue with her friend. Hers is a personal enactment of that "nineteenth-century association of reading with personal contact" of which Barbara Hochman has written.[43] She is responding not with empathy, though, but through her intellect and from her experience: a reply to *Shirley* that was to continue long after Brontë's death (is communicating with the dead analogous to communicating with those who are twelve thousand miles away?) in the pages of her own novel, *Miss Miles* (published 1890, but begun during her time in New Zealand), and in the articles which she wrote for the *Victoria Magazine* between 1865 and 1870: both novel and articles expound, in different ways, on the value and importance of work for women. To have taken the option of subjective identification with the novel's pages would have been to run the risk of inhabiting a solipsistic world of the imagination, in which the material and fictitious worlds meld into one whole. Acknowledging that *Shirley* is a novel of ideas, and that position-taking is demanded by it, was a means, for Taylor, of maintaining her former affective connection with Charlotte Brontë. To write a letter challenging the novel's premises was a means of reminding the author of the fact that they had shared in discussions of topical issues, and was a deliberate continuation of such discussions: as such, it was a means of asserting her actual and nonfictional identity, and of doing so, moreover, in a way that tacitly asserts the importance of location when it comes to the formulation of both relationships and identity. Without the imperative of work, and work of a kind that was more readily available as an emigrant to a woman of her class than it would have been at home, Mary Taylor would not have been in New Zealand in the first place, negotiating the complex ways in which language and narrative both intensify and collapse the distinction between "home" and the colonies.

In the case of Mary Taylor, we have a clearly articulated set of responses to the activity of reading, composed by one who actively appears to enjoy the self-scrutiny involved and its connection to global displacement. Yet other records of reading while away from home offer far less by way of evidence when it comes to assessing the way in which the books that accompanied the travelers were actually read. Take the example of Lucy Lyttelton, who married Frederick Cavendish on July 7, 1864. On their honeymoon, they traveled first to the Lake District, and then to Switzerland. A few days after her wedding, she wrote, "We have at last tackled to at some books F. chose for the honeymoon: rather an odd trio! Carlyle's 'Fr. Revolution,' Butler's 'Analogy,' and 'Westward Ho!' "[44] In the Alps, a month later, she records:

> We rode and walked in lovely weather to Camballas; there, having leisure, sat in the flowery long grass, and read "Westward Ho!" and had milk and bread and butter . . . Got into a bus at Martigny crammed with English folk, but they don't seem to overrun this hotel. Why does one hate and despise nearly all one's fellow-countrymen abroad?[45]

The reading subject who gives nothing away about her responses: a blank screen onto which a later reader may project speculations—based on what? Starting from where? From the circumstances of honeymoon reading?—already a displacement, for the new bride, in terms of role, and most probably—but how to write of this without composing a new conjectural narrative?—a relocation in terms of romantic and sexual experience.[46] Lucy Lyttelton was, as her diaries show, a confirmed and avid reader, and a sense of having her habitual freedom of choice taken away from her—submitting to the novelty of an imposition—comes across in her somewhat edgy remark about her new husband's choice. These are not newly published books. During the weeks that preceded her marriage, advertisements in the weekly journals such as the *Athenaeum, Spectator,* and *Saturday Review* center on sensation fiction: *Trevlyn Hold!* "by the Author of *East Lynne*"; Mary Braddon's *Eleanor's Victory; Maurice Dering,* by George Lawrence. Or the newlyweds could have furnished themselves with Part 1 of *Our Mutual Friend,* or caught up with chapters 17 and 18 of Braddon's *The Doctor's Wife* in *Temple Bar,* or Part VI of Trollope's *Can You Forgive Her?* or, if they had fancied something a little more challenging, George Meredith's *Emilia in England.* The publicity for new works was keen to emphasize the importance of being of the minute, breathlessly announcing NEW NOVELS; NEW LIST; NEW VOLUME: in this context, the reading material for the honeymoon trip looks safe and cautious, if not perversely serious and dutiful.

We may speculate about what lay behind Frederick Cavendish's choice of novel. Had he already read it, and was it something that he wanted to share, or was he merely hoping to catch up with a popular book from the previous decade (8,000 copies sold in the two years following its publication in 1855)?[47] How alert was he to the outrageously conservative gender politics of the novel? In its final pages, the novel's hero, Amyas Leigh, weeps in frustration at his blindness—and is consoled by the sudden reappearance of Ayacanora, whom he had met in the Amazon jungle: no native, but the daughter of an earlier explorer. She prostrates herself at his feet.

> "Oh, do not weep! I cannot bear it! I will get you all you want! Only let me fetch and carry for you, tend you, feed you, lead you, like your slave, your dog! Say that I may be your slave!" and falling on her knees at his feet, she seized both his hands, and covered them with kisses.[48]

It is impossible to tell whether Cavendish intended some marital semaphoring, or whether the newlyweds collapsed in helpless laughter at this point, or whether, indeed, they ever reached this episode: evidence of choosing a book as a printed traveling companion is no guarantee of its complete consumption. It is impossible, too, to calculate the impact of the book's incessantly patriotic message, and of the mismatch between its Devonian, Irish, and Amazonian settings and honeymooning in the Alps.

One might strongly suspect, nonetheless, that Lucy Cavendish would not have felt entirely at ease with Kingsley's racial views. Seven years later, when visiting Jamaica, she had no qualms in taking his descriptions in his travel book, *At Last* (1871), as the standard by which to assess the local scenery—an example of a common kind of utilitarian reading on the part of someone visiting a new setting. But she refers to a quite different author when, at a dinner party, she came face to face with the unpalatable, racist, complacent attitudes and policies that were being voiced at the table in the wake of the 1864–65 up-risings that Governor Eyre had so brutally suppressed. "I can't help a creep at the evident implication that 400 blacks may well die in revenge for 20 whites," she wrote: "it reminds one of the expression of Legree in 'Uncle Tom's Cabin': 'After all, what a fuss for a dead nigger!' "[49]

This response illustrates yet another way in which a text can travel with someone. Already lodged in one's memory, it may provide a personal point of reference—personal, yet this sentiment of compassionate outrage was one that linked Cavendish to many others. For like the writings of Scott that she herself so admired, Stowe's book traveled widely. Forty pirated editions ap-peared in Great Britain and the colonies within a year of its first publication; it was extensively translated, adapted for the stage, marketed through associ-ated products. In December 1852, George Sand wrote to the author that "it was in all hands and in all journals . . . the people devour it, they cover it with tears."[50] And the success of the speaking engagements that Stowe recounts in *Sunny Memories* bears witness to the capacity of this widely diffused work of fiction to create a community of readers. Although each individual's reading experience might depend on the striking of a particular and personal emo-tional chord, in the case of this novel, this is ultimately far less significant than the creation of a shared framework of reference. The sensationalism and sen-timentalism of *Uncle Tom's Cabin* were powerful factors in its popularity, sug-gesting the capacity of appeals to the emotions, together with the provision of mythic structures of success and survival, to travel across national and re-gional boundaries. As Cavendish's story demonstrates, it could form a part of the cultural matrix through which an individual might ground her sense of identity, but that identity, in turn, could be predicated upon feelings stimu-lated and consolidated by reading that encouraged their possessor to look outward, and to interpret the relatively unfamiliar. And yet, I would argue, *Uncle Tom's Cabin* serves, through its own mobility, to underscore the major point that I have been making. The idea that reading is an activity that both bonds us to a community and allows each one of us to develop our own indi-vidual identity is a well-established one by now. But for the novel read while traveling—as opposed to reading the novel that travels—that bonding is most likely to be with an absent community, and "home" provides the true location of an individual's imaginary escape.

To conclude: back to Brazil. At the end of *A Handful of Dust* (1934), Evelyn Waugh creates the antithesis of the traveling reader: a reader whose sadistic entrapment is underscored by his task of reading Dickens aloud to his captor, Mr. Todd. Deep in the Amazonas, in the swampy and uncertain borderlands between Brazil and Dutch Guiana, Mr. Todd hands the convalescing Tony Last a calf-bound book. "It was an early American edition of *Bleak House*."[51] He works his way through this, then through *Dombey and Son,* through *Martin Chuzzlewit*—in the pages of which Tony finds the ominous evidence of his predecessor's identical plight—through *Nicholas Nickleby, Little Dorrit,* and *Oliver Twist.* Mr. Todd's pleasure, apart from wielding power over another human, lies in the repetition of his responses: where he is habituated to laugh, he laughs (usually, it would seem, at passages depicting human misery); where he has cried before, he cries again. When Tony's potential rescuers turn up, Mr. Todd dopes the Englishman, dupes the visitors, and reharnesses his captive to his literary hell. " 'Let us read *Little Dorrit* again. There are passages in that book I can never hear without the temptation to weep.' "[52]

Tony and Mr. Todd's stasis enacts the imaginative straitjacket worn by the reader who consumes fiction only to confirm what he or she already knows. The escapism promised by a book can be a liberation, but it can also be an evasion, a refusal to encounter and think—whether pragmatically or inventively—about one's immediate circumstances. Repeatedly, the evidence furnished by a whole range of nineteenth-century sources links the consumption of the most popular, the best-traveled Anglophone texts to just such reading practices. Their very suitability as travel reading seems to rest on the sense of security that they deliver: security of narrative convention, of a resolved outcome, of moral certainties. The traveling reader who is prepared to challenge and resist, as well as engage in empathic involvement—like Mary Taylor—is as rare as she or he is welcome.

NOTES

A much earlier version of parts of this essay was published as "Libri in viaggio: Diffusione, consumo e romanzo nell'Ottocento," *Il Romanzo: I. La cultura del romanzo,* ed. Franco Moretti (Einaudi, 2001), 537–66.

1. Hélène Cixous, *Three Steps on the Ladder of Writing,* trans. Sarah Cornell and Susan Sellers (New York: Columbia University Press, 1993), 19.

2. Charles Dickens, *Martin Chuzzlewit* (1843–44; London: Penguin, 1986), 125.

3. Mrs. Alfred Higginson, *The English School-girl: her position and duties. A series of lessons from a teacher to her class,* 2nd edition (London: F. Norgate, 1879), 70.

4. Friedrich Nietzsche, *Ecce Homo: How One Becomes What One Is,* trans. R. J. Hollingdale (1908; London: Penguin, 1992), 43.

5. Herman Melville, *White-Jacket* (1850; Oxford: Oxford University Press, 2000), 168.

6. John Ruskin, Letter 20 (August 1872), *Fors Clavigera,* in *The Complete Works of John Ruskin,* ed. E. T. Cook and Alexander Wedderburn, 39 vols. (London: G. A. Allen, 1903–12), 27:346.

7. Agnes Repplier, "English Railway Fiction," in *Points of View* (Boston: Houghton and Mifflin, 1893), 209.

8. Elizabeth Gaskell, *The Letters of Mrs. Gaskell,* ed. J. A. V. Chapple and Arthur Pollard (Manchester: Manchester University Press, 1966), 373.

9. John Plotz, *Portable Property: Victorian Culture on the Move* (Princeton: Princeton University Press, 2008), 7, 12.

10. Wai Chee Dimock, *Through Other Continents: American Literature Across Deep Time* (Princeton: Princeton University Press, 2006), 4. For a discussion of imagination and the transnational, see Susan Sniader Lanser, "Compared to What? Global Feminism, Comparatism, and the Master's Tools," in *Borderwork: Feminist Engagements with Comparative Literature,* ed. Margaret R. Higgonet (Ithaca: Cornell University Press, 1994), 280–300.

11. Fragments, too, as Plotz notes, could be usefully portable and exportable: "The oft-noted Victorian predilection for quotation . . . derives partially from the sense that literary texts are designed to travel widely and hence ought to be useful in settings both congruous and incongruous" (Plotz, *Portable Property,* 4).

12. The phrase is from Lucien Febvre and Henri-Jean Martin, *The Coming of the Book: The Impact of Printing, 1450–1800,* trans. D. E. Gerard (1958; London: NLB, 1976), 167.

13. Some theoretical ramifications of this question are discussed in Fiona A. Black, Bertrum H. MacDonald, and J. Malcolm W. Black, "Geographic Information Systems: A New Research Method for Book History," *Book History* 1 (1998): 11–31.

14. Steven Mailloux, "Misreading as a Historical Act: Cultural Rhetoric, Bible Politics, and Fuller's 1845 Review of Douglass's *Narrative,*" in *Readers in America: Nineteenth-Century American Literature and the Contexts of Response,* ed. James L. Machor (Baltimore: Johns Hopkins University Press, 1993), 3.

15. Mary Lawton, *A Lifetime with Mark Twain: The Memories of Katy Leary* (New York: Harcourt, Brace, 1925), 55–57.

16. Emily Eden, *Up the Country: Letters from India* (1930; London: Virago, 1983), 157–58.

17. Eden, *Up the Country,* 286–87.

18. Eden, *Up the Country,* 174–75.

19. Caren Kaplan, *Questions of Travel: Postmodern Discourses of Displacement* (Durham: Duke University Press, 1996), 131.

20. For the discursive enablement of the woman traveler, see Dea Birkett, *Spinsters Abroad: Victorian Lady Explorers* (London: Victor Gollancz, 1991), and Janet Wolff, *Resident Alien: Feminist Cultural Criticism* (Cambridge: Polity, 1995).

21. See Meenakshi Mukherjee, *Realism and Reality: The Novel and Society in India* (Delhi: Oxford University Press, 1985), and Priya Joshi, *In Another Country: Colonialism, Culture, and the English Novel in India* (New York: Columbia University Press, 2002).

22. George Gardner, *Travels in the Interior of Brazil* (London: Reeve, Brothers, 1846), 468.

23. Quoted in Frank Luther Mott, *Golden Multitudes: The Story of Best Sellers in the United States* (New York: Macmillan, 1947), 66.

24. Machado de Assis, *Dom Casmurro,* trans. R. L. Scott-Buccleuch (1899; London: Penguin, 1992), 51.

25. Owen Wister, *The Virginian* (1902; Harmondsworth: Penguin, 1979), 86.

26. Susan Stanford Friedman, *Mappings: Feminism and the Cultural Geographies of Encounter* (Princeton: Princeton University Press, 1998), 115.

27. Thomas Carlyle, review of John Gibson Lockhart's *Life of Sir Walter Scott, Baronet, London and Westminster Review* 28 (1838): 293–45, rpt. in *Scott: The Critical Heritage,* ed. John O. Hayden (London: Routledge and Kegan Paul, 1970), 364.

28. Christopher Hardie, *Scotland and Nationalism: Scottish Society and Politics, 1707–1977* (London: Allen and Unwin, 1977), 132.

29. B. J. Tysdahl, "Sir Walter Scott and the Beginnings of Norwegian Fiction, and a Note on Ibsen's Early Plays," in *Scott and his Influence,* ed. J. H. Alexander and David Hewitt (Aberdeen: Association for Scottish Literary Studies, 1983), 477. This volume provides much valuable information about the diffusion of Scott's works, both in the original and in translation.

30. Harriet Beecher Stowe, *Sunny Memories of Foreign Lands* (Boston: Phillips, Sampson, 1854), 47, 49, 54.

31. Stowe, *Sunny Memories of Foreign Lands,* 69.

32. Plotz, *Portable Property,* 11.

33. Mary Taylor, *Friend of Charlotte Brontë: Letters from New Zealand and Elsewhere,* ed. Joan Stevens (Auckland: Auckland University Press and Oxford University Press, 1972), 97.

34. Charlotte Brontë, *Shirley* (1849; London: Penguin, 2006): 377.

35. Taylor, *Friend of Charlotte Brontë,* 73.

36. Taylor, *Friend of Charlotte Brontë,* 77.

37. Taylor, *Friend of Charlotte Brontë,* 108.

38. Taylor, *Friend of Charlotte Brontë,* 102.

39. *Wellington Independent* (July 31, 1850): 2.

40. Taylor, *Friend of Charlotte Brontë,* 73.

41. Taylor, *Friend of Charlotte Brontë,* 93.

42. Taylor, *Friend of Charlotte Brontë,* 93–94.

43. Barbara Hochman, "Disappearing Authors and Resentful Readers in Late-

Nineteenth Century American Fiction: The Case of Henry James," *English Literary History* 63 (1996): 181.

44. John Bailey, ed., *The Diary of Lady Frederick Cavendish,* 2 vols. (London: John Murray, 1927), 1:223.

45. Bailey, ed., *The Diary of Lady Frederick Cavendish,* 1:228.

46. For the emotional dynamics of the Victorian honeymoon, see Helena Michie, *Victorian Honeymoons: Journeys to the Conjugal* (Cambridge: Cambridge University Press, 2006).

47. Charles Morgan, *The House of Macmillan, 1843–1943* (New York: Macmillan, 1944).

48. Charles Kingsley, *Westward Ho!* (1855; London: Macmillan, 1899), 590.

49. Bailey, ed., *The Diary of Lady Frederick Cavendish,* 2:118.

50. Quoted in Mott, *Golden Multitudes,* 118.

51. Evelyn Waugh, *A Handful of Dust* (1934; Harmondsworth: Penguin, 1972), 209. This episode in the novel is a reworking of Waugh's earlier short story, "The Man Who Loved Dickens."

52. Waugh, *A Handful of Dust,* 217.

Reader's Block

TROLLOPE AND THE BOOK AS PROP

LEAH PRICE

Since *Don Quixote* at least, writers and critics alike have assumed that one defining feature of the novel lies in its investment in the act of reading. No other genre, this story goes, so inventively represents the act on which its own realization depends; none so ambivalently sketches out the pleasures and dangers of the absorption, the mediation, and the solitary selfhood that reading in general and fiction-reading in particular exemplify. My question, in this context, is what to do with the representation of unread books. Even those novels that we remember as full of scenes of reading, I contend, often turn out to contain something more negative: descriptions of unread books, depictions of characters pretending to read, or other verbs interposing in the place where we would expect "to read" to appear. In particular, I want to suggest that one strand of the mid-Victorian novel—including all of Trollope and much of Thackeray—elaborates a competing paradigm that could be called antiquixotic, one that values withdrawal over engagement and bibliographic or social surfaces over linguistic or psychological depths.

Start with the language in which some Victorian novels establish a character's position in relation to a book. That may sound circumlocutious, but my mouthful reflects the thesaurus-sized arsenal of circumlocutions the Victorian novel itself elaborates in order to avoid coupling its characters' names with the verb "to read."[1]

1. "The quarto Bible was laid open before him at the fly-leaf . . . Mr Tulliver turned his eyes upon the page."[2]
2. "said Mrs Tulliver, going up to his side and looking at the page."[3]
3. "He sat with a magazine in his hand."[4]
4. "The gentleman had his head bent over a book."[5]
5. "the pages of the magazine which he turned."[6]
6. "with which Mr Osborne spread out the Evening-paper."[7]
7. "Baxter's 'Saints' Rest' was the book [Mrs Glegg] was accustomed to lay
   open before her on special occasions"[8]
8. "having always at breakfast a paper or a book before him."[9]
9. "When he had done yawning over his paper . . ."[10]

The first two passages describe ocular gestures, the next four manual ones. The seventh and especially the eighth go farther, invoking spatial terms to describe the position of the printed object in relation to a person's body, but refusing to specify what that person is doing with his hand—let alone with his eye, much less his mind. The last uses "over" in a sense that could be either causal (the book is so boring that the man yawns while reading it) or purely spatial (in which case the yawn might indicate, on the contrary, that the book is not being read at all).

You could object that these ambiguities are of the literary critic's own making: that these quotations appear elliptical only because I've wrested them from their original contexts. In *Vanity Fair,* the description of Mr. Osborne spreading out his newspaper is immediately followed by the afterthought that "George knew from this signal that the colloquy was ended and that his Papa was about to take a nap." *The Mill on the Floss* makes us wait longer for that resolution: there, a hundred pages separate the initial refusal to specify whether Mrs. Glegg's laying open of the book forms a prelude to, or a substitute for, the act of reading, from the moment when the narrator remarks, a propos of something quite different: "If, in the maiden days of the Dodson sisters, their bibles opened more easily at some parts than others, it was because of dried tulip-petals, which had been distributed quite impartially, without preference for the historical, devotional, or doctrinal."[11] As "opening" becomes an intransitive verb, and as its agent shifts from Mrs. Glegg to the book itself, a character—as so often in *The Mill on the Floss*—becomes accessory to an inanimate object. At the same time, though, the strategic ambiguity of that "laying open" gives way to an unmistakably broad joke about the precedence that the material book takes over not only its human user, but its verbal content. (Any reader can tell that the "opening" of the Bible doesn't refer to Genesis.)

In other words, if an individual sentence leaves us to decide for ourselves whether to parse an ambiguous act as "reading," in the long run each novel as a whole makes perfectly explicit the gap between the presence of the book and its user's absence of mind. Yet the time lag between a passage that suggests what we're witnessing might count as reading, and a later one when that possibility is definitively ruled out, seems to me characteristic of a strategy by which Victorian novels spread out over time our doubts about the relation of persons to books. Thus, *The Mayor of Casterbridge* opens with Henchard and Susan walking "side by side in such a way as to suggest afar off the low, easy confidential chat of people full of reciprocity; but on closer view it could be discerned that the man was reading or pretending to read, a ballad sheet which he kept before his eyes."[12] No sooner does the hypothetical observer congratulate himself or herself on shattering the illusion that a human conversation is going on, than the impression that Henchard is communing only with a printed (and therefore non-"reciprocal") text is punctured, in turn, by the qualification that even physical proximity—whether "side by side" or "before his eyes"—provides no guarantee of mental engagement.

Characteristically, Hardy fudges the question of whose consciousness to locate that undecidability in: the passive voice leaves unclear exactly who is trying and failing to distinguish bodily actions from cognitive ones. In Trollope, though, our own uncertainty about what use a book is being put to is almost always projected onto observers who inhabit the fictional world. In fact, in the passages from his fiction that I quoted a moment ago, the act of reading (and I mean that in both senses) seems to respond to the presence of such a third party. Thus, *The Prime Minister* establishes the breakdown of a marriage by pitting Palliser's newspaper against Glencora's novel.

> Each was labouring under a conviction that the other was misbehaving, and with that feeling it was impossible that there should be confidence between them. He busied himself with books and papers,—always turning over those piles of newspapers. . . . She engaged herself with the children or pretended to read a novel.[13]

Meanwhile, in a parallel subplot, Lopez's quarrel with *his* wife leads to the same result: "he sat with a magazine in his hand."[14] The sentence stops there:

no need to spell out (as the narrator will when the scene recurs a hundred pages later) that "it may be doubted whether he got much instruction or amusement from the pages of the magazine which he turned."[15]

Along with foxhunting and electioneering, pseudoreading forms one of the set pieces that knit together the loose bagginess of the Palliser series. At its other end, *Can You Forgive Her?* already described the young Palliser "*reading, or pretending to read,* as long as the continuance of the breakfast made it certain that his wife would remain with him."[16] Bibliographic aggression spans lifetimes, bridges subplots, and unites enemies. In *The Claverings,* all that the two feuding brothers share is their use of the book. "At their meals [Sir Hugh] rarely spoke to [his wife],—having always at breakfast a paper or book before him, and at dinner devoting his attention to a dog at his feet." In a different household, his brother "was reading,—or pretending to read—a review."[17]

Reading or pretending to read: what's the difference between the two? Not much, Hardy's lack of punctuation suggests. Trollope's pileup of commas with dashes puts more distance between them, but the fact that one rarely appears without the other still reduces the book to a prop. In *The Small House at Allington* (if I can take one more Trollope example), the most economical way to signal two honeymooners' hatred for one another turns out to be a game of bibliographical chicken.

> He had the *Times* newspaper in his dressing-bag. She also had a novel with her. Would she be offended if he took the paper out and read it? The miles seemed to pass by very slowly, and there was still another hour down to Folkestone. He longed for his *Times,* but resolved at last, that he would not read unless she read first. She also had remembered her novel; but by nature she was more patient than he, and she thought that on such a journey any reading might perhaps be almost improper.[18]

His and hers, newspaper and novel: the railway carriage echoes the railway platform across which Johnny Eames and Adolphus Crosbie chased one another several chapters earlier, ending up at the W. H. Smith bookstall where Johnny "laid his foe prostrate upon the newspapers, falling himself into the yellow shilling-novel depot by the overt fury of his own energy."[19] Crushing each genre under the weight of a different combatant, the first scene introduces a face-off between newspaper and novel that the second will peg to sexual difference.

The Small House shows less interest in analogizing men's newspaper-reading to women's novel-reading, however, than in pairing unread copies of each. (One measure of this is that "remembered her novel" doesn't mean what I'd mean if I wondered, for example, whether you remembered *The Small House at Allington* well enough for me to dispense with plot summary: what's being remembered isn't the content of the text, but the location of book.) Even when Crosbie can no longer resist taking out his newspaper, "he could not fix his mind upon the politics of the day."[20] But however little impression the newspaper makes on its owner, it serves a more useful function for the woman in whose presence he's reading it (or not). What Crosbie needs to take off Alexandrina is his eye, not his mind. Where the national community theorized by Benedict Anderson depends on each reader's knowledge that his newspaper-reading is temporally coordinated with spatially distant strangers, here the newspaper can reconcile common spaces with emotional distance.[21]

What the newspaper covers isn't current events, but a body. Crosbie's conventionally agreed-upon signal for what Erving Goffman calls "civil inattention" is ratified in turn by the novel's refusal to tell us what exactly in the newspaper is going unread. "He could not fix his mind upon the politics of the day": neither can the narrator, who proceeds without transition to detail the thoughts that crowd out the news: "Had he not made a terrible mistake? Of what use to him in life would be that thing of a woman that sat opposite him?" and so on, for the space of a paragraph. We can see inside Crosbie's mind, not his newspaper. And the symmetry of this scene extends the paper's emptiness to the genre that frames it: the novel shows as little interest in the content of Crosbie's newspaper as Alexandrina shows in the content of her novel.

An obvious term of comparison: think back to the nineteenth century's most canonical variation on the quixotic theme. In *Madame Bovary,* physical gestures ("she turned the pages," "Emma greased her hands on the dust of reading-rooms," "delicately handling their fine satin bindings") function mainly to introduce the content of the books being read.

> *Pendant six mois, à quinze ans, Emma se graissa donc les mains à cette poussière des vieux cabinets de lecture. Avec Walter Scott, plus tard, elle s'éprit de choses historiques, rêva bahuts, salle des gardes at ménestrels.*[22]

[So, when she was fifteen, Emma spent six months breathing the dust of old lending libraries. Later, with Walter Scott, she became enthralled by things historical and would dream of oaken chests, guardrooms, and min-

strels.][23] [The remainder of the paragraph describes the plot and characters of a historical novel.]

On lisait [les keepsakes] au dortoir. Maniant délicatement leurs belles reli-
ures de satin, Emma fixait ses regards éblouis sur le nom des auteurs. Elle
frémissait, en soulevant de son haleine le papier de soie des gravures, qui se
levait à demi plié et retombait doucement sur la page. C'était, derrière la
balustrade d'un balcon, un jeune homme en court manteau qui serrait dans
ses bras une jeune fille en robe blanche.[24]

[The girls used to read [gift books] in the dormitory. Handling their
handsome satin bindings with great care, Emma stared in dazzled amaze-
ment at the names of the unknown authors, most of whom used a title—
count or viscount—when signing their contribution. She shivered as she
blew the tissue paper off each engraving; it would lift up half folded, then
gently fall back against the opposite page. There, beside the balustrade of
a balcony, a young man in a short cloak would be clasping in his arms a
young girl wearing a white dress.][25]

A table même, elle apportait son livre, et elle tournait les feuillets, pendant
que Charles mangeait en lui parlant. . . . Paris, plus vaste que l'Océan,
miroitait aux yeux d'Emma dans une atmosphère vermeille. . . . Le monde
des ambassadeurs marchait sure des parquets luisants, dans des salons lam-
brisés de miroirs, autour de tables ovales couvertes d'un tapis de velours à
crépines d'or. Il y avait là des robes à queue, de grands mystèeres, des an-
goisses disimulées sous des sourires.[26]

[She would even bring her book to the table and turn over the pages while
Charles ate and talked to her. . . . Paris, vaster than the ocean, shimmered
before Emma's eyes in a rosy haze. . . . The world of high diplomacy moved
about on gleaming parquet floors, in drawing rooms pannelled with mirrors, round oval tables covered by gold-fringed velvet cloths. It contained
dresses with trains, impenetrable mysteries, anguish concealed by
smiles.][27]

Like virtual speech tags, these descriptions of books warn the reader that
what follows should be attributed to another text. In Trollope, on the contrary, no paraphrase of textual content motivates or even follows the description of the hand or eye of the person holding the book.

Like any other object, books can be represented at varying degrees of resolution—not just in visual art, where, as Garrett Stewart has shown, print is conventionally recognizable but illegible, but also in words.[28] If you take Flaubertian pastiche as one extreme, the other might be Henry James's habit of withholding author and title but providing something like a descriptive bibliography: the color of the cover, the number of volumes, the size of the print. His references to "a small volume in blue paper"[29] or "three books, one yellow and two pink" make the book as empty as a patent pill.[30] Like Woolf describing Rachel Vinrace "stirring the red and yellow volumes contemptuously," James uses the visual to crowd out the verbal.[31] The narrator of "Greville Fane," too, dismisses the content of his friend's writing when he measures her rate of production by the fact that "every few months, at my club, I saw three volumes, in a green, in crimson, in blue."[32] Neither dismissal would have been possible in the era of loose sheets; now, bindings mark the mass production at once of the outsides of books and the interiority of readers. When the protagonist of *In the Cage* pulls out a novel "very greasy, in fine print and all about fine folks," the repetition of a single word in two opposed senses opens a gap between bibliographic form and mimetic content.[33] The contrast between cheap typographical characters and rich fictional characters reverses the equally doubled logic of James's large-leaded volume about the petty bourgeoisie. Trollope goes even farther, contenting himself sometimes with generic markers ("her novel"), sometimes with even more purely physical descriptions ("books and paper," "a paper or book"). These are phrases that an illiterate could have come up with.

James's telegraph girl reminds us that marriage is hardly the only human relationship to need a bibliographical buffer: books can be used to demarcate the lunch hour from the workday as easily as to shield commuters from strangers, parents from crying children, children from demanding parents, clubmen from one another. "Les Anglais ont une infinité de ces petites usages de convention," as one French contemporary remarked, "pour se dispenser de parler."[34] Yet at the moment when a human relationship has just been chosen—that is, the honeymoon—the book forms a particularly intrusive third party. Alexandrina's hunch about the shock value of newlyweds' reading is confirmed as late as 1904 in Sturgis's *Belchamber*, where a matchmaking mother pesters an eligible bachelor to recommend books for her daughter; the ploy works, but any hope of marital happiness disappears once we see the two reading on their wedding night. "Cissy sank deep in a big armchair, and appeared to be immersed in a novel she had brought with her. Sainty tried to read too, but his attention wandered; his eyes fell first on his

companion, . . . the hands flashing with new rings that held the gaudy book-
cover like a shield between her face and him." Terrified of going to bed with
the new husband who repels her, Cissy "professed a tremendous interest in
her book"—even though Sainty points out that she hasn't read a page in half
an hour.[35]

One explanation for the place of conjugal reading in the nineteenth-century novel, then, is that this trope turns the logic of courtship fiction inside
out. Unsurprisingly, Trollope's *non*fiction defines the relation of reading to
marriage in mimetic terms: that is, his reviews, lectures, and autobiographical writings assume that we go to books in general, and novels in particular,
in order to find out how to conduct a courtship.

> It is from them that girls learn what is expected from them, and what they
> are to expect when lovers come; and also from them that young men un-
> consciously learn what are, or should be, or may be, the charms of love,—
> though I fancy few young men will think so little of their natural instincts
> and powers as to believe that I am right in saying so.[36]

> The novelist . . . believes that the honest love of an honest man is a treasure
> which a good girl may fairly hope to win, and that, if she can be taught to
> wish only for that, she will have been taught to entertain only wholesome
> wishes. . . . There are countries in which it has been in accordance with the
> manners of the upper classes that the girl should be brought to marry the
> man . . . out of the convent—without having enjoyed any of that freedom
> of thought which the reading of novels will certainly produce; but we do
> not know that the marriages so made have been thought to be happier
> than our own.[37]

But if Trollope's essays cast the novel as the genre of courtship, his own novels are more interested in what comes after. And a corollary to that shift from
romance to realism is that his fiction upstages the texts that help their readers
to reach marriage with the books that help their holders to bear it. In that
sense, the deployment of reading to mark a loveless marriage neatly inverts
the age-old trope that makes the act of dropping the book a preamble to
courtship. Think of Paolo and Francesca.

> *Quando leggemmo il disiato riso*
> *esser basciato da cotanto amante,*

questi, che mai da me non fia diviso,
la bocca mi basciò tutto tremante.
Galeotto fu 'l libro e chi lo scrisse:
quel giorno più non vi leggemmo avante.

[When we had read how the desired smile
was kissed by one who was so true a lover,
this one, who never shall be parted from me,
while all his body trembled, kissed my mouth.
A Gallehault indeed, that book and he
who wrote it, too; that day we read no more.][38]

The erotic charge comes not from reading, but from stopping.

And that timeline may help explain why the honeymoon forms such a crucial moment in Trollope's novels. If they define novel-reading (or at least novel-holding) as a postmarital activity, this isn't because of novels' sexual content (as in those other countries where girls can read fiction only once marriage has released them from the convent), or closer to home, as in figure 1. Trollope shows interest in neither what the choice of reading material suggests about a character's morals or tastes (as, for example, in the contrast between Dorothea Brooke's high-minded appreciation of Pascal and Rosamond Vincy's middlebrow admiration for simpering verse), nor the mimetic logic in which a character's reading of a novel about love either causes, echoes, or foreshadows her falling in love herself, nor even some intertextual correspondence created by placing in the hands of his characters a text named and known to his own readers. When Emma reads opposite Charles at the table, Flaubert names names: the titles of periodicals (*La Corbeille, Le Sylphe des Salons*) and the authors of novels ("elle étudia, dans Eugène Sue, des descriptions d'ameublements"). For the space of two more pages, in fact, the narrator reproduces in free indirect discourse the content of the texts in front of her. In retrospect, the description of the breakfast table at which Emma is reading seems at best a lead-in to, at worst a pretext for, this uneasy mixture of pastiche and parody.

What interests Trollope, in contrast, isn't the relation between a person and a text so much as the relation, or lack thereof, that two persons can establish only in the presence of a bibliographic object. (Emma hates her husband because she reads romances, but Glencora reads romances because she hates her husband.) We usually assume that the printed text exists to provide

EMANCIPATION.

Young Bride of Three Hours' standing (just starting on her Wedding Trip).—"OH, EDWIN DEAR!
HERE'S 'TOM JONES.' PAPA TOLD ME I WASN'T TO READ IT TILL I WAS MARRIED!
THE DAY HAS COME . . . . AT LAST! BUY IT FOR ME, EDWIN DEAR."

Fig. 1. "Emancipation," *Punch* (London, December 5, 1891): 270.

a connection to a writer who is both personally unknown to the reader and
physically absent—even, in many cases, dead. In Trollope's parody of that
logic, the book offers disconnection from a known person, one who is all too
physically present and all too intimately known.

The same holds true for the novel that set out to "adapt" *Madame Bovary*
for English audiences, *The Doctor's Wife*, which Mary Elizabeth Braddon
published in the same year as *The Small House at Allington* (1864). During her
honeymoon, Braddon's heroine bears less resemblance to Emma than to
Alexandria Crosbie: for where Emma reads without even registering Charles's
proximity, Isabel (as befits a more straitlaced English bride) hesitates to read
in her new husband's presence: "There were no books in the sitting-room of
the family hotel; and even if there had been, the honeymoon week seemed to
Isabel a ceremonial period. She felt as if she were on a visit, and was not free

to read."[39] Like Alexandrina, Isabel wants to get out a book; like Alexandrina, she recognizes that desire as disrespectful to her husband. But there the similarity ends. Where Braddon makes the presence of another human being an impediment to reading, Trollope makes it the reason *to* read. Where Braddon contrasts self-indulgent reading with ceremonial visiting, Trollope parses reading itself as a ceremony.

Contrary to what sentimental celebrations of reading aloud might lead us to expect, then, reading becomes most social when it's least sociable. Maud Churton Braby's 1909 conduct book *Modern Marriage and How to Bear It* decrees that when a man is at his club, "the wife can have a picnic dinner—always a joy to a woman—with a book propped up before her, can let herself go."[40] In choosing a book as the marker of freedom from the husband's gaze, *Modern Marriage* sanitizes the fictional convention that made reading a symptom of marital breakdown. Yet its reasoning bears an equally uncanny resemblance to the 1857 conduct book (also quoted by Kate Flint) that advised women traveling alone that "civilities should be politely acknowledged; but as a general rule, a book is the safest resource for an unprotected female."[41] The oppressively intimate home mimics the excessively public railway carriage: in both cases, the opposite sex is what the book makes bearable.

Railways were not, of course, the only place where books functioned as shields. Bill Bell's study of ships bound for Australia shows reading serving both as a social cement and as a guarantor of privacy. Sociable, because passengers read aloud, exchanged books, and produced and circulated manuscript newspapers; but also antisocial, as when Elizabeth Monaghan welcomed a storm for eliminating the possibility of going on deck: "I can be so much more alone, get a book and shut myself up in my cabin quite cosy." The book can be used to mark territory even in its owner's absence: as a newsletter for passengers instructs, "When the cushions at the after part of the saloon are arranged in a particular inviting manner and a book or glove is placed thereon, it may be surmised that the occupant of the couch is absent temporarily and that if another were to take possession it would be an intrusion."[42]

Even if the mid-Victorian novel exchanged guilt about solipsistic reading for cynicism about rhetorical reading, therefore, the presence of parallel scenes in conduct books makes clear that this isn't the only genre or the only moment where cultural consumption looks like an avoidance tactic, any more than reading constitutes the only way to achieve that effect. On the one hand, the scene of a man fending off his wife with a newspaper would be cyclically redeployed in other genres and even other media. By the end of the

MARRIED FOR MONEY.—THE HONEYMOON.

"Now then, Darling, put away your paper, and we'll have a nice long walk, and then come back to Tea in our own little Cottage, and be as happy as two little Birds!" said the Fair Bride—   "Oh! Hang it!" mentally ejaculated the Captain.

Fig. 2. "Married for Money—The Honeymoon," *Punch's Almanack* (London, 1859): 8.

century, the conjugal newspaper had figured so regularly in *Punch* that a political cartoon could allude to the device in the confidence that readers would recognize it even at a second remove (see figs. 2–5). In the twentieth century, pre-Code Hollywood learned to cut between the husband unfurling his newspaper at breakfast to ward off his chattering wife and the wife, abandoned, staring blankly at a book in her solitary bed (see, for example, Clarence Brown's 1936 *Wife vs. Secretary*). In the twenty-first, the railway novels that represented commuters hiding behind newspapers have given way to in-flight catalogs depicting husbands cocooned in an audiovisual equivalent to Benedict Anderson's "lair of the skull."[43]

On the other hand, reading is not the only way for novelistic characters to carve out private space: witness Jeff Nunokawa's argument that George Eliot deploys "the sexual as the primal scene of social withdrawal," with reading a close second.[44] Trollope himself makes aggressive reading interchangeable with conspicuous sleeping: in *He Knew He Was Right*, for example, Colonel Osborne hides from his fellow traveler on the train by alternately "burying

THE HONEYMOON.

Wife (after a little "tiff"). "BUT YOU LOVE ME, DEAR"—*(sniff)*—"STILL?"
Husband ("Cross old thing!"). "OH LOR', YES, THE STILLER THE BETTER!"

Fig. 3. "The Honeymoon," *Punch* (London, May 17, 1884): 230.

himself behind a newspaper" and pretending to sleep.[45] When a Brontë character sleeps, she dreams; when a Trollope character sleeps, he shams.

In alternately flirting with and swerving from the question of what exactly it is that characters are reading, these fictions extend the traditional understanding of the novel itself as a placeholder or a blank. The reading *in* novels borrows its emptiness from the reading *of* novels. Put differently, novels pro-

A PERFECT WRETCH.

Wife. " WHY, DEAR ME, WILLIAM ; HOW TIME FLIES ! I DECLARE WE HAVE BEEN MARRIED TEN YEARS TO-DAY !

Wretch. "HAVE WE, LOVE ? I AM SURE I THOUGHT IT HAD BEEN A GREAT DEAL LONGER."

Fig. 4. "A Perfect Wretch," *Punch's Almanack* (London, 1851), 42.

ject onto the newspaper their own task of reconciling what Coleridge called "indulgence of sloth and hatred of vacancy."[46] Trollope himself (again, in a lecture rather than a work of fiction) complained of novel-readers' "listless, vague, half-sleepy interest over the doings of these unreal personages."[47] Yet reading differs from sleeping or sex—to state the obvious—in that it's also the activity on which those representations depend.

"THE WANING OF THE HONEYMOON."

Right Hon. Arth-r B-lf-r (*to himself*). "WHAT! IS SHE TIRED OF ME ALREADY?"

Fig. 5. "The Waning of the Honeymoon," *Punch* (London, August 1, 1896): 55.

Where the novel from its beginnings has tended to imagine reading as heroically antisocial, Trollope makes it reductively other-directed. (If oblivion to one's family can serve as a gauge for interest in a text, concentration on a book can just as well provide a yardstick for hatred of one's family.) As pseudoreading replaces overreading, the old fear that fiction might produce solipsism—as in a 1795 article in *The Sylph* that pictures mothers "crying for the imaginary distress of an heroine, while their children were crying for bread"[48]—finds its obverse in Trollope's understanding of silent reading as an interpersonal act (see fig. 6). Where the zero-sum logic of *The Sylph* imagines engagement as a limited resource—the more feeling we give textually mediated characters, the less is left over for our immediate surroundings—Trollope assumes the problem to be a surplus of attention. When Diderot described *Clarissa* as "a gospel brought onto earth to sunder husband from wife,

HOW TO MAKE A CHATELAINE A REAL BLESSING TO MOTHERS.

Fig. 6. "How to Make a Chatelaine a Real Blessing to Mothers," *Punch* (London, 1849): 78.

father from son, brother from sister," he measured the novel's power against the strength of the social ties that it could override.[49] Trollope merely substitutes means for end.

Translated into moral terms, this means that selfhood can shade into selfishness. In Elizabeth Sewell's Tractarian novel *Gertrude,* a girl asked to help her mother with some sewing immediately picks up a novel: "'Well, I will see about it presently,' replied Jane; and she went to fetch her book, and then, seating herself by the drawing-room window, forgot her mother's wishes."[50] Any Brontë reader will recognize the name and the window seat: the only difference lies in the value attached to solipsism by a didactic bildungsroman or an "antichristian composition."[51] Conversely, an 1894 conduct book trying to illustrate consideration for others can find no clearer ex-

ample than that of a girl refraining from reading. "You are sitting, let us sup-
pose, by a sleeping invalid, the third volume of your novel with its thrilling
dénouement is on the mantel-piece just out of your reach. Your boots creak,
or your dress rustles, you dare not stir; there you have to sit, perhaps in growing dusk, and you dare not light a candle. These are the kinds of little self-de-
nials that really touch us."[52]

In the midcentury novel *Susan Osgood's Prize* (of which my own copy is
inscribed as a Sunday-school prize), the heroine's fascination with a copy of
Edgeworth's *Simple Susan* given to her as a school prize instills two irrecon-
cilable desires: to find herself in her namesake and to lose herself in the book.
When her sister asks her to fill the kettle, "Susan was still busy over the picture, and was wondering which part of the story it described; she did not
move at first. 'Now, Susan, dear,' said her grandmother, kindly, 'be brisk, I see
you are not a "Simple Susan" yet.'" The desire to read exemplifies the desire to
ignore others: Susan reflects that she "had been put out when her father called
her from her book, to weed his flower beds." Conversely, we know that the
lessons of *Simple Susan* have been absorbed once Susan Osgood refrains from
reading it: "The little book looked tempting on the table by Grannie, but Susan could not get to it yet. There was 'washing up' to be done."[53] The logic is
mechanical but irrefutable: if reading makes you a bad wife (or mother or
daughter), then not reading must make you a good one.

The problem is not reading itself, however, so much as the place in which,
and pace at which, it occurs. The right circumstances can short-circuit its
moral dangers: Sarah Ellis, for example, recommends reading aloud because
"the habit of silent and solitary reading has the inevitable effect, in a family,
of opening different trains of thought and feelings, which tend rather to separate than to unite, and which naturally induce habits of exclusive, selfish,
and unprofitable musing."[54] More counterintuitively, the conduct literature
takes sustained attention to pose a particular danger. Getting to the middle
volume and stopping right there forms the bibliographic equivalent of the
withdrawal method: just as sex becomes acceptable when interrupted, so
reading is sanitized by discontinuity. If pacing one's reading by volume breaks
implies self-restraint and even "self-denial," conversely the narrative momentum that overspills its material containers can be equated with selfishness and
even aggression. The conduct book doesn't specify exactly what you risk doing to the invalid if you open a third volume the minute you close the second,
but a discussion of page-turning published two decades earlier provides a
hint. In 1873, James Greenwood opened an article on "Penny Awfuls" by in-

voking Harrison Ainsworth's Newgate novel *Jack Sheppard* (1839), whose highwayman hero was widely blamed for corrupting its readers. From the belief that texts *about* stealing cause boys to steal, however, Greenwood goes on to identify the stealing *of* books as the first step in a life of crime. Later in his article, a young thief testifies that his brother was first corrupted by reading *Tyburn Dick*—or rather, by *not* being able to read it. After gazing at a page-spread displayed in the shop window, whose conclusion is cut off by the page break, both boys lie awake "wonderin' and wonderin' what was over *leaf*." The brother "wasn't a swearin' boy, take him altogether, but this time he did let out, he was so savage at not being able to turn over."[55] Not content with word crimes, the brother steals a hammer to buy the desired number, the informant steals an inkstand to pay for the next, and a pattern is set.

Middle-class girls' reading might appear to pose a very different moral threat from working-class boys' literacy. What cuts across that divide between political and domestic registers, however, is a new awareness of the book as something more (and less) than a container. In both cases, the traditional model of imitative reading—in which a text *about* a crime (whether adultery or theft) is reproduced by its readers' real behavior—is upstaged by the possibility that the book itself might occasion antisocial behavior. For the traditional worry that the content of a text can corrupt its readers, Greenwood and the conduct book both substitute the fear that the material obstacles to narrative continuity—whether a page break or a volume break—can either test or overstrain the reader's self-control. Threatening an invalid's health or murdering a master: a multitude of sins can be blamed on the hunger to "turn over," or to see "what was over *leaf*." To surface on bibliographical cue is to deny oneself; to be absorbed in the text is to kill the other.

The wedge that novels drive between the outside of books and the interiority of readers, or between material cover and verbal content, forces them to choose between describing the look and feel of reading. I posited at the beginning of this chapter that any turn toward material media means a swerve away from both the text and the mind—as if the narrator needed to stake out a vantage point either inside the pages or outside the covers. In coding the handling of books as authentic and the reading of texts as a front, Trollope's comedies of manners upstage textually occasioned absorption by bibliographically assisted repulsion; but more crucially, they abdicate any attempt to measure psychological depth. Whenever the novel juxtaposes competing vocabularies in which to describe a printed object—whether it puns on "remembered her novel," or replaces *page* by *paper,* or substitutes the opening of a book for the beginning of a text—it stages basic questions about the relation of the inner life to the object world. But in making behaviorism to solipsism what book is to text, novelists of manners also prefigure the challenge facing historians of reading: how to observe an activity against which the social defines itself.

NOTES

1. Nicholas Dames observes that "the very straightforward gerund 'reading' is almost invisible in Thackeray who prefers the use of slightly imperfect synonyms which reflect discontinuity, such as 'subsiding into' or 'simpering over' a book; to 'turn over the leaves,' 'dip into,' or 'muse over' a volume; or the virtually constant use of 'peruse' or 'perusal' to stand in for any more continuous 'reading'" (Nicholas Dames, *The Physiology of the Novel: Reading, Neural Science, and the Form of Victorian Fiction* [Oxford: Oxford University Press, 2007], 108). Thanks to Melissa Shields Jenkins and Miruna Stanica for help with the research for this essay, and, for helpful suggestions, to Billy Flesch, Natalka Freeland, Deb Gettelman, Yoon Sun Lee, John Plotz, Matt Rubery, and Ramie Targoff.

2. George Eliot, *The Mill on the Floss*, ed. A. S. Byatt (Harmondsworth: Penguin, 2003), 274.

3. Eliot, *Mill on the Floss*, 274.

4. Anthony Trollope, *The Prime Minister* (Harmondsworth: Penguin, 1994), 383.

5. Henry James, "The Middle Years," in *Henry James: Collected Stories, 1892–1898*, ed. Denis Donoghue (New York: Library of America, 1996), 335.

6. Trollope, *Prime Minister*, 514.

7. William Makepeace Thackeray, *Vanity Fair*, ed. Peter L. Shillingsburg (1847–48; New York: Norton, 1994), 134.

8. Eliot, *Mill on the Floss*, 274.

9. Anthony Trollope, *The Claverings* (Oxford: Oxford University Press, 1959), 372.

10. Anne Brontë, *The Tenant of Wildfell Hall* (London: Dent, 1914), 164.

11. Eliot, *Mill on the Floss*, 284.

12. Thomas Hardy, *The Mayor of Casterbridge* (New York: Bantam, 1981), 1.

13. Trollope, *Prime Minister*, 361.

14. Trollope, *Prime Minister*, 383.

15. Trollope, *Prime Minister*, 514.

16. Anthony Trollope, *Can You Forgive Her?* (Harmondsworth: Penguin, 1972), 610; emphasis added.

17. Trollope, *Claverings*, 372, 114.

18. Anthony Trollope, *The Small House at Allington* (Harmondsworth: Penguin, 1991), 497.

19. On the relation between novel and newspaper in Victorian culture, see Richard D. Altick, *The Presence of the Present: Topics of the Day in the Victorian Novel* (Columbus: Ohio State University Press, 1991), and Matthew Rubery, "The Novelty of News," Ph.D. dissertation, Harvard University, 2004.

20. Trollope, *Small House at Allington*, 498.

21. Compare Goffman's study of the 1954 newspaper strike, which argues that its main impact was not on public access to information but rather on subway commuters' use of space. Erving Goffman, *Behavior in Public Places: Notes on the Social Organization of Gatherings* (New York: Free Press, 1963), 52. For an eloquent recent argument for Goffman's importance to literary interpretation, see Jeff Nunokawa, *Tame Passions of Wilde* (Princeton: Princeton University Press, 2003), 58–59. My understanding of the paradoxes of silent reading in public draws on Georg Simmel, *The Sociology of Georg Simmel*, ed. Kurt Wolff (New York: Free Press, 1950), 337, as well as on David Henkin's argument that reading in antebellum New York constituted a public performance, even—or especially—when silent (*City Reading: Written Words and Public Spaces in Antebellum New York* [New York: Columbia University Press, 1998], 110). David Vincent, too, associates privacy with "control" rather than with "isolation": "at one level it was the increasingly asserted right to determine what the outside world knew of your thoughts and actions; at another it was the freedom to make your own connections with that world" (*The Rise of Mass Literacy: Reading and Writing in Modern Europe* [Cambridge: Polity, 2000], 103).

22. Gustave Flaubert, *Madame Bovary*, ed. Bernard Ajac (Paris: Flammarion, 1986), 96.

23. Gustave Flaubert, *Madame Bovary*, trans. Margaret Mauldon (Oxford: Oxford University Press, 2004), 34.

24. Flaubert, *Madame Bovary*, ed. Ajac, 97.

25. Flaubert, *Madame Bovary*, trans. Mauldon, 35.

26. Flaubert, *Madame Bovary*, ed. Ajac, 118–19.

27. Flaubert, *Madame Bovary*, trans. Mauldon, 52–53.

28. Also see Michel Butor, *Les Mots Dans La Peinture* (Geneva: A Skira, 1969), 41–43.

29. Henry James, *The Awkward Age*, in *Novels, 1896–1899*, ed. Myra Jehlen (New York: Library of America, 2003), 934.

30. Henry James, *What Maisie Knew*, in *Novels, 1896–99*, ed. Myra Jehlen (New York: Library of America, 2003), 636.

31. Virginia Woolf, *The Voyage Out* (New York: Modern Library, 2001), 304.

32. Henry James, "Greville Fane," in *Henry James: Collected Stories, 1892–1898*, ed. Denis Donoghue (New York: Library of America, 1996), 233.

33. Henry James, "In the Cage," in *Henry James: Collected Stories, 1892–1898*, ed. Denis Donoghue (New York: Library of America, 1996), 119.

34. Edward Bulwer-Lytton, *England and the English*, ed. Standish Meacham (Chicago: University of Chicago Press, 1970), 23.

35. Howard Overing Sturgis, *Belchamber* (1904; New York: New York Review Books, 2008), 188, 219, 220.

36. Anthony Trollope, *An Autobiography,* ed. P. D. Edwards (1883; Oxford: Oxford University Press, 1980), 220.

37. Trollope, *Autobiography,* 42.

38. Dante Alighieri, *The Divine Comedy: A Verse Translation,* trans. Allen Mandelbaum (Berkeley: University of California Press, 1980), v:112–42.

39. Mary Elizabeth Braddon, *The Doctor's Wife,* ed. Lynn Pykett (Oxford: Oxford University Press, 1998), 108; see also Barbara Leckie, *Culture and Adultery: The Novel, the Newspaper, and the Law, 1857–1914* (Philadelphia: University of Pennsylvania Press, 1999), 147.

40. Quoted in Kate Flint, *The Woman Reader, 1837–1914* (Oxford: Clarendon Press, 1993), 100, 105. Many thanks to Kate Flint for suggesting these examples to me.

41. Quoted in Flint, *Woman Reader,* 100, 105.

42. Bill Bell, "Bound for Australia: Shipboard Reading in the Nineteenth Century," in *Journeys through the Market: Travel, Travellers, and the Book Trade,* ed. Robin Myers and Michael Harris (Folkestone New Castle, DE: St. Paul's Bibliographies; Oak Knoll Press, 1999), 136.

43. Benedict Anderson, *Imagined Communities: Reflections on the Origin and Spread of Nationalism* (London: Verso, 1991), 35. See also Dominus:

> When two people curl up on a couch, absorbed in their respective novels, that state of affairs seems somehow companionable, even if the two have been transported to opposite ends of the imaginative universe, with one traipsing down the lush green paths of a 19th-century English estate and the other checking out the interstellar sex in one of Frank Herbert's sci-fi novels. . . . Now the good people at Sharp have created yet another opportunity for multitasking togetherness. It's called the controlled-viewing-angle LCD: a screen—for either a computer or a television, or a combination of the two—that shows different images depending on the angle from which you view it. (Susan Dominus, "His—and—Her TV," *New York Times Magazine* [December 11, 2005]: 74.)

Unisar announces that its silent "TV ears" will "save your marriage"—and the gender of that "you" is made clear when the sebsite adds "No more arguments about watching TV in bed. And no more waking up your wife or baby because the TV is too loud." One satisfied customer on Amazon.com substitutes Unisar's product for the newspapers represented in Trollope, testifying that the "Marriage Saver" means that "He can watch TV in bed, while I can read in peace and quiet!" (http://www.amazon.com/gp/pdp/profile/A2YJORXMEWOXX5).

44. Jeff Nunokawa, "Eros and Isolation: The Antisocial George Eliot," *English Literary History* 69, no. 4 (2002): 839.

45. Anthony Trollope, *He Knew He Was Right* (Oxford: Oxford University Press, 1978), 219.

46. Samuel Taylor Coleridge, *Biographia Literaria,* ed. James Engell and W. Jack-

son Bate, 2 vols. (Princeton: Princeton University Press, 1983), 1:48–49n. On the problem of attention in the nineteenth century, see Jonathan Crary, *Suspensions of Perception: Attention, Spectacle, and Modern Culture* (Cambridge: MIT Press, 1999).

47. Anthony Trollope, "The Higher Education of Women," in *Four Lectures,* ed. Morris L. Parrish (London: Constable, 1938), 85.

48. *Sylph* 5 (October 6, 1795), quoted in John Tinnon Taylor, *Early Opposition to the English Novel: The Popular Reaction from 1760 to 1830* (New York: King's Crown Press, 1943), 53. Garrett Stewart's reading of one image of a reading woman as "the charged site of an almost primal exclusion: the return of the repressed moment when your mother's voice first went silent to you, her face angled away, as she entered a compelling world without you, a space of disconnection from which you were eventually to model your own interiority" ("Painted Readers, Narrative Regress," *Narrative* 11 [2003]: 141; see also Garrett Stewart, *The Look of Reading: Book, Painting, Text* [Chicago: University of Chicago Press, 2006], 105) is confirmed by the *Punch* cartoon entitled "The Chatelaine—A Blessing to Mothers" (fig. 9).

49. Denis Diderot, "Eloge De Richardson," *Oeuvres Complètes,* ed. Herbert Dieckmann, Jean Fabre, and Jacques Proust (Paris: Hermann, 1975), 1066, my translation.

50. Elizabeth Sewell, *Gertrude* (London: Longmans Green, n.d.), 7.

51. [Lady Elizabeth Rigby Eastlake], "*Vanity Fair, Jane Eyre,* and the Governess' Benevolent Institution," *Quarterly Review* 84 (1848): 451.

52. Elizabeth Wordsworth, *First Principles in Women's Education* (Oxford: James Parker, 1894), 11–12, quoted in Flint, *The Woman Reader,* 93.

53. Sophie Amelia Prosser, *Susan Osgood's Prize: A New Story About an Old One* (Boston: Henry Hoyt, n.d.), 20, 29, 22.

54. Sarah Ellis, "The Art of Reading Well, as Connected with Social Improvement," in *Victorian Print Media: A Reader,* ed. John Plunkett and Andrew King (Oxford: Oxford University Press, 2005), 252.

55. James Greenwood, "Penny Awfuls," *St. Paul's* 12 (1873): 10.

Mediated Involvement

JOHN STUART MILL'S
ANTISOCIAL SOCIABILITY

JOHN PLOTZ

*The peculiarity of poetry appears to us to lie in the poet's utter
unconsciousness of a listener. Poetry is feeling confessing itself
to itself in moments of solitude, and embodying itself in
symbols which are the nearest possible representations of the
feeling in the exact shape in which it exists in the poet's mind.
. . . All poetry is of the nature of a soliloquy.*[1]

*Society . . . practices a social tyranny more formidable than
many kinds of political oppression . . . penetrating much more
deeply into the details of life and enslaving the soul itself . . .
and compel[ling] all characters to fashion themselves upon the
model of its own [character].*[2]

Though direct moral teaching does much, indirect does more.[3]

John Stuart Mill struggled throughout his career to find a meaningful space
for individual autonomy and self-determination within a universe governed
by indisputable rational laws.[4] Mill's perennial worry that "society" threatens
to "compel all characters to fashion themselves upon the model of its own
[character]" can make his work seem deeply suspicious of *all* social structures, be they enabling or constricting.[5] Yet his systematic approach to the

69

"moral sciences" reveals that at the root of his fear of social coercion is a comprehensive and nuanced sense of how strongly all human action is shaped by well-nigh inescapable norms that cultures inevitably generate, and from which no individual can ever be entirely free.

This article proposes that scholars have systematically undervalued the role played by reading in Mill's effort to reconcile individual liberty with the strong role that cultural contexts, particularly of the face-to-face variety, play in generating and ordering any individual's actions and thoughts. Mill grew up devoted to a Benthamite strain of Enlightenment reason, but an early-adult turn toward Romanticism led him both to a more historical conception of Enlightenment universals and to an assertion of the distinctive role that subjectivity plays in constituting social relations.[6] That duality—reason on the one side, historically shaped subjectivity on the other—hovers over Anglo-American liberalism still.[7] My claim, though, is that scholars reckoning with that legacy have in some important ways undervalued Mill's profoundly unsettled attitude toward the various *forms* through which the individual receives a society's impress. Far from having forged a perfect union between the demands of social cohesion and those of free action, Mill's work reveals a constant search for new or reconfigured structures that might be able to shape—without rigidly fixing—individual character.[8] Mill's liberalism is in fact profoundly indebted to his theorizing about the role that reading can—and should—play in crafting character.

Mill hypothesized that the printed page would let individuals draw close to others in thought and feeling, while avoiding both the emotional homogenization and the gothic terror that face-to-face interaction can threaten to inflict on the vulnerable individual. For Erving Goffman, a century later, the individual's proper role within an omnipresent and inescapable social network is defined by *facework:* that is, by the inescapable duty of preparing one's face to fit one's world: "Face is an image of self delineated in terms of approved social attributes."[9] In Goffman's account society is not formed out of autonomous agents but rather out of an incessant flow of social transactions: "not, then, men and their moments. Rather, moments and their men."[10] Mill, I propose, is from 1833 onward in search of a formal alternative to such facework—a search that takes him through a variety of genres (among them lyric poetry, personal correspondence, the publicly circulating essay, and the dedication) in an attempt to locate the sorts of writing, and of reading, that best achieve the sort of mediated intimacy he requires.[11]

Florence Nightingale, Parallel and Counterexample

Mill's liberalism stands or falls on its capacity to navigate a tension between autonomy and solidarity. It is this tension that makes Mill acutely aware of the threat of "compulsion and control" over an individual posed not simply by the state monopoly on "physical force in the form of legal penalties," but also—more ominously because less openly—by "the moral coercion of public opinion."[12] Kwame Anthony Appiah has even described Mill as arguing for "the *unsociability of individualism*"; Mill suggests, by Appiah's account, "that political institutions, which develop and reflect the value of sociability, are always sources of constraint on our individuality."[13] I propose a different formulation: Mill is interested in grounding his defense of individualism in what might be called *antisocial sociability.* Mill wants to explore works that make others crucially present on paper in place of face-to-face contact; something like excusing oneself from a dinner with Bentham to go upstairs and read some Bentham. The role Mill envisions for reading, accordingly, is not a substitute for sociability, but a new form of social interaction.

Mill's passionate condemnation of the tyrannical qualities of the everyday social realm certainly does not put him in a Victorian majority—but neither does it make him a complete outlier. We might compare him, for instance, to another vehement opponent of social facework, Florence Nightingale. Nightingale's 1860 "Cassandra" (Mill acknowledges his debt to it in his 1869 *The Subjection of Women*) memorably describes the suffocating effect of the empty social rituals women must perform when they could instead be pursuing their real work elsewhere. Nightingale's denunciation of the evils of genteel society, however, is more vehement than Mill's. Nightingale loathes the vicarious escape into shared feeling that novels offer: being read to, she opines, "is like lying on one's back, with one's hands tied, and having liquid poured down one's throat."[14] "Cassandra" is permeated with disgust, horrified by the social world, desperately seeking ways to forsake the world of facework. By Nightingale's reading, though, reading is mere escapism. The chief fare for benumbed ladies is novels, which offer romantic fantasies of escape, while in actuality playing a key role in the gothic confinement that ladies suffer at the hands of their immediate families and society as a whole. Cultivated women trapped in the drawing room, Nightingale says, are "exhausted like those who live on opium of novels, all their lives—exhausted with feelings which lead to no action."[15]

By contrast, Mill's late political works are shot through with visions of an alternative to social conformity that does not involve, as Nightingale's ideal vision does, a simple plunge into hard work in the public world. Instead, in the 1850s and 1860s Mill returns to what in the 1830s had only seemed to him a feature of poetic texts, and discovers aspects of that same "feeling thought" in a range of speculative writing. Mill does not give up on a wide range of avenues to aesthetic experience—among them the reading of poetry and of novels—because he is searching for a way to retain all the benefits of solidarity and of community interaction in forms that will not impinge on individual autonomy. Mill is intrigued by the idea of a text-space endowed with all the positive features of ordinary social life—hearing others speak, making them mentally present, catching hold of their feelings, and responding to them inside one's own mind, prior to offering any public response.

We can begin to understand the distinction Mill implicitly erects between face-to-face and reading-mediated interactions by considering his memorable discussion, in *On Liberty*, of different ways an opinion may circulate.

> An opinion that corn-dealers are starvers of the poor, or that private property is robbery, ought to be unmolested when simply circulated through the press, but may justly incur punishment when delivered orally to an excited mob assembled before the house of a corn-dealer, or when handed about among the same mob in the form of a placard.[16]

It seems clear here that Mill posits a form of latent resistance built into printed opinions, a way that the medium encourages reasoned judgment by discouraging the possibility of immediate (shared) emotional response. Mill's liberalism is predicated in part, then, on establishing a distinction (much like Gabriel Tarde's and Robert Park's three decades later) between a "crowd" and a "public": that is, between inherently excitable forms of social aggregation, like mobs, and a reading public's inherent resistance to such affective intensification.[17]

However, Mill's concerns with the capacity of the printed word run deeper. Appiah's notion of unsociable individualism would suggest that Mill's political thinking is always predicated on establishing a secluded space in which the cool light of reason shines without the heat of passion. The problem with such an account, though, is that it disregards Mill's emphasis, early and late, on the times when retreat to such a cool, detached realm in fact engenders the most poignant sorts of feeling. The famous case for reading lyric that Mill makes in "What Is Poetry?" (1833), after all, is precisely predicated on the intense emotions that can only arise in acts of solitary reading: poetry is the "overheard" utterance that sparks in the reader the same feeling (or "feeling thought")[18] that had inspired the utterance in the author.

Mill's account of poetry may have little enduring interest as an account of the creative process, or as an account of the form of the lyric itself. But it has a great deal to tell us about the forms of receptive reading that Mill came in his political writings to see as deeply formative of the liberal subject. "What Is Poetry?" records the surprising discovery of an emotional upwelling within a reader—implicitly, within Mill himself, as the memorable passages on his own poetry reading in his *Autobiography* attest. It is crucial in Mill's account that the access of strong emotion is triggered not by any direct appeal but rather elicited indirectly. The reader's emotions are made available when the poet reveals to the reader her own inward nature, thus preceding her in giving utterance to her own deepest feelings. The reader's response to a poem is like neither the newspaper reader nor the mob member absorbing an opinion about corn-dealers. Or rather, the reader of a lyric utterance seems to possess qualities both of the mob member and of the newspaper reader. What circulates through magazines and books, then, need not be dispassionate; instead, some written words can function as the irreplaceable record of another's emotions, recollected not in tranquility but via a complete recall that unites the original speaker and the reader in a feeling that is deeply personal and yet not at all private.

This view of reading has immense implications when Mill comes to describe the ideal form of a liberal subject, formed by exposure to his or her social realm, yet capable of choosing how to express the character that had been cultivated by that exposure. In spending so much time with the potential emotional charge of poetry, Mill may be after something like an extension of the Kantian notion of "representative thinking," in which others are made present inside one's own internal version of the public realm, conjured up mimetically so that they can be properly understood and answered.[19] What his essay does not set out to endorse—what it seems pointedly to avoid contemplating—is the possibility of a visceral emotional response to an appeal made directly, person to person.

Feeling, Heartiness, and Spectral Bipeds: Carlyle versus Mill

Given the wide latitude that Mill is willing to give to feelings expressed through the medium of verse, Thomas Carlyle's ill-advised attempt, also in early 1833, to wring from Mill a more direct expression of sympathy makes for fascinating reading. Carlyle, most provoking of Victorian provocateurs, always knew how to get Mill's goat. Raised under the stripped-down Associationist psychology of Benthamite radicalism, Mill was, in the early 1830s, initially overwhelmed by Carlyle's appeals for his friendship. But the correspondence reveals that, as seriously as Mill took Carlyle's vision of a sort of empathic connection different from any friendship he had known, he also took seriously his own involuntary recoil from the most direct and explicit appeals that Carlyle made for that friendship.[20]

In an 1833 response to a letter in which Carlyle, feeling emotionally battered, pleads for sympathy and evidence of love, Mill effusively praises Carlyle's ability to feel passionately and to demand fellow-feeling from friends like Mill himself. However, he declares himself incapable of returning the kind of emotions in the way Carlyle might want: "You wonder at 'the boundless capacity Man has of loving . . . ' Boundless indeed it is in *some* natures, immeasurable and inexhaustible; but *I* also wonder, judging from myself, at the limitedness and even narrowness of that capacity in *others*."[21] Carlyle had asked that Mill speak to him with a "Man's" true feelings, rather than "Cackle" like a "mere spectral biped."[22] In response, Mill declares that he must lack the feeling heart that such declarations require.

> Truly I do not wonder that you should desiderate more "heartiness" in my letters, and should complain of being told my thoughts only, not my feelings; especially when, as is evident from your last letter, you stand more than usually in need of the consolation and encouragement of sympathy. But alas! when I give my thoughts, I give the best I have.[23]

The very fertility of thoughts that Mill elsewhere delights in has here become a deficit. If Mill had learned nothing else from his early education he had learned to trust the dispassionate turn toward cool calculation, which is just what Carlyle is seeking to deny him here.

Faced with the prospect, raised by Carlyle's demand on him, that he might be nothing but an emotionless calculating machine.[24] Mill instead conjectured that the best form of character building and the most reliable form of profound social interaction lay in what I'd like to call *mediated involvement.* By this I mean a form of absorption in the emotional content of poetry that depends on the readers' knowing that the emotions of others are accessible only through the print public sphere. Rather than being an impediment to emotional connection, then, the realm of print (here, lyric poetry, but in later writings other genres as well) becomes a way to experience others' necessarily private experience. The reader's distance—in space, in time, in possibility of reciprocation—from the lyric speaker whose feelings he or she understands so intimately is thus not a pitfall but, paradoxically, an asset.

Mill's enduring attachment and attraction to Carlyle, and to the strain of nationalist romanticism that he cautiously praises in "Coleridge" (1840), has deep roots. It stems from his conviction that Benthamite radicalism lacked a route to happiness and spiritual perfection—a conviction strengthened by his own misery and bouts of depression.[25] The burgeoning friendship with Carlyle in the early 1830s seemed to offer Mill a way to restore strong feeling to the ordinary current of life.[26] However, instead of meeting Carlyle's demands head-on, in 1833 Mill makes clear how far he is from being able to mount any articulate response, to respond to the claim directly. Far from finding a way to overcome this sense of deficit in his later writings, Mill conjures up out of this collision an innovative liberal aesthetics.

To return to "What Is Poetry?": here, Mill represents poetry as an oasis, a place to eavesdrop on others' words and feel their feelings—as Montaigne put it, to gather other men's flowers—secure in the knowledge that an enlightening return to one's private thoughts and feelings would follow. In his letters to Carlyle, Mill disavows the capacity to sympathize. Yet he treasures poetry because it can produce, by way of an operation that is part thought and part feeling, effusions that are at once private—one's own inescapably inward feelings—and public—exchangeable tokens in the common language of the world. Poetry, as the "overheard" art form, opens up the possibility of indirect, nonreciprocal communication with others, but seemingly only at the cost of forswearing any such direct appeals as Carlyle was making to Mill. True companionship can arise if the poet

> can succeed in excluding from his work every vestige of such lookings-forth into the outward and every-day world, and can express his emotions exactly as he has felt them in solitude, or as he is conscious that he should feel them, though they were to remain for ever unuttered, or (at the lowest) as he knows that others feel them in similar circumstances of solitude.[27]

This is the kind of detached involvement Mill craves—that the utmost in inward contemplation might also turn around and become a form of external address. The unuttered emotions of oneself or others thus become precious currency, precious because they are not originally intended for utterance in the public realm at all.

Mill is looking here for a way of understanding social interaction as something that may proceed most satisfactorily when the parties involved are not mutually present: when they do not share the same physical space, when they are not in dialogue with one another. It brings to mind Cato's apothegm "Never am I less alone than when by myself." Only in gaining poetic access to a feeling that is not my own but somebody else's can I actually understand what it means to have a feeling.

> Poetry is feeling confessing itself to itself in moments of solitude, and embodying itself in symbols which are the nearest possible representations of the feeling in the exact shape in which it exists in the poet's mind.[28]

By airing a feeling that is known as another's and yet recognized and felt as one's own, poetry manages to be at once subjective and objective, intimate and universal. Thus Carlyle's feelings, phrased as direct demand to Mill, can spark no response; but Wordsworth's, dangling there as an objectless appeal, can readily seem at home in Mill's mind.

Mill establishes, then, neither the serene realm of disinterested thought that Benthamite radicalism seems to prescribe, nor a Carlylean appeal to a deep authentic self, available only by way of feelings lodged in unplumbable interiors. Instead, he offers an innovative and implicitly recursive account of the role that recognizing the feelings of others plays in generating a self that only *seems* to have existed prior to the reading of the poem itself. Poetry calls into being the very feeling self that seems to preexist it. "Feeling confessing itself to itself" becomes material when, and seemingly only when, it is concretized in the poem. The result is that poetry makes visible, to itself, a self that would otherwise have no reliable grounds of existence.

Only when poetry has opened up the reader's own feelings as belonging, antecedently, to another person can that reader begin to delineate his or her own discrete self. Only in his *indirect* or mediated encounter with the highly wrought feelings of others can Mill discern his own. Poetry teaches Mill how to forge his character on the model of another, but only because that other is unaware of, and unchanged by the effect he or she has had upon Mill. It has often seemed tempting to critics to isolate the claims that Mill makes about poetry, to distinguish them sharply from his later accounts of the basis for interaction with others in the social realm. However, by my account Mill's later articulation of a new basis for liberal subjecthood actually begins here, in his description of how a reader can gain access to another's feelings—and his own—via the printed page. Meanwhile, personal correspondence is a genre that partakes of two sorts of intimacy at once: the potentially universal emotive appeal of lyric poetry and a much more tangible, direct, and accordingly unsettling, even disgusting, appeal that operates much more like face-to-face social interaction.

Correspondence, then, can elicit honest answers from Mill about the state of Carlyle's feelings or his own—but Mill pointedly denies that it can provide the sort of immediate succor that he feels Carlyle is calling for. This is a generic distinction, certainly, between two forms of writing. Yet for Mill it is also something more, a difference between the admirable, immediate, and transformative effect of lyric poetry's *indirect* appeal, and the unsettling but ultimately unmoving attempt of Carlyle's direct address. For further evidence that Mill continued to endow the readerly relationship with forms of mediated involvement not available elsewhere, we might begin by looking at Mill's autobiographical descriptions of his relationship to reading.

Mill among the Disciples

Our mode of communication with people implies a diminution of the active powers of the soul which, on the contrary, are concentrated and exalted by this wonderful miracle of reading which is communication in the midst of solitude. When we read, we receive another's thought, and yet we are alone . . . we are that other person and yet at the same time we are developing our own "I" with more variety than if we thought alone; we are driven by another on our own ways. In conversation even leaving aside the moral, social influences, etc., created by the presence of the interlocutor, communication takes place through the intermediary of sounds, the spiritual shock is weakened, inspiration, profound thinking, is impossible. Much more, thought by becoming spoken thought is falsified, as is proved by the inferiority as writers of those who enjoy and excel too much in conversation. . . . If all the dead were living they could talk to us only in the same way that the living do. And a conversation with Plato would still be a conversation, that is to say, an exercise infinitely more superficial than reading, the value of things heard or read being of less importance than the spiritual state they create in us and which can be profound only in solitude or in that peopled solitude that reading is.[29]

Half a century after Mill's death, the notion that reading might be *more* intimate than face-to-face communication may not have been an artistic commonplace, but it was certainly a viable hypothesis. In the description of the virtues of reading that Marcel Proust offers above, even talking with Plato comes to seem far inferior to reading him. Nothing suited Proust better, we might say, than the notion of finding in reading an absent presence, a happy substitute for the perils of ordinary sociability.

Proust's textophilia is certainly a far cry from Mill's fascination with moments in which textual mediation seems to bring with it inescapable immediacy, a text-borne solidarity that is unmatchable in textless sociability. It is vital to recall, after all, how fervently Mill remained engaged in crucial political and cultural battles of his own day, battles he could and would not have fought without a passionate investment and a firm belief in the inextricability of any human being from his or her cultural surroundings.[30] Nor did Mill's liberalism grow out of a notion of autonomy that favored reading over speech, or solitude over interaction. In fact, it is precisely the *interplay* of solitude and necessary interaction that has seemed to characterize Mill's chief innovation as a theorist of liberalism.[31]

Both early and late in his career, though, Mill is curiously fascinated by the possibility that a reading-based mediated involvement might prove the best way for the feelings of others to make their way into an individual's thoughts. In parsing written work, Mill argues, readers may come to make sense of emotional demands that are touching precisely because they are not directly addressed to oneself ("all poetry is of the nature of a soliloquy"). Nancy Youssef reads Mill's *Autobiography* as representing Mill wrapped so profoundly in solitude that he finds himself bereft even of the words with which to express loneliness.[32] But the ceaseless production of text about texts that defines the boyhood recollections in the *Autobiography* also suggests ways in which Mill's loneliness comes to be transfigured, transvalued even, by a mental solidarity that he arrives at only in his encounters with books.

In Mill's *Autobiography* (written and rewritten from the early 1850s onward), both the quantity and the quality of his encounters with books vastly overshadow the space and energy allotted to detailing face-to-face encounters. This begins with Mill's predictable recourse to books for tutorial in concepts—as when it takes reading a history of the French Revolution for Mill to gain a feeling for what liberty is and why it ought to be valued. In every meeting Mill records, moreover, the textual trace precedes and conditions mere social contact.[33] Mediated involvement begins to seem immediate—and immediate contact, irrelevant. When Mill fondly recalls meeting Saint-Simon, for example, he omits any personal description, instead avowing enthusiastically that "the chief fruit which I carried away from the society I saw was a strong and permanent interest in Continental Liberalism."[34] When Mill speaks of friends—Ricardo, Bentham, and the radical MP Joseph Hume—his descriptions are so buttressed by commentary on their writings that their "dearness" is inextricable from his responses to their oeuvres.[35] After having known Bentham his whole life, and repeatedly discussed his ideas with him, Mill has nothing to say about the man, but reports his near ecstasy when, on his first serious perusal of Bentham's writing at age eighteen, the greatest happiness principle "burst upon me with all the force of novelty."[36] By the same token, Mill registers nothing of his actual travels through Europe in early life—no Simplon Pass episodes, no Humboldt-like pleasure in the natural—instead, he details "mental eminences." When reading Bentham on "Painful and Pleasurable Consequences," for example, Mill recalls feeling "taken up to an eminence from which I could survey a vast mental domain, and see stretching out into the distance intellectual results beyond all computation."[37]

Mill's descriptions of his relationship with his father have long struck readers as the ne plus ultra of emotional chilliness, but Mill's curious descriptions of the nascent utilitarians who hung around James Mill and Bentham are equally revealing. Mill goes out of his way to proclaim a disjunction between those young men and his father. His initial motive is to refute the idea that a "school" of philosophical radicalism was brought together and drilled under Bentham and Mill.

> This supposed school, then had no other existence than what was constituted by the fact, that my father's writings and conversation drew round him a certain number of young men who had already imbibed, or who imbibed from him, a greater or smaller portion of his very decided political and philosophical opinions. The notion that Bentham was surrounded by a band of disciples who received opinion from his lips, is a fable to which my father did justice in his "Fragment on Mackintosh" and which, to all who knew Mr. Bentham's habits of life and manner of conversation, is simply ridiculous. The influence which Bentham produced was by his writings. Through them he has produced, and is producing, effects on the condition of mankind, wider and deeper, no doubt, than any which can be attributed to my father.[38]

Looking back at his youth, Mill again strikes the note that he struck in the 1830s: trust in the intimacy, the passionate connection, available only via the printed page. Ask for something more direct, and risk either mere nullity or the kind of irrecoverable intimacy that never achieves the poetic effect of lending itself to being overheard. In place of such directness, Mill continually seeks some form of laudable social (we might even want to call it *para*social) interchange, a site where thought and feeling can merge, so that what is felt as most personal can potentially be shared with any other person.[39] Nor does it seem to me that critics have been right to sequester Mill's thinking about poetic interchange, or about the pleasures offered by books, treating such claims as distinct from his thoughts on what forms of social interaction can best sustain a liberal polity. My claim, rather, is that in his mature works of political philosophy Mill remains dedicated to mapping text-based forms of solidarity (or communion, forms that can allow valuable kinds of intimacy while avoiding the dangers that "society's . . . moral coercion" poses.

On Liberty

By 1859, when he published *On Liberty,* Mill was ready to find in a remarkably wide range of readerly experiences the same kinds of associative intimacy that in 1833 he had cautiously discerned within poetry alone. The final few passages I want to examine all shed some light on the complicated ways that Mill works to explore forms of sustained and productive exchange of views with others from whom one may differ greatly not just in opinion but in beliefs and forms of feeling. A century and a half of critical work has been directed at Mill's ideas about how a diversity of views can be both produced and sustained within a modern democratic state. If we ask what paradigms Mill offers for how rival opinions and views can work on us to change our minds, his notion of mediated involvement begins to make more sense. He stresses the importance of the widest and most pervasive form of exposure to such divergent views. And what he seems to prescribe is exposure to the human beings who can attest to those views in the broadest range of ways—a diversity, that is, of living human disagreement.

> To do justice to the arguments or bring them into real contact with his own mind [the liberal subject] must be able to hear them from persons who actually believe them . . . he must feel the full force of the difficulty which the true view of the subject has to encounter and dispose of, else he

will never really possess himself of the portion of the truth which meets
and removes that difficulty.... [Beware of people who] have never thrown
themselves into the mental position of those who think differently from
them.[40]

Mill goes on to argue, however, that the actual existence of those who think
and believe differently from oneself is not at the crux of the exercise. The crux
is the capacity to think representatively, to make the ideas of others present in
unexpected ways.

So essential is this discipline to a real understanding of moral and human
subjects that, if opponents of all-important truths do not exist, it is indis-
pensable to imagine them and supply them with the strongest arguments
which the most skilful devil's advocate can conjure up.[41]

When Mill goes on to assert, "There are many truths of which the full meaning *cannot* be realized until personal experience has brought it home,"[42] he
means something less existential about "experience" than is generally assumed. "Personal experience" hinges simply on the capacity to "feel the full
force" of skillful arguments from another perspective, conjured up out of the
brain's ceaseless capacity to make other people and their views present to itself. As I argued above in parsing the differences Mill sees between lyric poetry and his personal correspondence with Carlyle, we ought to think about
what forms of mediated involvement various genres of writing can offer. And
in order to locate the sorts of distinctions that Mill makes between the various genres' reading experiences, it is worth turning to a portion of *On Liberty*
that, prominently placed as it is, is generally ignored altogether in parsing the
text: its dedication.

Mill opens *On Liberty* with a striking suggestion about where to find an
exemplary kind of "personal experience": in the composition of *On Liberty* itself.[43] Harriet Taylor Mill's death in 1858 may not have been the only precipi-
tating factor in the 1859 publication of *On Liberty*, but it is quite clear from
the dedication that she was on Mill's mind in more ways than one.[44] The dedication portrays her as beloved spouse, but also as the interlocutor of choice
in his writing projects—and something more.

To the beloved and deplored memory of her who was the inspirer, and in
part the author, of all that is best in my writings—the friend and wife

whose exalted sense of truth and right was my strongest incitement, and whose approbation was my chief reward—I dedicate this volume. Like all that I have written for many years, it belongs as much to her as to me; but the work as it stands has had, in a very insufficient degree, the inestimable advantage of her revision; some of the most important portions having been reserved for a more careful re-examination, which they are now destined never to receive. Were I but capable of interpreting to the world one half the great thoughts and noble feelings which are buried in her grave, I should be the medium of a greater benefit to it, than is ever likely to arise from anything that I can write, unprompted and unassisted by her all but unrivalled wisdom.[45]

Neither entirely muse nor ghostwriter nor actual author of Mill's works, Harriet is assigned a floating role—or rather, she moves between several roles.[46] First, she is "inspirer and incitement"—yet in that first phrase she has also become "in part the author." This might seem a conventional courtesy to the Muse—after all Mill still places his own name on the title page and reserves the right to dedicate the volume to her: coauthors are never dedicatees. The claim that "it belongs as much to her as to me" might similarly still seem to fit a simple model of grateful gift-giving—this volume in exchange for love or other pervasive inspiration. The second sentence though, locates another role for her: she is the reviser of his work, and it seems usually the re-reviser as well. Muse and editor, then, are oddly conjoined: she inspires Mill to write, and then also edits what he does write. In the final sentence, though, she becomes the fount from which both thoughts and feelings flow.

How can the person who edits his words also be the source from which they are derived? Mill thinks that two friends who are caught up in reading and writing together achieve involvement with one another through the realm of ideas—and with the realm of ideas through one another. Rather than the "audible thinking" Charlotte Brontë idealizes as the acme of conversation at the end of *Jane Eyre*, Mill has in mind a permanently mediated interplay between two reader/writers and the text that arises between them. The mutual interpretation that Harriet and John supply one another models one way in which thoughts and feelings can move within a realm larger than the individual mind, without threatening to exercise the tyrannical claim that society's "opinion" otherwise threatens to inflict.

In his reflections on the process of composition in the *Autobiography*, Mill continues the thought and sustains the ambiguity about where any particular thought or expression can be located.

With regard to the thoughts, it is difficult to identify any particular element as being more hers than all the rest. The whole mode of thinking of
which the book was the expression, was emphatically hers. But I also was
so thoroughly imbued with it that the same thoughts naturally occurred
to us both. That I was thus penetrated with it, however, I owe in a great degree to her.[47]

Rather than Mill deducing from Harriet Taylor Mill's influence a general duty
to be open to a variety of intellectual influences, however, he immediately
stresses that he was so "penetrated" by the thoughts that he shared with Harriet precisely because he was not overpenetrated with stray thoughts from
elsewhere. He credits her explicitly with making him a "thorough radical and
democrat" because she dissuaded certain kinds of suggestibility and openness
to new ideas coming from other quarters.

My great readiness and eagerness to learn from everybody, and to make
room in my opinions for every new acquisition by adjusting the old and
the new to one another, might, but for her steadying influence, have seduced me into modifying my early opinions too much.[48]

Mill praises Harriet, both as the opener and gatekeeper of his mind. That
praise might be thought of as a continuation of their practice of shared reading and writing. He conceived the applicability of that practice so broadly
that he also imagined it as belonging to any reader—any reader, that is, who
saw an avenue of intimacy in what to the unperceptive outsider might look
like little more than glorified copyediting.

Conclusion: Willful and Will-less

Lorraine Daston and Peter Gallison have recently argued that Kant's influence makes will come to seem the basis for subjectivity. This creates, they argue,
an ironic basis to the objectivity that emerges as the desideratum for scientific
research. In a world defined by "a scientific self grounded in a will to will-lessness at one pole, and an artistic self that circulated around a will to willfulness
at the other," objectivity is defined as the site where subjectivity is suppressed—
but suppressed *willfully*.[49] Scientific rigor is willed willessness [*sic*].[50]

I wonder whether we might read Mill's apology to Carlyle—"When I give
my thoughts, I give the best I have"—as the confession of a dispassionate sci-
entist bemoaning his unsuitability for the role of artist. Perhaps Mill—

whether because he is part of the first generation to attempt to translate Bentham's speculations into a living political credo, or simply by good timing as part of the first generation of scientists to value objectivity (or, more narrowly, to be one of the rare avowed social scientists among that generation)—finds it feasible to will will-lessness, but worries about his failure to be willful, in the Carlylean vein, when called upon. Mill comes to see himself, that is, as a depleted subject who is, in Carlyle's terms, nothing more than a pale empirical being suffering from a superabundance of thought and a lack of substance—"a mere Thinking machine" who turns out not "real Facts" but a "matrix of surds."[51] And yet, if this is the feeling that afflicts him, it is striking that he does not attempt to overcome it by *willing* himself back into a direct emotional address to this friend. Instead, in "What Is Poetry?" he describes a readerly capacity to discover one's own emotions as an echo of another's, which has the odd effect of making the feelings triggered by poetry seem at once willful and unwilled. Mill's 1833 recoil from Carlyle thus casts a revealing light on his passionate advocacy, in the same month, for the thought-shaping "feelings" that are concretized in poetry.

By my account, it is not until the major writing of the 1850s—as evidenced by that anguished dedication to *On Liberty*—that Mill comes to terms with the full implications of the aesthetics that is nascently outlined in 1833. Not only in his fervent denunciations of the power of "moral coercion" exerted by society, but also in his equally passionate avowal of his quasi-social debt to Harriet, Mill offers new ways to imagine reading as the reconciling term between societal pressure and individual liberty. Schematically, it may appear that in *On Liberty*, Mill is praising the idea of emotional contact, but with nobody living: wanting sociability, but without actual society. Yet that schematic formulation risks undervaluing the subtlety with which Mill approaches the problem of how "moral coercion" pours down on individuals from "society," while individual character simultaneously comes to be constituted out of that same individual's exposures to the rational norms that are only available through an ongoing, open-ended conversation with like and unlike minds.

The liberal aesthetics that Mill struggles toward as early as "What Is Poetry?" and partially constructs in *On Liberty* has therefore a great deal to tell us about Mill's perennial problem of reconciling the impetus toward individual autonomy with the impetus toward solidarity.[52] Rather than positing a public realm of action and thought, marred by a private realm of feeling, Mill's late writing seems to suggest both that thought flows readily through our private lives (how else to explain the poignancy of the dedication to Harriet?) and that feelings can come more thoroughly to life in the realm of letters than inside individual minds. If this is the case, then Mill's liberalism takes a Romantic notion of acute self-examination and inverts it: literature is never more moving to Mill than when it allows for the inspection of interior depths that belong to others even before they belong to oneself.

If this makes liberalism into a political belief system with a crucial place for feeling (and for willing), it also ensures that such feelings can register their claim only indirectly. Sartre describes literature as an *appeal* to the reader. We might say that for Mill, such an appeal strikes a chord, can strike a chord, only when the reader is certain of *not* being the text's addressee. A great deal of Mill's relationship with Harriet Taylor occurs in the realm of the face-to-face, and a great deal more in their correspondence. But in crucial ways, Mill proposes at the beginning of *On Liberty* that the reader need not imagine that face-to-face realm as meaningfully distinct from the textual intercourse that constituted much of the labor of her (and what he imagined to be his) final years. Mill believed he was most passionately involved with Harriet, and she with him, when they were together imagining, writing, and revising a text, ushering it into public circulation. To be involved with others is to be involved with their words, their reading, their thoughts. But it is equally true that to be involved with such reading, such thoughts, is also to be involved with the others who wrote or read those words. Mill conceives of an intercourse connecting a text's initial composition with its editing and rewriting, its publication and its eventual reception by readers who through it gain some mediated, indirected, almost antisocial sense of its author, earlier interlocutors, and other readers of its audience. And that intercourse may seem to him to be the most reliable form of involvement a liberal society affords.

In the larger project from which this piece is drawn, I argue that the mediated involvement that Mill experiments with in the 1830s through 1850s suggests an intriguing new genealogy for the relationship between political liberalism and the formal work of the European novel (especially in its English and French incarnations) from 1850 into the Modernist era. One reason for that link is implicit in the tension Donner identifies in Mill, between social connection and autonomy. Say that one aspect of Mill's thinking posits that autonomy, and maximum freedom from constraint, are the crucial desiderata of a society. What does that account leave for the realm of culture broadly, and for literature narrowly, to do?

Certainly there have been a range of attempts to redeem liberal autonomy and cultural cohesion both: notably Arnold's, which makes Mill seem a spokesman for a notion of character development that flows readily into the moral role attributed to the modern university. But perhaps the mediated involvement I have described in Mill—a way of making other minds present to oneself, "realizing them" in ways that go beyond cordial bodily encounters in some sanctioned public space—has an efficacy of its own, one that has proved attractive to certain writers suspicious of the direct moral claims levied by society. If so, then a common thread may link Nightingale's denunciations of society's impingements to George Eliot's withdrawn fascination with the lives of her neighbors (her belief that she could create typical "nobodies" who would become bearers of intense emotions without actually existing)[53] and link both in turn to Henry James's experiments with building novels that, like machines, could operate to deliver the idea of other people to readers without those other people having to exist. Perhaps all are experiments in an alternative form of sociability that makes lavish use of the passivity or suspended disbelief that novels paradigmatically demand, but that other kinds of reading also presume. Such sociability, a sort of willful willlessness, potentially offers a form of intersubjectivity to liberal subjects that operates as an alternative to the propulsively active and willed character-formation of the sort that Arnold, for instance, favors.[54]

Why might liberal subjects require this new kind of mediated involvement in others' lives, involvement that takes place through a new kind of reading? In the larger project, I aim to make the case that this tension arises at least in part because the Victorian subjects Mill addresses can take comfort neither from organic community nor from an intuitive shared knowledge of the noumenal world. And yet, even the children and acolytes of James Mill and Bentham plainly lack confidence in the radical truism that purely objective social-scientific knowledge can alleviate social woe. Perhaps we should think about an alternative history of liberalism, one that begins with Mill deciding that thinking of poetry as "overheard speech" is the only way both to preserve and to share knowledge about inner states in a form that is at once personal and potentially applicable to all mankind. If Mill begins to look as connected to Proust as he is to the Liberal party that declared itself the rightful heir to his legacy, that altered genealogy may follow from taking seriously Mill's durable ambivalence about the promise and the pitfalls of coming to know the world through texts.

NOTES

1. John Stuart Mill, "What Is Poetry?" in *Collected Works of John Stuart Mill*, ed. J. M. Robson (Toronto: University of Toronto Press, 1963–) 1:341–67, 348. This essay was originally published in the January 1833 *Monthly Review* and was reprinted in 1867 as the first half of *Thoughts on Poetry and Its Varieties.*

2. John Stuart Mill, *On Liberty*, in *Collected Works of John Stuart Mill*, ed. J. M. Robson (Toronto: University of Toronto Press, 1963–), 18:220.

3. John Stuart Mill, *Autobiography*, in *Collected Works of John Stuart Mill*, ed. J. M. Robson (Toronto: University of Toronto Press, 1963–), 1:49.

4. Cf. Janice Carlisle, *John Stuart Mill and the Writing of Character* (Athens: University of Georgia Press, 1991).

5. This is the aspect of Mill's thought that Appiah criticizes on the grounds that it "can lead us to think that the good of individuality is reined in by or traded-off against the goods of sociability so that there is an intrinsic opposition between self and society" (Kwame Anthony Appiah, "Liberalism, Individualism, and Identity," *Critical Inquiry* 27 [Winter 2001]: 319).

6. Cf. John Stuart Mill, "Coleridge," in *Collected Works of John Stuart Mill*, ed. J. M. Robson (Toronto: University of Toronto Press, 1963–), 10:117–64. Some recent critics stress Mill's deep roots in Benthamite utilitarianism, while others argue that his debt to Anglo-German romanticism makes Mill value "autonomy" and the development of character as goods superior even to happiness itself. Cf. Nicholas Capudi, *John Stuart Mill: A Biography* (Cambridge: Cambridge University Press, 2004). There is also a recent interest in exploring Mill's affinities with Hegelian historicism. Cf. John Skorupski, "The Philosophy of John Stuart Mill," *British Journal for the History of Philosophy* 15, no. 1 (February 2007): 181–97. For a telling analysis of the overall trajectory of Mill's reputation in Britain, see Stefan Collini, "From Sectarian Radical to National Possession: John Stuart Mill in English Culture, 1873–1945," in *A Cultivated Mind: Essays on J. S. Mill Presented to John M. Robson*, ed. Michael Laine (Toronto: University of Toronto Press, 1991), 242–72.

7. Wendy Donner has aptly described Mill's liberalism as born out of the tension between an almost monadic conception of human autonomy and a palpable yearning toward strongly knotted social ties (*The Liberal Self* [Ithaca: Cornell University Press, 1991]). And Nancy Youssef has recently argued that the tension in Mill's liberalism between autonomy and the necessity for sociability was never resolved, and that it resulted in a split intellectual project. "The limited impact of Mill's seemingly profound valuation of sociality," she argues, is evidenced by the tension between his openness to the "light of other minds" and his craving for poetry, understood as a categorically private form of utterance (*Isolated Cases* [Ithaca: Cornell University Press, 2004], 172). Even critics who blame Mill for his role in the formation of modern Anglo-American liberalism (most recently, Uday Singh Mehta, *Liberalism and Empire: A Study in Nineteenth-Century British Liberal Thought* [Chicago: University of Chicago Press, 1999])

respond to what they see as his reconciling of Enlightenment ideals with objection-able versions of Romantic historicism, cultural nationalism, or teleological racism. Thus, Habermas's influential critique of Mill's liberalism argues that Mill took the positive step, absent in other theorists of democracy, of arguing for the necessary rather than the contingent exclusion of the working class from suffrage. Jürgen Habermas, *Structural Transformation of the Public Sphere: An Inquiry into a Category of Bourgeois Society* (1962; trans. Thomas Burger with the assistance of Frederick Lawrence [Cambridge: MIT Press, 1989]).

8. Perhaps trying to have it two ways at once, Mill asserts that society "both does its duty and protects its interests" principally by *not* imposing its stamp on its indi-vidual members: "A person whose desires and impulses are his own—are the expres-sion of his own nature, as it has been developed and modified by his own culture—is said to have a character. One whose desires and impulses are not his own has no char-acter, no more than a steam engine has a character" (*On Liberty*, 264).

9. Erving Goffman, *Interaction Ritual: Essays on Face-to-Face Behavior* (Garden City, NJ: Anchor Books, 1967), 5.

10. Goffman, *Interaction Ritual*, 3.

11. An earlier version of the argument in the following few paragraphs is also ad-vanced in John Plotz, "Antisocial Fictions: Mill and the Novel," *Novel* 42:5 (forthcom-ing, 2010).

12. Mill, *On Liberty*, 223. The word *moral* there (as in Mill's *Logic of the Moral Sci-ences*) is not an ethical but a ethnographic term; Mill uses it to refer to the "self-evi-dent and self-justifying" rules that make "custom" a "second nature . . . continually mistaken for the first" (Mill, *On Liberty*, 220). Far from being normative, then, the "moral" instructions that society issues are liable to mold others into society's homo-geneous blueprint. The "moral freedom" that Mill advocates in *A System of Logic*, by the same token, consists of recognizing the ways in which one was trained, but know-ing oneself capable of discarding that training should it prove inconsistent with rea-son: "a person feels morally free who feels that his habits and temptations are not his masters, but he theirs" (John Stuart Mill, *Logic of the Moral Sciences*, ed. J. M. Robson [Toronto: University of Toronto, 1963], 7:841).

13. Appiah, "Liberalism, Individualism, and Identity," 319; emphasis in original.

14. Florence Nightingale, "Cassandra," in *Cassandra and Other Selections from Suggestions for Thought*, ed. Mary Poovey (New York: New York University Press, 1992), 213.

15. Nightingale, "Cassandra," 219. It is worth noting that although she often rep-resents novels as enervating vessels of escapist fantasy, occasionally Nightingale will turn to the plots of novels as proof that women do in fact dream of something better than domestic confinement (cf. especially Nightingale, "Cassandra," 226).

16. Mill, *On Liberty*, 260.

17. Gabriel Trade, *L'Opinion et la Foule* (1901; Alcan: Paris, 1904). Cf. Robert Park, *The Crowd and the Public and Other Essays* (1903; trans. Charlotte Elsner [Chicago: University of Chicago Press, 1972]).

18. Or "thought [waiting] upon feeling" (Mill, *Autobiography,* 357).

19. Cf. the extended discussion of Kantian representative thinking in Hannah Arendt, *Lectures on Kant's Political Philosophy,* ed. Ronald Beiner (Chicago: University of Chicago Press, 1982).

20. Amanda Anderson has discussed Mill's commitment to the sympathy and imagination he found lacking in Bentham, the necessity of "deriving light from other minds." Anderson describes Mill's final effort to reconcile the twin aspirations of justice and intersubjective sympathy as "a complex dialectic of detachment and engagement; ethical and epistemological process achieved through the flexible agency of sympathetic understanding" (*The Powers of Distance: Cosmopolitanism and the Cultivation of Detachment* [Princeton: Princeton University Press, 2001], 17).

21. John Stuart Mill, letter to Thomas Carlyle (March 9, 1833), in *Collected Works of John Stuart Mill,* ed. J. M. Robson (Toronto: University of Toronto, 1963–), 12:143.

22. Thomas Carlyle, letter to John Stuart Mill (February 22, 1833), in *Collected Works of John Stuart Mill,* ed. J. M. Robson (Toronto: University of Toronto, 1963–), 12:328–29.

23. John Stuart Mill, letter to Thomas Carlyle (March 9, 1833), in *Collected Works of John Stuart Mill,* ed. J. M. Robson (Toronto: University of Toronto, 1963–), 12:144.

24. Which is how Carlyle once described Mill in a letter to his brother John.

25. In the "mental crisis" chapter of the *Autobiography,* Mill describes the despair he felt "to know that a feeling would make me happy if I had it, did not give me the feeling" and his discovery that "the habit of analysis has a tendency to wear away the feelings" (*Autobiography,* 141).

26. Compare with Raymond Williams: "We are concerned with means and values as they are actively lived and felt . . . specifically, affective elements of consciousness and relationships: not feelings against thought, but thought as felt and feeling as thought" (*Marxism and Literature* [Oxford: Oxford University Press, 1977], 132).

27. Mill, "What Is Poetry?" 349.

28. Mill, "What Is Poetry?" 348.

29. Marcel Proust, *On Reading Ruskin,* trans. and ed. Jean Autret, William Burford, and Philip J. Wolfe (New Haven: Yale University Press, 1987), 147–48.

30. I am grateful to Lauren Goodlad for a vigorous response (Notre Dame, March 2008) to an earlier version of this paper, which pushed me to clarify the tension that I locate in Mill's conflicted and often contradictory dual commitment to the realm of reading and that of direct political action.

31. Lisa Gitelman's notion of the *negotiation* that occurs at moments of paradigm shifts between media helps clarify how profoundly anti-Modernist Mill is in one key regard. He conceives of lyric utterance as a pure conduit between the author's feelings and the reader's. He sees lyric poetry not as capable of noting and responding to its own materiality, but as a genre in search of *divested,* immaterial intimacy. Lisa Gitelman, *Always Already New: Media, History, and the Data of Culture* (Cambridge: MIT Press, 2006).

On the interplay of solitude and necessary action, see Donner's discussion of "the intersubjective dimension" of Mill's thought (Donner, *Liberal Self*).

32. Youssef, *Isolated Cases*, 170–97.

33. Mill, *Autobiography*, 45. The portions of the *Autobiography* describing Mill's early years were written between 1851 and 1853 but were then extensively edited and revised by Mill and Harriet Taylor Mill together, in 1854 (her penciled notes are all over the manuscript) (John M. Robson and Jack Stillinger, "Introduction," *Collected Works of John Stuart Mill*, ed. J. M. Robson [Toronto: University of Toronto Press, 1963–], 1:xix–xxv). It was also extensively revised in 1861, two years after Harriet's death, at which point many of the more personal details were edited out (Robson and Stillinger, "Introduction," 1:xxv–xxvii). One effect of this is to make the *Autobiography* as published seem oriented a great deal more toward books, and away from personalities, than earlier versions. However, some of the revisions actually have the effect of concealing how strongly, in the 1851 version, Mill had identified himself with his experience as a reader. For example a notable passage in the 1851 manuscript, in which Mill boastfully compares himself to Plato, is revised into a general statement about the Platonic method for the 1873 edition (*Autobiography*, 24–25).

34. Mill, *Autobiography*, 44. This is reminiscent in some ways of Cobbett, for whom every natural detail he glimpses reminds him of some political debate raging at the time: crows look like unscrupulous bankers, starlings remind him of the royal pensioners who eat up the national budget, etc. William Cobbett, *Rural Rides* (1822–26; London: Penguin, 2001).

35. The correspondence with Carlyle provides another useful way to think about Mill's odd views of friendship and the role letters or printed matter could play in it. Carlyle regretted the fact that their friendship had to be carried on by letter: "We are so like two Spirits to one another, two Thinking-Machines" (Thomas Carlyle, letter to John Stuart Mill [September 24, 1833], in *Collected Works of John Stuart Mill*, ed. J. M. Robson [Toronto: University of Toronto Press, 1963–], 6:445). By contrast Mill, in his correspondence with Carlyle and with other friends, as well as in the *Autobiography*, sees letters and essays as the logical medium for forging a friendship; even a debate that takes place in articles published in rival journals he frequently depicts as a kind of friendly chitchat with a kindred spirit.

36. Mill, *Autobiography*, 46.

37. Mill, *Autobiography*, 47.

38. Mill, *Autobiography*, 103, 105.

39. Mill's attachment to the give-and-take of political magazines, for example, seems bound up with his interest in a medium that records indirect interactions even with one's intimates. His correspondence often records him writing to friends as if their latest articles had been personally addressed to him—and at times he tells correspondents that he does not see the need to say to them in a personal letter what he had already published in an article he presumes they have read.

40. Mill, *On Liberty*, 245.

41. Mill, *On Liberty*, 245.

42. Mill, *On Liberty*, 249.

43. I also analyze this passage in Plotz, "Antisocial Fictions."

44. Mill's *On Liberty*, like his *Autobiography* and *Utilitarianism*, was begun in the early 1850s, when Mill and Harriet both thought they had little time left to live, and then completed many years later. *On Liberty* came first, in 1859; *Utilitarianism* and *Considerations of Representative Government* followed in 1861; the *Autobiography* did not appear until after his death in 1873. "The death of Harriet, on 3 November, 1858 drove Mill to consider it [*On Liberty*] almost as a memorial to her that should never be altered by revision" (John M. Robson, "Textual Introduction," *Collected Works of John Stuart Mill*, ed. J. M. Robson [Toronto: University of Toronto Press, 1963–], 18:lxxxiii). For a reconstruction of the relationship that posits a yet stronger role for Harriet in composing the works of the 1850s, see Jo Ellen Jacobs, *Voice of Harriet Taylor Mill* (Bloomington: Indiana University Press, 2002).

45. Mill, *On Liberty*, 216.

46. Cf. Mill's more explicit discussion of the various technical and inspirational roles that she played in the composition of the book (*On Liberty*, 252–60). He is particularly explicit about the composition of *On Liberty*: "The *Liberty* was more directly and literally our joint production than anything else which bears my name, for there was not a sentence of it that was not several times gone through by us together, turned over in many ways, and carefully weeded of any faults. It is in consequence of this that, although it never underwent her final revision it far surpasses, as a mere specimen of composition, anything which has proceeded from me either before or since" (Mill, *On Liberty*, 257–59).

47. Mill, *On Liberty*, 259.

48. Mill, *On Liberty*, 259.

49. Loraine Daston and Peter Gallison, *Objectivity* (New York: Zone Books, 2007), 38–39.

50. Daston and Gallison also argue that this spawns a genre of apologia in which scientists boast of their capacity to will themselves absent from their own thoughts—or tearfully confess their moral weakness in remaining a meddling, too-subjective presence in their experiments.

51. Thomas Carlyle, letter to J. S. Mill (September 24, 1833), in *Collected Works of John Stuart Mill*, ed. J. M. Robson (Toronto: University of Toronto, 1963–), 6:445.

52. If one key overlooked component of Mill's liberalism may be precisely the weight that it places on the possibility of indirect emotional affiliation between seemingly disengaged subjects, then Mill's approach may have some links to the late Kantian idea of *Teilnehmung* (i.e., participation, rather than mere sympathy) that Kevin McLaughlin suggests is more present in Victorian thought than is generally acknowledged. Kevin McLaughlin, "Culture and Messianism: Disinterestedness in Arnold," *Victorian Studies* 50, no. 4 (Summer 2008): 615–39.

53. Cf. Catherine Gallagher, "George Eliot: Immanent Victorian," *Representations* 90 (2005): 61–74.

54. Cf. Barthes for an attempt to theorize a more complete withdrawal from ac-

tive conversation. Roland Barthes, *The Neutral: Lecture Course at the Collège de France (1977–1978)*, trans. Rosalind E. Krauss and Denis Hollier (New York: Columbia University Press, 2005). For an argument that the novel offers a novel linguistic form in which the speaker and the originator of speech are potentially unlocatable, see Anne Banfield, *Unspeakable Sentences: Narration and Representation in the Language of Fiction* (Boston: Routledge, 1982).

Reciting Alice

WHAT IS THE USE OF A
BOOK WITHOUT POEMS?

CATHERINE ROBSON

This essay approaches the topic of Victorian reading at a very elementary level and asks the following question: how might we begin to understand the relationship between the nineteenth century's dominant modes of literacy instruction and the structures of learners' minds? To narrow a potentially huge area of inquiry, I focus upon just one of the period's pedagogical practices, the memorization and recitation of poetry by young children; further, I explore the representation of this practice within a single text, *Alice's Adventures in Wonderland* (1865).[1]

Carroll's famous heroine has played the role of poster girl for a hundred and one burning issues in both Victorian and contemporary studies; for the purposes of this essay, she serves as an icon of the reciting child. While readers and critics have long enjoyed the verses Alice performs, analysis of *Wonderland*'s recitation scenes has rarely stretched beyond the poems' contents and the twists they inflict upon those of their source texts. Here I switch the emphasis from content to form; attention to the presence and function of verse in *Alice's Adventures in Wonderland,* I maintain, reveals the fundamental disciplinary importance of poetic structure to Victorian culture and subjectivities alike.

My argument proceeds along two main axes. First, the simple act of plac-

93

ing the *Alice* books in their correct formal genre is illuminating; *Wonderland* and *Through the Looking Glass* (1871) join a wide array of other texts that may be chiefly written in prose but find it impossible to keep poetry out of their pages. Second, I establish that the cultural omnipresence of such generic hybrids is unsurprising, given the key position of poetry in prevailing juvenile pedagogies. Restoring the history of verse memorization and recitation to the *Alice* books in particular and nineteenth-century life in general allows us to see that this mode of literacy instruction created not only different types of reading, but different kinds of readers altogether.

The recitation scenes in *Alice's Adventures in Wonderland* and *Through the Looking Glass* have long attracted critical comment. Florence Milner's essay "The Poems in *Alice in Wonderland*," published in 1903, inaugurated the investigation of the source texts of Carroll's parodies; others, most notably Elsie Leach, Donald Rackin, and Ronald Reichertz, have continued the work, widening the angle of approach to consider not only the specific targets of Carroll's wit, but the contours of didactic children's literature of the period more generally. The impetus behind these labors is straightforward: scholars explain that they are simply bringing back into view that which was in plain sight for the *Alice* books' first readers. Milner maintains that the originals of Carroll's verses had already dropped out of common currency just four decades after *Wonderland*'s first publication: "in order to search them out," she writes, "it has been necessary to beat the dust from many a forgotten volume in a library's unmolested corners."[2] Milner accounts for her recovery mission as follows.

> Those who read the book when it was first published found in it a delight which the child of today misses. Fifty years ago certain poems appeared in every reader and were read over and over again until the child was stupid indeed who did not unconsciously learn them by heart. . . . All the poems in *Alice in Wonderland* are parodies upon these familiar rhymes. Scattered lines of the poems cling to the minds of older people; they remember being once familiar with them; they recognise the metre and can sometimes repeat two or three opening lines, but the complete poem eludes them, and the author they probably never did know. The children of today do not know the verses at all, and as a parody ceases to be a parody without the original poem as a background, the trouble of gathering these originals seems worth while.[3]

The idea of the child's delight in perceiving the difference between what she had committed to memory and what she read in his book was important to Carroll: writing on the topic of possible translations of *Alice,* he worried that "the verses would be the great difficulty . . . if the originals are not known in France, the parodies would be unintelligible: in that case they had better be omitted."[4] The author may seem overanxious to us now (readers, young and old alike, appear perfectly capable of enjoying "How doth the little crocodile" and "You are old, Father William" without any knowledge whatsoever of the poems' originals), but editions such as Martin Gardner's *Annotated Alice* (1960) have ensured that scholars and enthusiasts, at least, have the source texts close at hand. Faced by the pious originals and Carroll's transgressive revisions, critics usually comment upon the grim potentialities of *Alice's* poems. James R. Kincaid, for instance, welcomes the vision they grant of "the darkest parts of Alice's mind."[5] As part and parcel of their attack upon the "anti-comic stuffiness and prudence" of poems by Isaac Watts, Robert Southey, and William Wordsworth,[6] the poems of the *Alice* books are deemed to deliver cruelty and killing, an emphasis upon devouring or being devoured.

To turn from the content of the poems—of either the originals, or the parodies—to the issue of their placement within both the text and Alice's experience is to embark, however, on a different kind of critical enterprise. There are three signal occasions in *Alice's Adventures in Wonderland* when the heroine attempts to produce the hard-earned fruits of her poetic education; I wish ultimately to argue that close analysis of these scenes allows us to retrieve traces of the lost discipline of pedagogical recitation, as it was felt in the mind and the body. But at this point in the investigation it is too early to cordon off Alice's three recited poems from all the other verses that are scattered through the pages of *Wonderland* and *Through the Looking Glass.* Alice herself confides to her kitten in the last chapter of this latter work that she has heard "such a quantity of poetry" in her long day's travail (*LG,* 217); although it would be misleading to describe the *Alice* books as primarily a collection of poems with a little prose inserted in and amongst, this exaggeration is of momentary use if it helps train our eyes on specifically formal issues. Exactly how do we register the push and pull between indented and nonindented text in these books? What, indeed, do we call a work that is written in both prose and verse? What kind of assumptions do we have about how such a work might behave, and for whom it might be intended?

These questions bear relations to numerous scholarly discussions. Much has been written about the interplay between verse and prose in the context of dramatic genres—most notably, in relation to the Shakespearean play, and the rank-laden question of who gets to speak which kind of language. In addition, analyses of those species of texts that tend to alternate between prose and poetry also exist: in recent years, historians of the book have directed increasing attention to the commonplace book, the miscellany, the magazine, and (perhaps of greatest relevance to *Alice*'s case) the anthology and educational reader. But the exact form of the *Alice* books—a continuous narrative that proceeds in both prose and verse—requires a more specialized categorization. Fortunately this strange beast, neither fish nor fowl, does indeed have a name, for there is a fabulous monster in the world of genre called the *prosimetrum:* a work, quite simply, that contains both prose and verse.[7] To classicists and medievalists, the prosimetrum is a familiar phenomenon, their favorite examples being, respectively, Menippean satire and *Aucassin et Nicolette,* a thirteenth-century French romance. There are some disagreements about its exact constitution—is the ratio of prose to verse important? does the poetry have to be original to the work to count?—but if these fine distinctions are disregarded, I believe that the prosimetrum is a general concept that deserves to be known and used more widely by literary scholars of other eras as well.

For Victorianists, a willingness to recognize the prosimetric yields interesting results, helping to shake up (particularly pedagogical) predilections for filing verse in one place and prose in another. We have long been familiar, of course, with habitual generic boundary straddlers, such as Thomas Hardy and Rudyard Kipling, who insist on forcing their way into courses on both the novel and poetry. We are also well attuned to those peculiar emanations of the mid-Victorian period, verse novels such as *Aurora Leigh, Idylls of the King,* and *The Ring and the Book,* or verse novellas like *Amours de Voyages* and *Modern Love.* But although such works make it plain that there is no chance of keeping the novel out of Victorian poetry, less attention has been paid to the fact that it is also impossible to keep poetry out of the Victorian novel—or, indeed, out of practically any text that could reasonably be called a novel since the very inception of the form, whenever this is dated.[8] Inasmuch as poetry has been part of everyday life, then it has also been part of the novel, the genre of everyday life.

Most immediately noticeable are the prefatory verses and poetic chapter epigraphs that often stand in appositional relationships to the vast swathes of prose that constitute a novel's bulk. But more interesting, perhaps, is the poetry in and among that prose, poetry in every imaginable form, and intro-

duced into the text for a dizzying variety of reasons. For the sake of conve-
nience, it is perhaps useful to divide the novel's interpolated poems into two
rough categories—on the one hand, we have the drafting of an extant, and
frequently deliberately recognizable, or attributed, poetic text into service; on
the other, the appearance of an original, or nonce, composition, often presented as springing from the fertile brain of a created character, or less commonly, a narrator. In other words, the novel gives us quoters and quotations,
and verse makers and verses, and in all cases, the material set forth on the
page can range from the most rarefied of sonnets to the lowest of ragtag
rhyming riddles.

Throughout the history of the novel, authors have rarely restricted themselves to one type of poetic interpolation or another. Daniel Defoe, for instance, provides a good example of a verse composition scene when a suitor
for the hand of Moll Flanders "pulls off his diamond ring, and writes upon
the glass of the sash . . . this line."

> *You I love, and you alone.*
> I read it [says Moll], and asked him to lend me the ring with which I
> wrote under it, thus:
> *And so in love says every one.*
> He takes his ring again, and writes another line thus:[9]

And so they continue, for another eight alternating lines of what Moll calls
"this poetic scribble,"[10] which is presented as created especially for the occasion. Just as likely, though, is she to quote another character's proverbial cou-
plet ("Where love is the case, / The doctor's an ass")[11] or share with us a cell-
mate's "piece of Newgate wit."

> If I swing by the string
> I shall hear the bell ring,
> And then there's an end of poor Jenny.[12]

Other eighteenth-century novelists are similarly eclectic in their inclusion of
the ready-to-wear and the bespoke. Samuel Richardson's Lovelace can barely
get through a letter to his friend Belford without a good ten or twelve of generally attributed lines from Howard, Otway, Cowley, Shakespeare, Milton, or
Dryden (this last his particular favorite); Clarissa, in her delirium, covers a
paper with scraps of verse from more or less the same group of writers.

Pamela, in contrast, is called a "pretty *rhimester*" and praised by Mr. B. for some "simple verses" of her own,[13] which she then proceeds to set down in her letter (that the verses were probably composed not by Richardson but by one of his circle adds further complexity to the mix). All in all, it is harder to find a prose narrative that never declares poetry's—or at least verse's—presence by those telltale indented passages than to call to mind novelists who have a positive mania for the prosimetrum. That other boundary straddler, Sir Walter Scott, is perhaps the prime example, the Scottish bard who finds more excuses than any other author to slip in a song, smuggle in a ballad, or sneak in a rhymed prophecy. Yet Jane Austen, too, will find occasion both to furnish lines from Pope, Gray, Thompson, and Shakespeare when she tells us that Catherine Morland had "read all such works as heroines must read to supply their memories with those quotations which are so serviceable and so soothing in the vicissitudes of their eventful lives,"[14] and to show us how the limited poetic gifts evident in Mr. Elton's "Courtship" charade are still sufficient to inspire Emma Woodhouse's moderate admiration and Harriet Smith's utter confusion. And the vast majority of novelists in the years between Austen and the *Alice* books are no less prone to the diverse pleasures and possibilities of the interpolated poem or versified interlude.

It is tempting to accumulate further examples, but I am sure the point about the prevalence of verse in novels is clear already. In addition, it should be more than apparent that juvenile literature had no special claim on prosimetrum in the years before *Alice's Adventures in Wonderland*. This is not to say, of course, that such literature did *not* make use of its opportunities: from *The History of Little Goody Two Shoes* of 1765,[15] which closes with verses composed extempore by a young gentleman affected by Margery's tomb, to the lines on the metamorphosis of the bee into an elephant that delight Lucy in Maria Edgeworth's *Harry and Lucy* in 1801,[16] storybooks that came into children's hands were highly likely to serve up some verse with their prose. Further, the ever-increasing vogue to package folk and fairy tales and fables specifically for children also ensured the prominence of the prosimetric: these genres' fondness for waxing poetical for curses, riddles, spells, and moments of high tension was as marked then as it is today ("Do what you can to get away, / Or you'll become the Giant's prey"; "Welcome, Beauty, banish fear / You are queen and mistress here").[17]

Religious and didactic literature also had a special investment in the form. Anyone who has endured the full course of Mrs. Sherwood's *History of the Fairchild Family* of 1818 will recall that each chapter sticks to a wearyingly reg-

ular form: a narrative of Lucy, Emily, and Henry's goings-on, or a tale recounted to them; then an apposite prayer, and then around four or five verses
of a similarly relevant hymn. As Rackin notes, the repeatedly reprinted
Fairchild Family is a particularly appropriate text to place alongside the *Alice*
books, for it seems highly likely that Carroll has this story and its tiresome
cousins in his sights, both in his general satire of "improving" moral literature
and on more specific occasions in his text. For example, when Alice behaves
according to the precepts of such works, because "she had read several nice
little stories about children who had got burnt, and eaten up by wild beasts,
and other unpleasant things, all because they *would* not remember the simple
rules their friends had taught them" (*W*, 5), the awful fate of Miss Augusta
Noble in Sherwood's tale may be front and center in her mind—the Miss Noble who "had a custom of playing with fire, and carrying candles about,
though Lady Noble had often warned her of the danger of this."[18]

Further, *The Fairchild Family* functions as an important source, or comparative, text for the *Alice* books because its hymn verses are frequently from
the pen of Isaac Watts, and sometimes directly from his volumes for children.
Indeed, on one of the rare occasions when the form of the book admits some
variation from its usual narrative/prayer/hymn sequence, we encounter the
first two stanzas of Watts's Divine Song 16, "Against Quarrelling and Fight-
ing," *within* the opening prose section. Lucy's doll, the innocent cause of
much mayhem in the Fairchild household, is the bone of contention between
the fractious siblings.

> Lucy tried to get the doll away from her brother; but Emily ran in between
> them, and the two sisters began to fight. Lucy bit Emily's arm, and Emily
> scratched her sister's face; and, if Mr. Fairchild had not run in and seized
> hold of them, I do not know what they would have done to each other; for,
> when Emily felt the bite, she cried out,
>   "I hate you! I hate you with all my heart, you ill-natured girl!"
> And Lucy answered,
>   "And I hate you too; that I do!"
> And they looked at each other as if what they said was true, too; for
> their faces were as red as fire, and their eyes full of anger. Mr. Fairchild
> took the doll away from Henry; and, taking a rod out of the cupboard, he
> whipped the hands of all the three children till they smarted again, saying:
>
>   "Let dogs delight to bark and bite,
>   For God has made them so;

Let bears and lions growl and fight,
   For 'tis their nature too:

But children, you should never let
   Such angry passions rise:
Your little hands were never made
   To tear each other's eyes."[19]

This episode from *The History of the Fairchild Family* is also useful here because it helps to crystallize an important point about the *Alice* books. Within Carroll's work, it is not just the fact of the prosimetric that is interesting, but rather the fact of the embedded parody—the presentation within prose of not just a poem, but a transformed poem, a version of something that we all know (or knew), something *altered* to suit its precise placement within the forward narrative flow. What the *Alice* books furnish, then, are examples of the crossing-over point of the extant poetic text and the nonce composition. Still more specifically, we are presented with the lampooning, for comedic purposes, of the morally improving literature that Alice has had to memorize in her lessons. Or, to put this another way, and to focus particularly on two of the three poems that Alice recites, we witness the transformation of a "Divine Song" into a secular song. Once again, medievalists have a name for something similar, or, rather, for exactly the opposite process—when religious lyrics were sung to worldly tunes, then the resultant pieces were known as *contrafacta*. Carroll could therefore be classified as an aficionado of a specialized form of reverse *contrafactified prosimetra*.

But whatever words we might choose to describe Carroll's practice, there are clear precursors. Richardson, once more, is a good source. Afflicted by low spirits, Pamela tells us that "remembering the 137th psalm to be affecting, [I] turned to it, and took the liberty to alter it somewhat nearer to my own case, as follows:

When sad I sat in Brandon-hall,
   All guarded round about,
And thought of ev'ry absent friend,
   The tears of grief burst out."[20]

And so on, for nine more verses. Or, if we are less concerned to find the rewriting of the divine, then there are numerous good examples of novels with embedded poetic parodies—though these are often parodies of generic types rather than specific originals. Who could forget Mrs. Leo Hunter's "Ode to an Expiring Frog" in *The Pickwick Papers*?[21] Yet even though earlier authors may give us something along these lines, it seems to me that the precise combination of prose and parodic poetry in *Alice's Adventures in Wonderland* and *Through the Looking Glass* achieves different and unprecedented effects, or rather, allows us to see with clarity something that other, similar, works only imply.

We turn, at last, to Lewis Carroll's texts. As already mentioned, the heroine's three recited poems in *Wonderland* join a wide variety of poetic flights in the *Alice* books. Interestingly enough, Alice also recites three times in *Through the Looking Glass:* there she repeats the three nursery rhymes, "Tweedledum and Tweedledee," "Humpty Dumpty," and "The Lion and the Unicorn," and on each occasion gets the words unfailingly correct. In addition to Alice's six recitations, other verses pop up in the two narratives under a broad range of pretexts; if we put to one side the prefatory, and in *Looking Glass*'s case, valedictory poems that frame the texts, there are still some fourteen further interpolated patches of poetry—verses that are presented variously as lullabies, songs, an explanatory history, courtroom evidence, a poem read in a book, recitation pieces, and riddles.[22] But the following fact, is, I think, important: while some of these stretches of verse are identifiable parodies, none of the speakers is castigated, as Alice is, for getting the words wrong. To this observation, it might seem logical to counter that in Wonderland, or through the looking glass, getting it wrong is getting it right—from this point of view, in singing or reciting nonsense variations of "Speak gently" or "Resolution and Independence," the Duchess and the White Knight are actually presenting verses congruent to their native habitats. (The closest thing to a criticism of his or her performance a *Wonderland* or *Looking Glass* character receives is when Alice meekly observes that she has "heard something like" the Mad Hatter's "Twinkle, twinkle, little bat" before [*W*, 54].) Alice, however, is held strictly accountable to her poetic originals both by herself and by the listening Wonderland characters, and thus she is judged to have delivered three failing recitations.

Let us examine exactly how this happens. For one thing, Carroll makes it clear that Alice doesn't just lapse into poetry in any casual or haphazard manner. As critics and readers have always noticed, we are aware of Alice's relation to books from the very first, and almost as quickly are we acquainted with her sense of herself as a model student. Falling down the rabbit hole, she begins to parrot her stock of schoolroom facts, both for her own pleasure at her accomplishment and because, the narrator implies, she identifies fully with the structures of her pedagogical training—"though this was not a *very* good opportunity for showing off her knowledge, as there was no one to listen to her, still it was good practice to say it over" (*W*, 3). After one surprising, not to say disturbing, experience follows another, Alice, in chapter 2, returns to the same storehouse of acquired information, but this time for an altogether more urgent reason. To prove to herself that she is still the same person she used to be (and not poor despised Mabel, who is both her academic and social inferior), Alice decides to "try if I know all the things I used to know" (*W*, 10). Multiplication goes badly; Geography no better; Poetry then follows as the ultimate testing ground of identity.

> ". . . I'll try and say '*How doth the little* —,' " and she crossed her hands on her lap as if she were saying lessons, and began to repeat it, but her voice sounded hoarse and strange, and the words did not come the same as they used to do:
>
> > "*How doth the little crocodile*
> >   *Improve his shining tail,*
> > *And pour the waters of the Nile*
> >   *On every golden scale!*
> >
> > "*How cheerfully he seems to grin,*
> >   *How neatly spreads his claws,*
> > *And welcomes the little fishes in,*
> >   *With gently smiling jaws!*
>
> "I'm sure those are not the right words," said poor Alice, and her eyes filled with tears as she went on, "I must be Mabel after all, and I shall have to go and live in that poky little house, and have next to no toys to play with, and oh, ever so many lessons to learn!" (*W*, 10–11)

On the next occasion when the question of her identity arises, Alice returns to the damning evidence of this deviant performance in her attempt to explain to the Caterpillar why she believes she has changed. Although she also mentions that she has been finding it hard to "keep the same size for ten minutes together," the Caterpillar is only interested in her statement that she " 'ca'n't remember things as I used.' "

"Ca'n't remember what things?" said the Caterpillar.

"Well, I've tried to say '*How doth the little busy bee*,' but it all came different!" Alice replied in a very melancholy voice. (*W*, 33)

It is this admission that prompts the obdurate grub to insist that Alice "'repeat "*You are old, Father William,*"'" which results in another incorrect performance.

"That is not said right," said the Caterpillar.

"Not *quite* right, I'm afraid," said Alice, timidly: "some of the words have got altered."

"It is wrong from beginning to end," said the Caterpillar, decidedly; and there was silence for some minutes. (*W*, 33–35)

A third and final loop is formed when Alice is asked to tell the Gryphon and the Mock Turtle about her adventures.

Her listeners were perfectly quiet till she got to the part about her repeating "*You are old, Father William,*" to the Caterpillar, and the words all coming different, and then the Mock Turtle drew a long breath, and said, "That's very curious!"

"It's all about as curious as it can be," said the Gryphon.

"It all came different!" the Mock Turtle repeated thoughtfully. "I should like to hear her try and repeat something now. Tell her to begin." He looked at the Gryphon as if he thought it had some kind of authority over Alice.

"Stand up and repeat '*'Tis the voice of the sluggard*,'" said the Gryphon.

"How the creatures order one about, and make one repeat lessons!" thought Alice. "I might just as well be at school at once." However, she got up, and began to repeat it, but her head was so full of the Lobster-Quadrille, that she hardly knew what she was saying; and the words came very queer indeed. (*W*, 80)

Once again, the Wonderland characters are highly critical of Alice's performance.

"That's different from what *I* used to say when I was a child," said the Gryphon.

"Well, *I* never heard it before," said the Mock Turtle; "but it sounds un-common nonsense."

Alice said nothing: she had sat down with her face in her hands, wondering if anything would ever happen in a natural way again. (*W,* 80)

In the interlinking of these three scenes, the narrative proceeds in the manner of a chain stitch in needlework—a reference back to a failed instance of identity-confirming recitation generates a demand for a new recitation, and thus further failure. It is a fascinating repeating structure, and certainly constitutes the most regular and firmly fused arrangement of prose and poetry that I have discovered in my investigation of the prosimetric. But back to Alice—the fact that the heroine, thanks to Carroll's brilliance, has on these three different occasions delivered up wickedly witty verses is neither here nor there to Alice or her Wonderland audiences. According to their lights, all she has retained of her education is the *literary form* of the poems, into which she has inserted these mangled contents.

In any investigation of what these scenes show, the fact that the opening and closing poems in the sequence are parodies of works by Isaac Watts is certainly important. The *Divine Songs* had long constituted the most widely disseminated series of verses for children. First published in 1715, the little book attracted interest from the first, gaining its greatest popularity in the period between 1775 and 1850; individual Watts poems also found themselves frequently co-opted into schoolroom anthologies, at least up until the middle of the nineteenth century.[23] For children from comfortable homes in this period, the *Divine Songs* stood unrivaled as their first texts for memorization, their first "lessons" to be learned by heart and "repeated" (this, not "recited," being the correct term in Britain for the activity in an educational context, as the *Alice* books clearly show). On occasion it appears that exposure to these little verses came before a child began to read. From the *Papers and Diaries of a York Family,* for instance, we learn the following of Margaret Gray's education, which started in the first decade of the nineteenth century: "As soon as she was able to speak, she was taught to commit to memory Dr. Watts' *Divine Songs for Children;* at the age of four she could read the Bible and repeat the Church Catechism; and from that period for some years she regularly committed to memory the Gospel for the day."[24]

Whether or not this child was unusually gifted is hard to ascertain, but the ordering of her first texts is nevertheless revealing. In the *Divine Songs'* "Preface to all that are concerned in the education of children," Watts emphasizes

the importance of the early introduction of his religious verses into the receptive minds of very small children. He appears to have considered it equally
appropriate for his verses to be spoken, or sung; to facilitate the latter, he
writes, he has "confined the verse to the most usual psalm tunes," and he
imagines children both "sing[ing] over" one of his Divine Songs "to themselves" and performing them "in the family" in "their daily or weekly wor-
ship."[25] The point of the poetic form, he stresses, is twofold. In the first place,
it makes the child's work fun: "There is something so amusing and entertaining in rhymes and metre, that will incline children to make this part of their
business a diversion."[26] In the second place, and more important, "what is
learnt in verse is longer retained in memory, and sooner recollected. The like
sounds, and the like number of syllables exceedingly assist the remembrance."[27] The goal, he insists, is secure installation. Far from picturing the
child picking up the book, and turning from her reading of one poem to another, Watts suggests as book-free a model of internalization as possible.

> You may turn their very duty into a reward, by giving them the privilege
> of learning one of these songs every week, if they fulfil the business of the
> week well, and promising them the book itself when they have learnt ten
> or twenty songs out of it.[28]

Only once the child has the verses in her head does she get to keep hold of the
book; Margaret Gray's memorization of the poems before she could read,
then, may well have been the normative model. In any eventuality, what is important here is the establishment of permanent presence, an unwavering
monitor to ward off evil, the potential that "an emptiness of mind" could
later on be filled by "the loose and dangerous sonnets of the age."[29] The
verses, states Watts, are to be "a constant furniture for the minds of children,
that they may have something to think upon when alone."[30] The religious
content of that furniture is of course of supreme importance to Watts, but
there are indications in his Preface that he is aware that versification has a
power in and of itself. "It may often happen," he writes, "that the end of a
song, running in the mind, may be an effectual means to keep off some temptations, or to incline to some duty when a word of scripture is not upon their
thoughts."[31] If the regular thump of chiming pious thoughts can trump even
Holy Writ itself as an effective deterrent, how then can one be sure exactly
where form ends and content begins? When children memorize poems, do
they internalize a shape or a meaning?

It would be inaccurate to credit Watts with the introduction of memorization and recitation as pedagogical methods; learning by rote has, if not a distinguished, then a long and persistent history in education the world over. Yet it is fair to say that his production of religious verses explicitly tailored in form and diction to the infant mind did inaugurate a new phase in juvenile instruction, a phase that would eventually see the memorized poem become a standard element of mass pedagogies in both Britain and the United States.[32] By that stage of the game, however, the *Divine Songs* themselves were for the most part so many dead letters. But at the time of the first publication of *Alice's Adventures in Wonderland,* Watts's poems still retained much of their longtime hold over a substantial tranche of middle- and upper-class nursery life. That these works were indeed part of the mind's "constant furniture" for the well-to-do from childhood and into adulthood is proved over and over again by the large numbers of parodies they inspired; when Carroll picked up his pen to mock the little busy bee, he was once again joining a well-established tradition. In the 1850s alone, *Punch* carried at least three burlesques —"How doth the ever busy wasp"; "How doth the busy Russian bee" (a particularly unfunny *jeu d'esprit* on the Crimean War); and "How doth the dizzy Disraeli"[33]—while in *Bleak House,* Harold Skimpole inveighed against the "overweening assumptions" of the bee, "buzzing about the world," making "such a merit of his tastes."[34] Dickens had already stolen the march on Carroll when it came to the interpolated parody as well, for in the previous decade's *Old Curiosity Shop,* Miss Monflathers, schoolmistress to genteel young ladies, had proved herself to be, if not an inspired improviser, at least well-attuned to social distinctions.

"The little busy bee," said Miss Monflathers, drawing herself up, "is applicable only to genteel children.

"In books, or work, or healthful play"

is quite right as far as they are concerned; and the work means painting on velvet, fancy needle-work, or embroidery. In such cases as these," pointing to Nell, with her parasol, "and in the case of all poor people's children, we should read it thus:

'In work, work, work. In work alway
    Let my first years be past,
That I may give for ev'ry day
    Some good account at last.' "[35]

Closest to Carroll in intent, however, is an Emily Dickinson poem written in 1852; literally enlisting the contents of her education, "Sic transit gloria mundi" delivers a brilliant attack on prevailing pedagogical exercises. I quote the first four lines only, but each stanza is formed by the same nonsensical juxtaposition of isolated lines from Dickinson's schoolroom experiences.

> "Sic transit gloria mundi,"
>   "How doth the busy bee,"
> "Dum vivimus vivamus,"
>   "I stay my enemy!"[36]

But by embedding his parody of Watts's poem in a prosimetric narrative that both stages and critiques the act of recitation, Carroll makes the point still more forcefully: *Alice's Adventures in Wonderland* demonstrates that when pedagogical systems installed rhymed and rhythmic poems within children, they did not only, and perhaps did not primarily, install content, or meaning, into their heads. They also installed shapes, the *forms* of poetry; and just as the pages of the *Alice* books are laid out according to the diverse arrangements of prose and verse, so the mind of a child, trained in this manner, received the structure of verse, as well as the pattern of prose, deep down inside.

At the same time that Charles Dodgson was first telling the stories that were to become *Alice's Adventures in Wonderland*, Robert Lowe, the chairman of Britain's Committee of Council on Education, began implementing a series of measures that would ultimately ensure that the memorization and recitation of poetry became for many years a mandatory part of the lives of millions of children in Britain. But while the empire of the memorized poem came to spread in this way beyond the realm of the privileged classes, the selection of works recited in the classroom shifted away from the juvenile standards that Carroll's book had so deftly mocked. The practice that Alice performs ultimately became entirely familiar to a mass population; the originals of the poems she parodied did not. Over the Atlantic, pedagogical recitation held a secure foothold in thousands and thousands of schoolhouses across the United States long before and after the two *Alices* were published; "reciting" the passages of text one had committed to memory from the textbook constituted the standard practice of "learning" most subjects in the curriculum anyway, but regularly in the school week, usually on a Friday afternoon, the memorized text was a poem.[37] And thanks to the runaway success of a

limited number of school readers, tremendous numbers of children were exposed to exactly the same passages of text and thus learned by heart the same
poems, again and again and again. The most successful series, the McGuffey
brothers' *Eclectic Readers,* sold some 122 million copies between 1836 and
1920, and thus formed a hugely important educational and cultural phenomenon.[38] And what poems did they present to generations of children across
the expanding nation? A certain work by Robert Southey about an aged gentleman appeared in early editions, but did not hold its place for very long;[39] a
scrap of Watts makes it into Lesson 47, "Advantages of Industry," in the *New
Fourth Reader* of 1866, not as a stand-alone poem for recitation, but in this
prosimetric combination.

> But perhaps some child who reads this, asks, "Does God notice little chil-
> dren in school?" And if you are not diligent in the improvement of your
> time, it is one of the surest evidences that your heart is not right with God.
> You are placed in this world to improve your time. In youth, you must be
> preparing for future usefulness. And if you do not improve the advantages
> you enjoy, you sin against your Maker.

> With books, or work, or healthful play,
>   Let your first years be past;
> That you may give, for every day,
>   Some good account, at last.[40]

Although the educational justifications for poetry recitation in the classroom underwent numerous shifts over the decades, the practice continued for
many years in Britain, with a remarkably unchanging selection of poems, until measures introduced by the 1944 Education Act brought its mass application to an end. In the United States, the memorized poem held sway for a little longer. And the practice has still not died out altogether: when I ask my
undergraduate classes who can recite a poem memorized at school, a fair
number of hands are raised. In Britain today fewer children undergo the experience, but thanks to the efforts of a minority of diehard teachers on two sides
of the Atlantic, poetry recitation—especially at the primary, or elementary,
school level—still persists. Ironically enough, one of the poems that seems especially popular as a text for memorization these days begins like this.

'Twas brillig, and the slithy toves
    Did gyre and gimble in the wabe

All mimsy were the borogoves
    And the mome rathes outgrabe. (LG, 117)

Yet because large numbers of Britons and Americans are no longer trained in early childhood to internalize rhymed and rhythmic material as a matter of course, apprehension of some aspects of the *Alice* books cannot be immediate. These readers must now reconstruct after the fact what the stories tell us about the place of recitation in the everyday life of the Victorians.

Not so long ago, I was having dinner with a guest speaker at my university; three of my companions happened to be from India, academics who had come to the United States for their graduate education and then stayed. In the course of the evening, I was asked what I was working on: "Children and recitation," I replied. Barely were the words out of my mouth before the three Indians, without looking at each other, gripped their hands together in front of their bodies at midchest height, threw back their shoulders, and held their heads erect. "What are you doing?" I asked. "That's what you do when you recite a poem at school," said Parama. And as I looked at them, still holding their hands locked in that automatic gesture summoned up from their Indian classrooms of thirty, forty years ago, I remembered that Carroll also happens to show us that recitation is a bodily pose as much as a mental exercise.

> "I'll try and say '*How doth the little* —,'" and she crossed her hands on her lap. (*W*, 10)

> "Repeat '*You are old, Father William*,'" said the Caterpillar.
> Alice folded her hands, and began. (*W*, 33)

These are small enough moments in the text, but for all that, they take us back vividly to the lost quotidian, the endlessly repeated minutiae of everyday experience that seem too insignificant to be set down in any kind of formal manner, but that can become irretrievable when the practice that prompts them falls out of fashion. I have read countless sentences of exhortatory instruction in elocution manuals and prefaces to schoolroom readers about what we might call the high style of declamatory gesture—the management of the eyebrows for satirical effect, the throwing out of the arm for moments of intense drama—but no one thinks to comment in these texts on the simple practice of having children cross their hands if sitting, or fold them if standing, for everyday recitations at school or at home.[41] Confirming that this is the kind of snippet of information that must be found in the storehouse of living memory rather than on the printed page, a Lewis Carroll society member mentioned some twenty years ago that he had discussed the recitation "passages with a retired primary school headmaster . . . who confirmed" the accuracy of these representations.[42] Of course it is common sense to lock those hands down—Watts makes it clear in the "little busy bee" poem that "Satan finds some mischief" for them otherwise—but it is precisely the common detail that is most likely to drop out of the historical record.

By repeatedly presenting Alice's recourse to what her education has given her, Carroll shows that he is acutely aware that a child's mind is a constructed entity. And while the destabilizing tendencies of Wonderland, which afflict Alice's interior as profoundly as they affect her exterior being, make merry with what she has learnt, forcing already arbitrary assemblages of facts and figures into ever more ridiculous combinations, it is noticeable that the shapes and structures of her acquired stock of knowledge remain with her. Alice may not be able to reproduce the content of the poem she memorized, but with her hands crossed in her lap she will reproduce its form. The song remains the same, though the words may alter. The tune, we learn in *Through the Looking Glass*, is never our own invention. With the passing of the pedagogical drills of early childhood memorization and recitation, many of us have lost not only the ability to recognize the old standards of the nursery or the classroom, but also any easy way of connecting to the states of mind and body created by these practices. The three recitation scenes in *Alice's Adventures in Wonderland* allow us to see that the educational practices of the past created vast numbers of properly prosimetric individuals—selves that were structured according to the forms of poetry as well as prose.

NOTES

1. Lewis Carroll, *Alice's Adventures in Wonderland* (1865; New York: Bantam Classic, 1981). This and *Through the Looking Glass* (1871; New York: Bantam Classic, 1981) are hereafter abbreviated *W* and *LG*, and cited in the text.

2. Florence Milner, "The Poems in Alice in Wonderland," in *Aspects of Alice: Lewis Carroll's Dreamchild as seen through the Critics' Looking-Glasses, 1865–1971*, ed. Robert Phillips (New York: Vanguard Press, 1971), 252.

3. Milner, "The Poems in Alice in Wonderland," 245–46.

4. Quoted in Donald Rackin, "Corrective Laughter: Carroll's *Alice,* and Popular Children's Literature of the Nineteenth Century," *Journal of Popular Culture* 1 (1967): 243.

5. James R. Kincaid, "Alice's Invasion of Wonderland," *PMLA* 88 (1973): 96.

6. Kincaid, "Alice's Invasion of Wonderland," 96.

7. *Prosimetrum: Cross-Cultural Perspectives on Narrative in Prose and Verse* (Suffolk: D. S. Brewer, 1997), a collection of essays edited by Joseph Harris and Karl Reichl, offers a useful starting point for further exploration.

8. Tricia Lootens addressed this topic in her keynote lecture for the Victorian Institute's conference on the "Nine Lives of Victorian Poetry" at the University of North Carolina, Greensboro, Spring, 2005. Leah Price also makes a brief mention of the difficulty of taking seriously "the hackneyed scraps of verse that litter eighteenth- and nineteenth-century novels" (*The Anthology and the Rise of the Novel* [Cambridge: Cambridge University Press, 2000], 2).

9. Daniel Defoe, *Moll Flanders* (1722; London: Penguin, 1989), 125.

10. Defoe, *Moll Flanders,* 65.

11. Defoe, *Moll Flanders,* 90.

12. Defoe, *Moll Flanders,* 351.

13. Samuel Richardson, *Pamela* (1740; Harmondsworth: Penguin, 1985), 514.

14. Jane Austen, *Northanger Abbey* (1817; Harmondsworth: Penguin, 1972), 39.

15. Anon., *The History of Little Goody Two Shoes* (1765; London: T. Carnan and F. Newbery, 1777).

16. Maria Edgeworth, *Harry and Lucy* (1801; Boston: Cummings and Hilliard, 1813).

17. Examples of such couplets abound in volumes published in the mid-Victorian period. For these specific instances, see James Orchard Halliwell-Phillips, *Popular Rhymes and Nursery Tales* (London: J. R. Smith, 1849), 65, and Robert Dudley, Thomas Bolton, Walter George Mason, and William Luson Thomas, eds., *Old Nursery Tales and Popular Stories* (London: Ward, Lock, and Tyler, 1869), 14.

18. Mary Martha Sherwood, *The History of the Fairchild Family* (1818; London: J. Hatchard, 1818), 155.

19. Sherwood, *The History of the Fairchild Family,* 53–54.

20. Richardson, *Pamela,* 179.

21. Alas, given the 1885 publication date of *The Adventures of Huckleberry Finn,* we cannot count in any search for antecedent works the morbid effusions of Mrs. Hunter's poetic heiress Emmeline Grangerford.

22. Here is a rapid summary of the other verses and the circumstances of their appearances in the *Alice* books. In *Wonderland,* the mouse tells his tale "Fury said to / a mouse"; the Duchess sings a lullaby ("Speak roughly"); the Mad Hatter recounts his singing of "Twinkle, twinkle, little bat!"; the Mock Turtle sings "Will you walk" and "Beautiful soup"; the White Rabbit reads "The Queen of Hearts" and "They told me" in court. In *Through the Looking Glass,* Alice reads "Jabberwocky" in a book; Twee-

dledee recites "The Walrus and the Carpenter"; Humpty Dumpty recites "In winter when the fields are white"; the White Knight recites "An aged, aged man"; the Red Queen sings a lullaby ("Hush-a-by lady"); the verses of "To the Looking-Glass world" are sung by "a shrill voice" at the banquet, with "hundreds of voices" joining in for the chorus (*LG*, 208); the White Queen tells a rhymed riddle ("First, the fish must be caught").

23. See Ian Michael, *The Teaching of English* (Cambridge: Cambridge University Press, 1987), 167–69.

24. Cited in Amy Cruse, *The Englishman and His Books in the Early XIXth Century* (London: G. G. Harrap, 1930), 75.

25. Isaac Watts, *Divine and Moral Songs* (1715; Derby: T. Richardson, Friar-Gate; London: Hurst, Chance, 1829), ix.

26. Watts, *Divine and Moral Songs,* viii.

27. Watts, *Divine and Moral Songs,* viii.

28. Watts, *Divine and Moral Songs,* viii.

29. Watts, *Divine and Moral Songs,* ix.

30. Watts, *Divine and Moral Songs,* ix.

31. Watts, *Divine and Moral Songs,* viii.

32. For an account of the progress of the memorized poem in mass British and American educational systems, see part 1 of my *Heart Beats: Everyday Life and the Memorized Poem* (Princeton: Princeton University Press, forthcoming).

33. Reprinted in Walter Hamilton, ed., *Parodies of the Works of English and American Authors* (London: Reeves and Turner, 1884–89), 207. *Punch* published these anonymous contributions on September 25, 1852; October 10, 1857; and June 19, 1858.

34. Charles Dickens, *Bleak House* (1853; London: Penguin, 1996), 116.

35. Charles Dickens, *The Old Curiosity Shop* (1840–41; London: Penguin, 2000), 73.

36. This version of the poem appears in *Letters of Emily Dickinson,* ed. Mabel Loomis Todd (Boston: Roberts Brothers, 1984), 1:140. Angela Sorby has an enlightening discussion of the work in her *Schoolroom Poets: Reading, Recitation and Childhood in America, 1865–1917* (Lebanon, NH: University of New England Press, 2005), 141, 159.

37. See Sorby, *Schoolroom Poets,* passim; Joan Shelley Rubin, "'Listen, My Children': Modes and Functions of Poetry Reading in American Schools, 1800–1850," in *Moral Problems in American Life: New Perspectives on Cultural History,* ed. Karen Halttunen and Lewis Perry (Ithaca: Cornell University Press, 1998), 261–83, and Joan Shelley Rubin, "'They Flash upon That Inward Eye': Poetry Recitation and American Readers," in *Reading Acts: U.S. Readers' Interaction with Literature, 1800–1950,* ed. Barbara Ryan and Amy Thomas (Knoxville: University of Tennessee Press, 2002), 259–80.

38. See Joel Spring, *The American School, 1642–1985: Varieties of Historical Interpretation of the Foundations and Development of American Education* (New York: Longman, 1986), 141.

39. I have been unable to establish whether the McGuffey brothers chose to drop

"You are old, Father William" because *Alice's Adventures in Wonderland* had brought the poem into disrepute.

40. W. H. McGuffey, ed., *The New Fourth Eclectic Reader* (Cincinnati: Wilson, Hinkle, 1866), 155.

41. My article, "Standing on the Burning Deck: Poetry, Performance, History," pays attention to the bodily dimension of poetry recitation, focusing particularly on the ways in which children may have responded physically to the experience of performing under duress; my *Heart Beats: Everyday Life and the Memorized Poem* considers questions of habitus more generally. Catherine Robson, "Standing on the Burning Deck: Poetry, Performance, History," *PMLA* 120 (2005): 148–62; Robson, *Heart Beats*.

42. Quoted in Selwyn H. Goodacre, "A Quizzical Look at *Alice's Adventures in Wonderland*," *Jabberwocky* 2 (1982): 35.

Over Worked, Worked Over

A POETICS OF FATIGUE

HERBERT F. TUCKER

Poetic fatigue, within the nineteenth-century tradition, comes in waves.[1] So does its obvious but also defining opposite, poetic afflatus. The complementarity between the two was a theme that Victorian poets embraced—exhaustion as exhilaration's telos, high purpose broken down into depressive ennui—because, I shall argue here, these complementary terms offered a coordinate system on which to plot the sensations that poets aimed to induce in readers. Behold William Morris stretched out, on a lounge chair of his own design, apologizing for *The Earthly Paradise* (1868–70) in borrowed drag as the "idle singer" of a modern day that is as empty as it is long. "I have no power to sing" (line 1), he confides, not even about "The heavy trouble, the bewildering care / That weighs us down" (lines 15–16); "rather," Morris advises the reader, "when aweary of your mirth" consult this poem for "a tale not too importunate / To those who in the sleepy region stay, / Lulled" (lines 8, 26–28).[2] The languid modesty of all this makes it most improbable that Morris should ever have bestirred himself to write, as in point of fact he had just done with efficiency and stamina, one of the longest poems in the English language. His prefatory posture of enervation, we suspect, merely belonged to a formula that underlay what success a nineteenth-century best seller like *The Earthly Paradise* might strive to enjoy: Work hard to make it look easy.

Poets who disdained such a formula did so at their risk, which is why if we

114

want to find the contrary to such studied easefulness—creative initiative, confessed in full rippling surge—we must seek it among the century's market-shy nonstarters: Robert Browning, for example, beside himself with the thrill of embarking on *The Ring and the Book;* or the relentlessly pulsing advances of A. C. Swinburne's amorous "Anactoria."[3] Behind these and other Victorian enthusiasts gleams what is the *locus romanticus* for bardic estrus in conception: Samuel Taylor Coleridge's would-be rock-star cynosure, the poet planted on the ground zero of a fantasized public outcry. "Beware! beware! / His flashing eyes, his floating hair!" (lines 49–50).[4] Hot stuff, and just about as designedly hot as Morris's stanzas are designedly cool. To test this rough estimate of thermal parity calls for, not the anachronism of stroboscope or oscilloscope, but the humbler measure of a Victorian metronome. For, be it zing or yawn, what we would gauge in the poets' mood is wave output. The undulations of flashing eyes and floating hair, gone acoustic and vocal in the spell-casting chant "Beware!" meet their match in the purling drawl of Morris's idler, who also had rhythm on the brain, albeit quite differently cadenced: "Why should I strive to set the crooked straight? / Let it suffice me that my murmuring rhyme / Beats with light wing" (lines 23–25).

In the currency of verse these two passages express complementary, high and low degrees of a heat that flowed along literary channels parallel to the nineteenth century's feats of caloric measurement in engineering and physics. The Victorian provers of cannon and casters of heavy equipment, and in their wake those dauntless theorists of thermodynamic entropy whose imagination plumbed subvisible matter all the way down to the shimmering of atoms, bequeathed to posterity not only the BTU but also a conceptual predisposition to think about that Victorian coinage *energy* (which only gradually superseded the earlier favorite *heat*) in terms of frequency and amplitude of oscillation. From steel poured at the mill to silver electroplated onto the soup spoon: their studies back then of metal fatigue provide an entrée for our study now of *mental* fatigue, which is the kind in which Victorian poets took preponderant interest.[5]

That poetry might entail hard work—not just the craftsmanlike, Ben Jonsonian writing of verse, but the prestige-accruing, elite-distinguishing, honorific *reading* of it as well—is an idea whose all-but-modernist time had come once Hopkins sprung rhythm from its padded cell and the Browning Societies started convening to probe their great pretender's elliptical monodramas for hidden truth.[6] But the idea behind those developments of the 1880s had been

surprise / reorientation of perspective

in incubation for a long while. They ratified anticipations that were half a century old, to look no further back than Browning's early work from the 1830s,[7] or, what the ostentatious difficulty of that work can occlude, the steepening curve of challenge on which even popular poets like Elizabeth Barrett Browning and Alfred Tennyson embarked when upgrading their legacy from Lord Byron, Felicia Hemans, and Letitia Landon, who had ruled the market in which the first Victorians came of authorial age. As Tennyson and Barrett Browning—the two figures who will chiefly occupy us here—raised to a new level the demand that mainstream Victorian poetry placed on its reader, they had to learn pretty fast, if they weren't to lose that reader, something that it took Robert Browning much longer to figure out: how to cushion the rise in difficulty with a matching rise in facilities and service.

This meant, in the first instance, acknowledging that the mental fatigue which the newly difficult modern poetic induced was a reality; that it entrained an affect of lassitude which, in contradistinction to old-fashioned Sensibility-era indolence, resulted from the very expenditure of effort that modern attentiveness exacted. Not just Tennyson's Mariana but her 1830 reader might well have become "aweary, aweary" by the time the poetic day was done,[8] and "the slow clock ticking" in the final stanza had topped off a sense-engrossing hyperaesthesia that was a far cry either from the adroitly lubricated clichés in which Hemans dealt or, on a distant other hand, from the diverting variety show lately broadcast by *Don Juan* (1819–24) or Tom Moore's sitcom *Fudge Family* (1818). The confession of weariness into which Mariana's refrains run down also speaks for the reader, who has shared with her an exhausting immersion in details that require the fullest attention if the poem is to be properly read at all. This obligatory fixture and dilation of mind were the reverse of tiresome, as readers have attested ever since Arthur Henry Hallam and John Stuart Mill first hailed Tennyson's achievement on the spot.[9] Still, by defaulting on the narrative incentives that a more ordinary ballad-based tetrameter poem of the era might have offered, the technique of mere dwelling on images does have a way of tiring the imagination out. Precisely because the details of "Mariana" are so enigmatic in their import, they remain relentlessly sensuous in presentation. Precisely because they don't mean but are, their brilliant procession fatigues that virtual body-in-the-mind which it is the privilege of verse to exercise.

7   This generic point is so nearly axiomatic as to defy proof, but its assertion can at least be clarified by reference to verse's defining opposite, prose. Few will deny that reading 1830s Carlyle is a lot like having your brain pummeled,

or that reading 1830s Dickens is a lot like having it tickled. By common testimony we laugh heartily, and bodily, at the latter; and I for one have known
the former's angular and labyrinthine English to call forth, from out my
reader's crouch over the book, twists and hearkenings of a body-English
worked up in aid of the mind's effort to follow some Teufelsdröckhian articulation home. What happens in reading verse, though, is different in kind
from these frankly physical responses to textual content (which is the com-
modity that the prose vehicle as such is charged to deliver).[10] It is poetry's
special charge to *perform* its meaning, to *incarnate* what it declares, in a pros-
thetic verbal physique compounded through the multisensory appeal that
imagery and prosody make to the inward eye and ear and tongue. The
artificiality of poetic language per se throws into relief the peculiarly virtual
nature of the embodiment it effects, and thus the quota of mental energy that
we expend in helping to bring the somatic illusion on and keep it up.

The physical properties of the verse medium will never let us forget—as
all told it is the prose fictionist's or essayist's business to make us forget—the
brokerage of the signifier. Precisely because it is more insistently mediated
than the prose sentence or paragraph, the poetic line or stanza is more immediately present to consciousness, which therefore includes a derivative, accompanying awareness of the mind's cooperative role in eliciting that partial
imaginative faith which Coleridge named the "willing suspension of disbelief."[11] Witness again Mariana, who in that moated grange of hers *does* next to
nothing, 24/7; nothing, that is, except move, at metered pace, through a world
of intense percepts coextensive with those that the reader of Tennyson's
poem, in perceiving, half-creates. What is this constitutive negotiation like?
Mariana tells us and tells us: "I would that I were dead!" "Oh God that I were
dead!" It's murder out there, she cries; and, if we have risen adequately to the
poem's occasion, before long the strain on our attention gives a tolerable idea
of what she is talking about.

It was all very well for Blake to announce that he would not cease from
mental fight.[12] Like Browning he was an artist who gave no quarter in the attention wars, and for cutting readers no slack both poets paid the stiff career
price of going largely unread. Tennyson knew better. Ever reader-solicitous,
he knew what it was to grow "half sick of shadows": the Lady of Shalott
(1832), sick and tired of gazing at the "mirror clear / That hangs before her all
the year," crumples under the sustained effort of imagination itself (lines 71,
47–48). She grows sick, I would propose, *because* she grows tired: laid low by
the curiosity-fatigue that besets the detail-oriented, all the more so in cases

like hers—or Browning's Andrea del Sarto (1855), or notoriously Tennyson himself from an early age—where the cursed gift of a superlative artisanal fluency frees technique to run itself, more or less, and accordingly consigns the artist mind to all but unremitting absorption in the image before it. A good part of Tennyson's signature melancholia in the early collections may be more primally an expression of the fatigue such immersion brought on. Thus Oenone (1832) is "all aweary of my life" (line 32), the eternally vigilant Hesperides can hardly chant themselves awake, and Saint Simeon Stylites (1842) must "clamour, mourn and sob" (line 6) because after all those years on the pedestal he is dead beat. "O well for the fisherman's boy, / That he shouts with his sister at play" ("Break, Break, Break," lines 5–6); and, while the salty tykes are at it nearby, matters are no better further offshore: "O well for the sailor lad, / That he sings in his boat on the bay!" (lines 7–8). These peripheral distractions, as drillingly continuous in their claim on attention as the progress of "the stately ships" that never do stop their ongoing goings-on (line 9), are enough to drive a poet crazy.

Reading early Tennyson is like eavesdropping on the autumnal spirit who haunts the year's last hours in his exquisite lyric of 1830.

> A spirit haunts the year's last hours
> Dwelling amid these yellowing bowers:
>   To himself he talks;
> For at eventide, listening earnestly,
> At his work you may hear him sob and sigh
>   In the walks;
>   Earthward he boweth the heavy stalks
> Of the mouldering flowers:
> Heavily hangs the broad sunflower
>   Over its grave i' the earth so chilly;
> Heavily hangs the hollyhock,
>   Heavily hangs the tiger-lily.
>   ("Song" [1830], lines 1–12)

For all his sobbing and sighing, this garden-dweller knows Adam's curse, that we must labor to be beautiful: "at his work" is where we find him. No Sensibility loiterer he—although at first glance he looks like one—the spirit assumes the classic posture of Victorian attentiveness: "listening earnestly." Each of its words nearly the other's anagram, the phrase hovers in patterned stasis between competing syntactic attachments, to the described spirit and to

the addressed reader, "him" and "you," for both persons are absorbed in parallel toils of minding. Much as the spirit "boweth the heavy stalks / Of the
mouldering flowers" (lines 7–8), so we imagine him bowing, also, to the un-
ending task of care renewal. And we may imagine this the more readily by
hunkering down sympathetically too over the text, bent on what we, listening
earnestly for our part, may glean of Tennyson's delicate, heartbroken music.
No, wait a minute, it's not real *work*, we may say, shaking off the spell, sitting
up straight, rubbing a stiff neck and looking about us. Yet it is work, all the
same, albeit work that is at most accidentally connected to occupational sco-
liosis. Poetry's work for the participant spirit is, again, virtual rather than
practical; it is the imaginative posturing we engage in for beautiful verses'
sake, and on their literally disembodied but figurally hypersensuous grounds.
Among the considerations that earned Tennyson the laureateship were his
conviction that these were the grounds of Victorian poetic art, his recognition that cultivating beauty was a tough row to hoe, and his solicitude to accommodate us just as we get to the point, in a poem of any length that has
achieved a modern intensity, where we could really use a break, break, break.

That Tennysonian trademark repetition leads to the next division of my
topic, which is what the Victorian poet, having acknowledged the ingredience
of mental fatigue within the experience of reading, might do about it in practice. Why, *be very interesting*, runs an unconsidered first response; yet on second thought this panacea for imaginative fatigue proves no more useful than
T. S. Eliot's feline advice to the method-hunting critic to *be very intelligent*.[13]
Just ordinary intelligence, trained on experience, will show that a poet's being
very interesting will not in fact suffice to keep drowsy reader-emperors
awake. The time comes when we want, instead of something that's more interesting, or interesting in a new way, something that's other than interesting.
The strain of too much or too prolonged an interest, after all, is what tires us
out. What the reader actually needs is to have fatigue not just acknowledged
but treated; and that means, since it is poetry we are talking about, to have fatigue anticipated in the flexion of the verse. A tall order, yet the good news is
that it's an order traditional verse is ideally suited to fill. The multiply repeti-
tive effect that is constituted by stanzaic conformity, echoing rhyme, alliteration, the rise and fall of metric pattern, and, surmounting that pattern, the
rule-constrained play of rhythmic variation from it, forms a complex weave
of recurrence on which Victorian poets were quick to seize for the purposes
of attention control.

Not compulsion, mind you, just control. The tissue of Victorian verse in-
corporates a calisthenic of focus and relaxation, study and recess—or, to get
a bit ahead of ourselves, labor and leisure[14]—without whose permissive in-
termittency the length to which Victorian poetry often ran would make it
quite unreadable. There has long been talk of poetic justice, but thankfully
there is also such a thing as poetic mercy. Splitting the difference, we might
call it poetic equity, a bar to which the Victorian reader's appeal was not made
in vain. The equity of fatigue poetics works like this: against a concentrated
imperative to attract and rivet the mind it balances a relieving impulse to let
the mind go; a process without whose reciprocation of catch and release we
would all lose our grip in no time.[15] It's the same in the library as at the gym:
execute, recover, repeat. The regimen that keeps us in Hygieia's good books
rules poetry books too. Exert a muscle (or, by analogy: lock onto a receptive
neural configuration), hold it, and then give it a rest. Omit that rest, and you
will find it visited on you anyhow, with an unwelcome awkwardness; for what
a posture overstrained or mental content held too long leads to is that wob-
ble by which muscles or minds rise up, against the will, to get their own back.
Even once physical overexertion has ended, a residual twitch will often set in:
this isn't so much a protest against abuse as it is an act of restitution in the
making. By a trivial yet authentic version of processes on which trauma studies have shed a welcome light, the body quivering with after-exertion under-
goes a disorderly, jagged, but equitable performance of the proper sequence
of effort and remission that was denied it, but that it still needs to have had.[16]
Respite yourself or grind away and spite yourself: the choice is yours. But
shudder you must.

As the muscles, so the Muses, when we look to the complex of reciprocation that is verse embodiment. The cresting, troughing wave of attention fatigue being inevitable, the poets' art rehearses that wave, over the comfort
threshold then under, and then over and under again, bestowing upon it an
ordering form and pressure that make it, not just tolerable, but a source of
positive pleasure. Ask William Wordsworth about the efficacy of meter "in
tempering and restraining the passion by an intertexture of ordinary feeling";
nay, ask his deep-inhaling sidekick Coleridge in the *Biographia Literaria*
about verse's "medicated" atmosphere.[17] Prosodists don't call stress *stress* for
nothing; indeed, they might as well, on good Victorian premises, go further
and call prosody itself *stress management*. So central is the pleasure of managed verse recurrence—entailing not the abolition of fatigue, which cannot

be, but fatigue-maintenance, which had better be—that at times a poet will
thematize tiredness itself for sheer joy.

> There is sweet music here that softer falls
> Than petals from blown roses on the grass,
> Or night-dews on still waters between walls
> Of shadowy granite, in a gleaming pass;
> Music, that gentlier on the spirit lies,
> Than tired eyelids upon tired eyes.
>
> (lines 46–51)

That's Tennyson again, in the opening lines of the Choric Song from "The Lotos-Eaters" (1832), a vigorous farewell to vigor whose long-winded vow of silence is paradoxical in a manner wholly consistent with the self-regulatory
poetics of fatigue I am trying to illuminate.[18] Given three similes here for the
easy-listening soundtrack that pervades Lotos Land, the third time proves the
charm, because in it the plushest orchestration is confected from the fewest
elements of sound. In the last two lines the quick ingratiating click of a cou-
plet, as against deferred quatrain rhyme in the lines before, is part of the
scheme to please, but only part. Feel, besides, how the tongue fitting snugly
against the lid of the mouth in "gentlier" relaxes but only to come right back
for more of the same in "spirit lies," and then how the phonemes of this latter
phrase return, lightly tossed, in the middle of the next line. "Spirit lies": "eye-
lids up-." Again the anagrammar of phonemic recombination, like "listening
earnestly" in the 1830 "Song," pleases no less deeply for operating subcon-
sciously. If Tennyson's early master Keats was right that "Heard melodies are
sweet, but those unheard / Are sweeter,"[19] the reader's pleasure may run
deeper when cognition's street-level traffic with meaning is thus undermined
unawares. The mind's workaday grapple with grammar may be sweetened—
unawares, and the "gentlier" for that—by anagrammatic rumors from down-
stairs in the unnoted continuo part.

Tennyson took some pride in the word "tired," "making the word," as he
said, "neither monosyllabic nor disyllabic, but a dreamy child of the two."[20]
Nineteenth-century philology meets the nuclear family! One parent, the en-
forcer, stickles for two syllables in the name of pentametric law, while the in-
dulgent other parent, plumping for unconditional love, lets the darling grow
up with a drawl. The cunning way Tennyson's verbal spoiled child "tired"

plays one parent off the other, and not once but twice, puts the labor/leisure dialectic in a nutshell. Meanwhile the kernel in the nutshell may actually be another word entirely, the preposition "upon," the runt of the line but full of mischief: an iamb according to the dictionary, a trochee according to the meter, and in recitation an elusive changeling I don't know quite how to pronounce. An unsung keystone, "upon" holds up its line, sustains it by delay, in a hesitant pause that refreshes.

The halfwayness of this tuned-in, mellowed-out passage epitomizes the alternately stimulant and narcotic properties of the Choric Song itself, veering as it does between the odd-numbered strophes' absorption into the natural here-and-now, and the even-numbered strophes' complementary wandering after thoughts of elsewhere: past toil, eventual death, memories of home, visions of the gods. One suspects that Ulysses's marine band wants neither of these conditions but rather what their alternation makes available, the habitual sine wave of arousal and satisfaction that is managed fatigue.

> How sweet it were, hearing the downward stream,
> With half-shut eyes ever to seem
> Falling asleep in a half-dream! . . .
>
> To lend our hearts and spirits wholly
> To the influence of mild-minded melancholy.
>
> (lines 99–109)

"To lend . . . wholly" makes strange economy. A *whole loan* is no more an actual gift than a "half-dream" is an actual trance or, indeed, than "to seem / Falling asleep" is actually to slumber. The mariners mean, after all, to keep calling in the loan of heart and spirit so as to lay it out again at interest, a pun I tender as fully underwritten by Tennyson's arresting infinitive in line 108. The mariners teach us here to want something quite like what they want; to catch themselves nodding in the act, halfway between flagging and snapping-to; and thus to stay at the tipping point of a fatigue deliciously prolonged. That point is the place of reverie where images swim up in the vividness of the surreal only to recede, placing no flat-out demand on the mind but instead entertaining a fluctuant alertness to "half-forgotten things" (line 123) in a *perpetuum mobile* of pulsing consciousness.

"And deep-asleep he seemed, yet all awake, / And music in his ears his beating heart did make" (lines 35–36). That music is the song of life itself; for finally it is the property of Tennyson's lotos speedball to keep the mind on edge indefinitely, by exploiting fatigue rather than either succumbing or standing up to it. An alternating current of focus and blur, thesis and arsis, message and remission, keeps saying goodbye hello goodbye.

> Fresh as the first beam glittering on a sail,
> That brings our friends up from the underworld,
> Sad as the last which reddens over one
> That sinks with all we love below the verge;
> So sad, so fresh, the days that are no more.
>
> ("Tears, idle tears," lines 6–10)

As with the gathering but unshed tears that Tennyson's lyric of 1847 made famous, repetition rightly orchestrated can cross novelty on the familiar, and find comfort in the strange, by poising memories on the very verge of apprehension. "New things and old co-twisted" thus, as the Laureate would remark of King Arthur's throne in the 1872 *Idylls of the King*, and as anyone who has sat up way too late may confirm, can so derange the temporal sense as to make it seem "As if Time / Were nothing" (II.222–23).

When the mariners say they crave "death, dark death" (line 98), they no more deserve belief than Tithonus does when he takes up the same cry in Tennyson's greatest dramatic monologue. What they all want is what Keats wanted when he lay swooning "half in love with easeful death,"[21] namely, the "dreamful ease" of rocking nonstop between going and coming, *fort und da*, fading and quickening life. This radical reciprocation helps explain why mariners who taste of the lotus experience their own weariness as a property less dwelling in themselves than diffused across the scenery: "evermore / Most weary seemed the sea, weary the oar, / Weary the wandering fields of barren foam" (lines 40–42). It is also what makes it impossible to know whether you're supposed to take a hit of lotus in order to heal fatigue or to induce it; because you're feeling bad or feeling badly: feeling clumsily, that is, imprecisely, fumblingly, anaesthetically. In either case, hurt or numb, lotus is good for what ails you because it makes you, in either sense of the phrase, *feel better*. "Let us alone" (lines 88, 90, 93) means *Let us be:* the thrice-repeated injunction articulates a Nietzschean will to repeat, a phenomenologist's petition for perceptual reinstatement at the threshold of mere sensate being.

This will to expand life's interval with the pulsations of a quickened, multiplied consciousness—that of course is Walter Pater talking—furnished the theme song of the Victorian fin de siècle, when poets bred on the aestheticism Morris had heralded became too exquisitely tired to aspire to more than minority. The late-Victorian cultural field is sown thick with figures of speech that bespeak the metropolitan figures cut by the poets who printed them, and who occupy a spectrum coextensive with the associations that attached to fatigue in the 1880s and 1890s, from seductive languor on one side to, on the other, clinical misgiving about the degeneracy of a wasted national stock. So pervasively overwrought was literary Decadence, not just on its face but down in the subcutaneous lyric tissue, that its brand of Victorian fatigue still passes in public literary history for the fatigue of Victorianism itself. It wasn't that; it was an often brilliant reprise of Tennysonian romanticism, undertaken as part of the cultural division of labor that typified the fin de siècle at large; and the Decadent movement in verse hummed with specialist refinements on those energy-saving devices that I have tried to show were ingredients all along in the poetics of fatigue. Thomson's "City of Dreadful Night" (1874), the one that really never sleeps, pumps anemic iron all its own; the ekphrases and imitations of Michael Field keep surprising an affect of world-weariness amid the ferment of the early Quattrocento, nay on Sappho's primal Lesbos; Dowson and Johnson and Wilde and Symons all find themselves by collapsing fastidiously into a Lost Generation.

Investigating the poetics of fatigue at the fin de siècle is enough like shooting fish in a barrel to send us back for better sport into the bounding main of the mid-century, though with honorable salutes en route to Hopkins's anatomy of accidie in the terrible sonnets of the mid-1880s; to the way Augusta Webster made "weary" mean *wired* in her "Circe" (1870); to the ingenuity with which Swinburne coupled exhaustion with climax and fused an extreme physiology with an entropic physics.[22] Rewind, then, to the 1840s, a decade as Tired as it was Hungry, when the manic boom of the bourgeoisie was built on the depressed condition of the first proletariat, and when *labor* and *fatigue* had quite specific social referents for whoever cared to notice. One poet who cared was Elizabeth Barrett Browning, and in "The Cry of the Children" (1843) she called attention to the neglected abuse of juvenile workers in Victorian mines and factories.[23] With signal imaginative reach, she propounded that something like the deficit in social attention that perpetuated this systemic abuse got replicated in the nervous system of the children it victimized: an attention-deficit syndrome, *avant la lettre*. And she gave poetic form to this syndrome through a specifically industrial experiment in the poetics of fatigue.

Barrett Browning's experiment isn't always happy in execution, but its brilliant and daring conception deserves more consideration than it has received. Here is how the poem opens.

> Do ye hear the children weeping, O my brothers,
>   Ere the sorrow comes with years?
> They are leaning their young heads against their mothers,
>   And *that* cannot stop their tears.[24]

The meter is evidently trochaic, alternating six- with four-foot lines. If in the intransigence of this meter the contemporary undergraduate hears *Oompa Loompa Willie Wonka Oompa Loompa*, the more seasoned Victorianist should hear what Roald Dahl (born 1916 in Cardiff) may actually have been recalling when he wrote *Charlie and the Chocolate Factory* (1964): the piston-pushing, time-clock-punching din of heavy steam machinery. Barrett Browning's meter cranks out a staccato recurrence to whose tune Ruskin in "The Nature of Gothic" (1853) saw the factory operatives of his day obscenely dancing, "their hands vibrating with a perpetual and exquisitely timed palsy."[25] It is a meter less compelling than compulsory, hardly bearable for more than a few lines. Indeed, my ear insists on halving the time signature and counting the trochaic 6 and 4 as a paeonic 3 and 2. (I would defend this as a humane and cordial rescue by the same prejudice that makes us hear a one-note clock say *tick-tock,* in wholesome abatement of mechanical monotony through preconscious acoustic interpretation.)

Be that as it may, it's surely the unbearability of Barrett Browning's chosen meter that leads her to contrive, in a master stroke of prosodic invention, that her poem's voiced rhythm, its actual *cry,* shall rebel against the meter. Already in line 3 above, the metrically prescribed "**their** young **heads**" has to be spoken as "their **young heads**"; and, in the line that follows, the syncopation thus opposed to mad metrical overdrive garners an official poetic endorsement with the countermetrical italicization of "*that.*" The mechanical trochaic juggernaut may be unstoppable, like the children's tears it extorts, but that it is at least resistible becomes the burden of the next lines, where in every instance but one the key word "young" calls for and gets a stress that strict meter would forbid.

> The young lambs are bleating in the meadows,
>   The young birds are chirping in the nest,

The young fawns are playing with the shadows,
   The young flowers are blowing toward the west—
But the young, young children, O my brothers,
    They are weeping bitterly!
They are weeping in the playtime of the others,
    In the country of the free.

                    (lines 5–12)

The way meter's Oompa Loompa kicks back in for the closing three lines shows how, across the middle of the stanza, repeated truancy from the pre-scribed stress order has been transmitting a prosodic SOS. Sick of itself, the versification strips its own gears.

Worse, this distress in the body of the poem mimics that in the damaged bodies and minds of the child laborers whom the poem ventriloquizes.

"For oh," say the children, "we are weary,
   And we cannot run or leap;
If we cared for any meadows, it were merely
   To drop down in them and sleep.
Our knees tremble sorely in the stooping,
   We fall upon our faces, trying to go."

                    (lines 65–70)

Fatigue gives the children the shakes, and it shortly brings on that surreal workaholic delirium tremens which we have seen Tennyson render as an agreeable heart-throb, Ruskin as a grim palsy.

"For all day the wheels are droning, turning;
   Their wind comes in our faces,
Till our hearts turn, our heads with pulses burning,
   And the walls turn in their places:
Turns the sky in the high window, blank and reeling,
   Turns the long light that drops adown the wall,
Turn the black flies that crawl along the ceiling:
   All are turning, all the day, and we with all.
And all day the iron wheels are droning,
   And sometimes we could pray,
'O ye wheels' (breaking out in a mad moaning),
   'Stop! be silent for to-day!'"

                    (lines 77–88)

Nothing is more pathetic—and the fellow-felt nausea these verses prosodi-cally induce justifies that adjective literally—than to realize that the industrial vertigo here enacted is an automatically triggered coping mechanism whereby the children's nervous system defends itself against unremitting sen-sory onslaught. Their group hallucination is fatigue's natural recoil against intolerable stress, the desperately shimmying mind's last stand against an en-vironment that overload has drilled into meaninglessness. This compen-satory recoil or endorphin rush, moreover, Barrett Browning's versification proposes to us as a vicariously shareable *pleasure,* which subsists in one sense beside our moral outrage and in another sense despite it.[26] The woozy gratification of the slue-footed, out-of-kilter prosody communicates some-thing that feels addictively good in the dizziness the children's reflexes impose to baffle the hard factory facts. Their altered state thus inhabits the same con-tinuum of occupational hazard on which the idled, addled Mariana's mur-murous vision of things defines an opposite extreme. Not for nothing does Ruskin call the timing of the industrial laborer's palsy "exquisite": it is balked reverie's revenge, within a day-shift economy that cuts daydreaming no slack. Ditto the funhouse-minded magic lantern show that, in Barrett Browning's nightmarish poem, young imagination projects with insuppressible abandon onto the shop wall and ceiling. Where you can't quit—and children, the least free of laborers, can't—then the most you can do is take leave of your senses in the semantic furlough of a "mad moaning." In fact, and in defense of hu-man dignity, going thus wild may be the *least* you can do. So Barrett Brown-ing's imaginative prosodic investment in the distressed virtual body suggests, pitting an early-Victorian sympathy poetics against the early-industrial specter of compassion fatigue.

Stop! be silent for today! I will, after one closing speculation. Among the public developments that the Victorian poetics of fatigue rehearsed in print—pending its social implementation in decades ahead—may have been the organized work stoppage as such, together with the many labor accom-modations to which determined use of the stoppage and the strike would eventually lead. Shorter hours, weekends off, paid holidays and leaves be-came, writ large and written into law, the unstressed syllables of an industrial life sentence. "The Cry of the Children" appeared in 1843, just one year after the revised "Lotos-Eaters," whose lines of strophic peroration can sound, in an 1840s context, strikingly like the rhetoric of the union hall: "We will no longer roam" (line 45), "Why should we only toil?" (line 69), and "Oh rest ye, brother mariners, we will not wander more" (line 173). And 1843 was the very year Carlyle opened *Past and Present* with the vision of a British workforce paralyzed as by the charm of incantation, which is to say by empowered words rhythmically uttered: "They sit there, pent up, as in a kind of horrid enchantment; glad to be imprisoned and enchanted, that they may not perish starved."[27] The Bartleby principle that *not* to labor might be a good work— might be, as we say, a labor action—formed one part of the High Victorian argument in poetic form that we have been considering.

NOTES

1. At least in poetry it does—though the case of Paul Dombey, drifting to early death, suggests that the phenomenon obtains more broadly. Dickens makes a leitmoif in *Dombey and Son* of little Paul's fluctuation between preternatural attentiveness and supernatural intimation. On one hand, "he never seemed to know what weariness was, when he was looking fixedly at Mrs. Pipchin" (Charles Dickens, *Dombey and Son* [1844–46; London: Penguin, 1985], 164). On the other hand, the access of world-weariness comes to Paul routinely with "the noise of the rolling waves" that are "always saying something. Always the same thing" (171). To the accompaniment of Florence's singing, "the many things he had had to think of lately, passed before him in the music; not as claiming his attention over again, or as likely ever more to occupy it, but as peacefully disposed of and gone. A solitary window, gazed through years ago, looked out upon an ocean, miles and miles away; upon its waters, fancies, busy with him only yesterday, were hushed and lulled to rest like broken waves" (264). And at the last: " 'I hear the waves! They always said so!' Presently he told her that the motion of the boat upon the stream was lulling him to rest" (297).

2. William Morris, *The Earthly Paradise: A Poem,* 4 vols. (London: Longmans, 1905), 1:1–2.

3. "A spirit laughs and leaps through every limb, / And lights my eye, and lifts me by the hair" (lines 776–77; Robert Browning, *The Ring and the Book,* ed. Thomas J. Collins and Richard D. Altick [Peterborough: Broadview, 2001], 34–35). "And my blood strengthens, and my veins abound"; "mine eyes / Burn as that beamless fire which fills the skies / With troubled stars and travailing things of flame" (lines 4, 227–29) ("Anactoria," in Algernon Charles Swinburne, *Major Poems and Selected Prose,* ed. Jerome McGann and Charles L. Sligh [New Haven: Yale University Press, 2004], 93–98).

4. Samuel Taylor Coleridge, "Kubla Khan," in *The Complete Poems,* ed. William Keach (Harmondsworth: Penguin, 1997), 250–52.

5. See pertinent discussions of Victorian energy physics in Daniel Brown, *Hopkins' Idealism: Philosophy, Physics, Poetry* (Oxford: Clarendon Press, 1997); and Alice Jenkins, *Space and the "March of Mind": Literature and the Physical Sciences in Britain, 1815–1850* (Oxford: Oxford University Press, 2007).

6. "Sprung Rhythm," in its correspondence with "that irregularity which all nat-

ural growth and motion shews," forms the topic of the "Author's Preface" to the posthumous edition of Hopkins's poems edited by Robert Bridges in 1918: rpt. in *The Poems of Gerard Manley Hopkins,* 4th ed., ed. W. H. Gardner and N. H. MacKenzie (London: Oxford University Press, 1967), 46. On the proliferation of Browning Societies after 1881 see William S. Peterson, *Interrogating the Oracle: A History of the London Browning Society* (Athens: Ohio University Press, 1969).

7. See David E. Latané, Jr., *Browning's* Sordello *and the Aesthetics of Difficulty* (Victoria: University of Victoria English Literary Studies, 1987).

8. This and subsequent citations of Tennyson are to *The Poems of Tennyson,* ed. Christopher Ricks (London: Longmans, 1969).

9. Arthur Hallam's "On Some of the Characteristics of Modern Poetry, and on the Lyrical Poems of Alfred Tennyson," *Englishman's Magazine* (1831), is reprinted in *The Writings of Arthur Hallam,* ed. T. Vail Motter (New York: Modern Language Association, 1943), 182–98. Mill reviewed Tennyson's 1830 and 1832 collections for the *London and Westminster Review* in July 1835; rpt. John Stuart Mill, *Literary Essays,* ed. Edward Alexander (Indianapolis: Bobbs-Merrill, 1967), 79–108.

10. As soon as prose evades this charge, or flourishes it, we start to deem it poetic. The late-century development of the "prose poem" instructively gamed this medial distinction, famously in France, but in Britain too when the prose format thickened up in writers from De Quincey to Pater and beyond—a development ratified on high when W. B. Yeats opened his 1936 *Oxford Book of Modern Verse* with a free-verse lineation of Pater's ekphrasis of Leonardo's Gioconda from *The Renaissance* (1873). A stylistic analysis that complemented mine in this chapter might find, in Pater's prose, rhythms of focus and remission that sponsor a more equitable account than, say, Catherine Gallagher's in "Formalism and Time," *Modern Language Quarterly* 61 (2000): 229–51. The ascetic regimen of "sprinting across a series of bright peaks" (242), which Gallagher convincingly proposes as *The Renaissance*'s prescription for successful living, in effect drains ordinary experience off as so much "dross, a dead thing" (243). Thus, no doubt, Pater's ruthless content in crystal extract. But his prose style, honed in part on the century's best poetry, may tell a gentler tale in the pooling of its appositions, the elaborations of its form. (See, for a head start along these lines, note 15 below.)

11. The phrase comes from chapter 14 of *Biographia Literaria* (1817); rev. ed. George Watson (London: Dent, 1971), 169.

12. "I will not cease from Mental Fight, / Nor shall my Sword sleep in my hand" (*Milton: A Poem* [1804; rpt. Boulder: Shambhala, 1978], plate 2).

13. "There is no method except to be very intelligent" (T. S. Eliot, "The Perfect Critic," in *The Sacred Wood: Essays on Poetry and Criticism* [London: Methuen, 1920], 10).

14. Glending Olson, *Literature and Recreation in the Later Middle Ages* (Ithaca: Cornell University Press, 1982), 96, finds a comparable cultural logic in place as early as Aquinas's rather reluctant concession, when commenting on the *Nicomachean*

Ethics, that by way of "recreation and rest for the soul," and provided it be "well-tempered," "application to play is lawful" (*Summa Theologica* 2.2). Aristotle's *Ethics* was a favorite Victorian school text set, e. g., for the top form at Thomas Arnold's Rugby.

15. For suggestive analogues in prosaics—fiction and nonfiction alike—see Stephen Arata, "On Not Paying Attention," *Victorian Studies* 46 (2004): 193–205. Arata sets Morris's ideal of "repose amidst of energy" (*News from Nowhere,* 1890) in relation to the industrial paradox that, for blue- and white-collar workers on and off the factory line, "paying attention was essential but often nearly impossible," as "the very nature of their tasks fostered *in*attention" (196).

16. Cathy Caruth, *Unclaimed Experience: Trauma, Narrative, and History* (Baltimore: Johns Hopkins University Press, 1996).

17. William Wordsworth, "Preface" to *Lyrical Ballads* (1800), in *Poetical Works,* ed. Thomas Hutchinson and rev. Ernest de Selincourt (London: Oxford University Press, 1904), 739; Coleridge, chap. 18, *Biographia Literaria,* 207.

18. David Shaw, "Tennyson and Zeno: Three Infinities," *Victorian Poetry* 47 (2009): 90–91, makes a resonant correlative point about "The Lotos-Eaters."

19. "Ode on a Grecian Urn" (lines 11–12), in John Keats, *Complete Poems,* ed. Jack Stillinger (Cambridge, MA: Belknap Press, 1978), 282.

20. Quoted in Ricks, ed., *Poems of Tennyson,* 431.

21. "Ode to a Nightingale" (line 52), in Keats, *Complete Poems,* 281. See also, in this regard, Keats's great late sonnet "Bright Star."

22. Swinburne, *Major Poems,* passim.

23. See my "Tactical Formalism: A Response to Caroline Levine," *Victorian Studies* 48 (2006): 85–93, for a more detailed prosodic analysis of this poem than is given here.

24. *The Poetical Works of Elizabeth Barrett Browning,* ed. Harriet Waters Preston (1900) and rev. Ruth M. Adams (Boston: Houghton Mifflin, 1971), 156.

25. *The Stones of Venice,* ed. L. March Phillipps, in 3 vols. (London: Dent, 1907), 2:152.

26. Wordsworth's 1800 insistence (see note 17 above) on the general point Barrett Browning here resumes was proportionate to his unease at its perverse amorality: metered language imparts pleasure no matter how repulsive the content which that language refers to. The intertextural, "tempering and restraining" power that metered verse exerts on else overwhelming passion involves, very curiously, a species "of feeling not strictly and necessarily connected with the passion"; as a result "more pathetic situations and sentiments, that is, those which have a greater proportion of pain connected with them, may be endured in metrical composition, especially in rhyme, than in prose" (739).

27. *Past and Present,* ed. Richard D. Altick (New York: New York University Press, 1965), 8.

The Impersonal Intimacy of Marius the Epicurean

STEPHEN ARATA

Has any reader ever wept over the death of Marius, the epicurean? I bet not. A conscientious survey of the critical literature, supplemented by a thoroughly informal polling of friends and acquaintances, shows without much doubt that readers of Walter Pater's 1885 novel have seldom if ever gotten emotionally worked up over its protagonist's untimely demise. Evidently it is just not that kind of relationship. Surely, though, we might wonder at our—call it unintended—heartlessness. Even casual readers of Victorian novels possess a rich experience of responding vicariously to the narrated deaths of unreal people. Why then don't we care more for Marius? Readers readily acknowledge that he is presented in a positive light and that his life story possesses intrinsic interest. Yet Pater's narrative seems designed precisely to block all avenues to readerly identification. That is, our interest in Marius is never allowed to become personal. We are not encouraged to sympathize with him, even when he dies, and so as a character he does not seem quite "real"—and so the text he inhabits does not seem quite to be a novel, since Victorian novels are conventionally built on just the kinds of interpersonal identifications that Pater in this narrative largely dispenses with.

To say that *Marius the Epicurean* operates at some distance from the conventions of the realist novel is not a startling claim. Too often, though, the tacit assumption among critics is that that distance in effect marks the limits of Pater's competence. Whatever his other virtues as a writer, this argument goes, he was a lousy novelist. We do better to begin by assuming, if only provisionally, that the book's departures from convention are motivated and then to ask what Pater wants to accomplish by way of them. How does *Marius* ask to be read? What forms of attention does it solicit, and to what ends? In what ways might our responses to this text alter our sense of what a fictional narrative is and what it does?

How to comport oneself in the presence of aesthetic objects: thinking through the complexities of this topic is arguably the central concern of Pater's writings from the beginning of his career to the end. Those writings focus most often on painting, sculpture, and poetry, though the category of "aesthetic objects" is for Pater a capacious one. It includes not only ideas but entire traditions of thought, which can captivate, even ravish, in precisely the way that art objects do. It also includes people, whose aesthetic appeal is sometimes due to physical beauty but is more frequently bound up with the quality and intensity of their inner lives. Pater returns over and again to the claims other people make on us and the effects they produce on us, and it is here that his concerns meet up with those of the Novel. If *Marius the Epicurean* is an eccentric example of the genre, its off-centeredness is due in large part to Pater's unconventional notions not simply of what it means to be a person but also of what it means to be a person-in-a-book. Pater seems to have felt with some urgency the need to distinguish between our emotional responses to other people and our emotional responses to the people we encounter in texts.

Put this way, such a position may seem unremarkable to the point of banality. Nevertheless it places Pater at odds with most theorists of the novel in the nineteenth century (and with many since), whose justifications of the genre almost invariably center on the importance of readers responding to fictional characters as if they were real human beings. Pater by contrast insists that we see fictional characters—including, perhaps most importantly, the fictional character we now refer to as the implied author of a text—as aesthetic objects made from words. In his essay "Style," Pater compares language to the marble a sculptor works with.[1] The comparison allows him to underscore a central claim of the essay: the artifact created from words, like the completed sculpture, is a materialization of human subjectivity, not its equivalent. We easily recognize that sculptures are at once intimately expressive of their makers and autonomous from them. Though it may provoke powerful emotional responses, we do not think to "sympathize" with a statue. In like manner, for Pater the intensity of engagement with verbal artifacts is grounded in the recognition of them *as* artifacts. Midway through "Style," Pater considers the kinds of readers "to whom nothing has any real interest, or real meaning, except as operative in a given person" (*A*, 27). Such readers are drawn to texts whose stylistic mastery takes the form of producing the illusion of "immediate contact" with the author (*A*, 25). "They seem to know a *person,* in a book" (*A*, 27; emphasis in original). What they instead know, Pater suggests, is a person-in-a-book: an artful arrangement of words that indexes rather than reproduces a particular subjectivity. No human subjectivity can be fully transposed into words. The person-in-a-book "does but suggest what can never be uttered," which is that human "plenary substance of which there is only one phase or facet" expressed in the verbal object (*A*, 27).

Ideally, in Pater's view, we confront aesthetic objects in an attitude of "impassioned contemplation." The conceptual tension in the phrase is instructive. To be impassioned and contemplative is to be at once engaged and detached. It requires us to enter into an emotional relation with the aesthetic object while also standing apart from both object and emotion. When the artifact in question is a person-in-a-book, our relation to that figure is best described as one of impersonal intimacy.[2] Pater devotes the last third of "Style" to a consideration of the century's consummate stylist, Gustave Flaubert. The first lesson Pater draws from Flaubert's example is the truth of "the well-known saying, 'The style is the man'" (*A*, 35). The second is that "if the style be the man, . . . it will be in a real sense 'impersonal'" (*A*, 37). We will need eventually to parse more fully this teasing formulation. For now, we can posit that the cultivation of impersonality is in Pater's view the prerequisite for certain forms of emotional immediacy and intimacy. So long cast as the apostle of a merely hedonistic subjectivity, Pater has recently figured prominently in critical accounts of Victorian ideals of detachment, objectivity, and impersonality.[3] It remains, though, to consider how those ideals might inflect the writing and reading of prose fiction. The distinction Pater draws between people and their representations has significant consequences for his practice in *Marius the Epicurean,* most notably in the range of techniques he employs to create his idiosyncratic version of what Garrett Stewart calls "the conscripted reader."[4] If that reader does not think to weep when Marius dies—after all, what's Marius to her, or she to Marius?—it may be because she knows that Pater has entrusted her with other duties.

The issue of the duties we owe to others is one that presses on Marius himself throughout his life. It emerges most forcefully in the aftermath of the death of his friend Flavian, felled by plague at the close of the narrative's first part. In his final illness Flavian is attended by Marius with what the narrator calls "an absolutely self-forgetful devotion."[5] So moved is Marius by his friend's plight that he "almost longed to take his share in the suffering" (*M,* 101). At the very last, Marius lies down beside Flavian in an effort to lend him some warmth. He then utters what is, improbable as it seems, his sole line of dialogue in the entire book. "Is it a comfort that I shall often come and weep over you?" To which Flavian, in *his* only line of recorded dialogue, replies bluntly: "Not unless I be aware, and hear you weeping!" (*M,* 101).

On the one hand, this is Pater reminding us that Flavian is a pagan whose cosmology does not entail belief in an afterlife. On the other hand, I want to suggest, this is Pater also reminding us that Flavian is a fiction, not a person, and challenging us as readers to justify, if we can, the emotional capital we typically spend so lavishly on such creatures. In *Marius the Epicurean* Pater consistently uses the dead as figures for those not-alive yet strangely present beings called fictional characters. I will have more to say on that conjunction shortly. For now, I simply point out that Marius's response to Flavian's impending death is described in terms that echo those frequently used by Victorians to describe the absorbed novel reader. Marius is "absolutely self-forgetful," his affective life so thoroughly wrapped up in the contemplation of another's fate—a fate he is emotionally entangled in but can in no way control—that he momentarily loses all sense of self. At the same time, in his longing to "share in the suffering" of another person Marius is caught up in the same dynamics of sympathetic identification that, from the late eighteenth century forward, are invoked in nearly every theoretical account of what ethically responsible novel readers do. Finally, in his promise to weep when Flavian dies, Marius again implicitly puts himself in the company of "good" readers, the intensity of whose emotional investments vouch for both the authenticity and the value of their reading experiences. In Garrett Stewart's terms Marius has, in this scene in which no reading occurs, nevertheless taken on the figuration of a reader.[6]

Marius's relation to his friend Flavian thus figures in a different register our relation to what, following Roland Barthes, we might call the "semic bundles" gathered in Pater's narrative under the proper name "Flavian." In this context, Flavian's response becomes all the more striking. "Is it a comfort that I shall often come and weep over you?" "Not unless I be aware, and hear you weeping!" If Marius mimics typical readers in their inclination to weep for those who cannot be aware of their weeping, then Flavian in effect demands to know of those same readers what, exactly, they think they are doing. To what end do we weep? This is more or less the question that Marius poses to himself after Flavian dies. "Flavian was no more," the narrator tells us, unequivocally (*M*, 105). Faced with this fact—that "the earthly end of Flavian" involves "nothing less than [his] soul's extinction"—Marius ponders the range of appropriate responses (*M*, 105). What do we owe the dead? Not our tears, it turns out. Impelled by what the narrator (perhaps punningly) calls "a novel curiosity" (*M*, 105), Marius looks into the teachings of various schools of philosophy and religion regarding the afterlife of the soul. In doing so he is nearly seduced into "an enervating mysticism" (*M*, 105), which the narrator disparages for leading to emotional sloppiness. To shed tears for the dead is self-indulgence at best, since the dead cannot benefit from our grief. It is to be (these again are the narrator's terms) "theatrical" and "melodramatic," and Marius finally has "a hatred of what is theatrical" (*M*, 105). Opting instead for the eminently Paterian virtues of "clearness of thought" and "a cold austerity of mind," Marius speculates that, if divinity can be said to exist, it is "most likely to be found a resident" in "vigorous intelligence" (*M*, 105). Honoring the memory of Flavian becomes for Marius primarily an exercise in self-discipline, an opportunity to attend diligently to what is required for the proper conduct of life.

Marius's response to Flavian's death is one instance of a larger pattern in the novel. Marius's affective life is intimately bound up with his responses to the dead, who are always "present" to him despite his reluctant suspicion that, being dead, they exist nowhere except in his consciousness. Committed even in boyhood to fostering "that secondary sort of life which we can give the dead, in our intensely realized memory of them," Marius conscientiously performs the ritual acts prescribed by his religion so that his deceased father may enjoy, in the narrator's reiterated wording, "that secondary existence, that warm place still left, in thought at least, beside the living, the desire for which is actually, in various forms, so great a motive with most of us" (*M*, 47). The ambiguous status of the dead in Roman theology makes Marius's position credible, yet, as Pater makes clear, that position remains substantially unchanged even after he comes under the sway of Christianity.

Indeed, regardless of the more or less continual changes in his beliefs—philosophic, aesthetic, religious—Marius all through life retains his initial skepticism concerning the existence of an afterlife. Because the dead "exist" only in his memory, the problem for Marius is always one of commemoration. Marius's life is marked at frequent intervals by occasions on which he must address anew the question of his relation to the dead. In each case, his motive desire is to secure for them the warmth of a "secondary existence" within his consciousness. That desire remains strong to the end: one of Marius's final acts is to refurbish his family crypt in order to assuage "a vain yearning . . . still to be able to do something" for his departed ancestors (M, 287). He realizes, though, that "such doing must be, after all, in the nature of things, mainly for himself" (M, 287), which is to say that his "doing" is ultimately in the service of personal commemoration, which in turn is aligned for Marius with the rigors of self-culture. In this context, we note too that Marius is moved by his first experience of the Christian Mass because to him it seems "a service, which was, before all else, from first to last, a commemoration of the dead" (M, 249).

For Marius as for Pater, to commemorate the dead is in effect to incorporate them into oneself. It is to make them into what Pater in a closely related context calls "objects known to memory" (M, 61). Thus incorporated, the dead occupy a different position in Marius's emotional economy than the living do. What Marius comes to believe is that the dead forfeit their status as persons. The claims they make on him differ in kind from the claims made by living people. To the living—to life itself, "that mysterious essence which man is powerless to create in even the feeblest degree"—Marius adopts an attitude "which had in it something of religious veneration" (M, 48). That veneration expresses itself through the cultivation of "sympathy," which Marius defines in ways that make him sound more like a nineteenth-century Briton than a second-century Roman. Near the end of the novel we are given a lengthy extract from Marius's journal (that he keeps a journal is "one of his modernisms" [M, 269]) that culminates in an extended meditation on the "power of sympathy" (M, 274). Marius believes that the exercise of sympathy can alleviate, in part, our essential isolation from one another just as it can assuage, in part, the human suffering resulting from "a certain necessary sorrow and desolation" woven into the fabric of existence (M, 274). His invocation of the tears in things—sunt lacrimae rerum—points back to Virgil, but Marius's argument on behalf of the sympathetic imagination is consciously forward-looking. "The future will be with those who have most of it," he writes (M, 274). There is, Marius claims, "something in that pitiful contact" between persons made possible by the exercise of sympathy "which, on a review of all the perplexities of life, satisfies our moral sense, and removes that appearance of unkindness in the soul of things themselves" (M, 275).

In such conclusions we can hear, as presumably many of Pater's first readers did, echoes of the tradition of moral philosophy associated with the names of Adam Smith and David Hume, whose work was instrumental in putting sympathy at the center of Victorian conceptions of moral sense. That sympathy was also at the center of Victorian conceptions of aesthetic response is likewise due to that same tradition. A key legacy of Scottish Enlightenment philosophy for the nineteenth century is just this entanglement of moral character and aesthetic sensibility. The pages on sympathy that open Smith's *Theory of Moral Sentiments* (1759), for instance, casually conflate persons and their representations. Sympathy is a universal human response— "In every passion of which the mind of man is capable, the emotions of the bystander always correspond to what, by bringing the case home to himself, he imagines should be the sentiments of the sufferer"[7]—yet because such "fellow-feeling" results from the exercise of the imagination, it is called forth as easily by enacted emotions as by real ones. We suffer or rejoice as readily, and as genuinely, with "those heroes of tragedy or romance" as we do with real people.[8] Smith feels no need to argue for the claim that the same feelings are awakened in us by witnessing a man in pain as are awakened when we watch an actor pretending to be in pain. The connection seems self-evident to him, as indeed it did to most eighteenth-century commentators. As Adela Pinch notes in the context of her discussion of Hume's *Treatise of Human Nature* (1739), a work that deeply influenced Smith among others, in common usage "sympathy described not only interpersonal relationships but also relations between persons and representations."[9]

It is easy to see why such a position was seized on in the nineteenth century by those eager to make a case for the social utility of an art form traditionally considered frivolous at best and morally corrupting at worst, namely, the novel. The cultivation of right feeling in readers was, for the Victorians who cared most about the genre, precisely what the novel is *for*. And the cultivation of right readerly feeling, which George Eliot memorably called "the raw material of moral sentiment,"[10] occurs primarily by means of sympathetic engagement with fully realized, psychologically complex, and socially embedded fictional characters. It was this foregrounding of the links between sympathy, right feeling, and the moral education of the reader that helped make the realist novel the preeminent popular art form of a liberal humanist Victorian culture. Later novelists such as Meredith, Hardy, and James moved partly away from the program of moral education while retaining a belief in the transformative power of sympathy, which was now credited with bringing readers into closer proximity with the essential energies of "life." James's essays on the novel thus turn repeatedly to the vital importance, for writers and readers alike, of treating fictional characters as if they were real people. His famous exasperation with Anthony Trollope in "The Art of Fiction" (1884) hinges on just this issue. Trollope's acknowledgment that he is "only 'making believe'" when he creates his characters strikes James as "a betrayal of a sacred office," even "a terrible crime,"[11] precisely because it robs the novel of the feature that does most to justify its existence.

Pater can hardly be accused of a Trollope-like "making believe" in *Marius the Epicurean,* though the novel does foreground its own fictionality to a degree unusual in the period. More important is the fact that Pater implicitly dissents from the claim that we should respond to fictional characters as if they were real people. As the extracts from Marius's journal suggest, Pater recognizes the claims of sympathy in governing the relations between people. But in his view fictional characters cannot make similar claims on us as readers. Indeed, Pater puts enormous pressure on the assumption that good reading is grounded in the cultivation of certain emotional states—that readers, when they are reading well, feel with or for characters and, by living vicariously through them, sharpen and refine their own moral or aesthetic sensibilities.

In fact, Pater is at times straightforwardly suspicious of vicarious experience. Consider the only moment in *Marius the Epicurean* that alludes explicitly to the novel as a genre. The second section of the narrative ends with Marius in attendance at the amphitheater in Rome for a festival in honor of Artemis. The festival consists mostly of the mass slaughter of animals in the name of entertainment, a spectacle Marius finds morally repugnant. His revulsion is fully endorsed by Pater's narrator, who likewise deplores "a show, in which mere cruelty to animals, their useless suffering and death, formed the main point of interest" (*M,* 168). Nearly as appalling to the narrator, though, is the fact that "people watched their destruction, batch after batch, in a not particularly inventive fashion" (*M,* 168). The slaughter must be made ever more theatrical, ever more spectacular, precisely in order to "make up . . . for the deficiencies of an age" in which experience comes primarily in vicarious form (*M,* 168). The narrator then ups the stakes by reminding his readers that Marius would have seen human beings publicly sacrificed in similarly theatrical ways had he lived a little earlier or a little later in history. The whole episode leads up to a comparison that, I think it is safe to assume, few readers anticipate. "The long shows of the amphitheatre were, so to speak, the novel-reading of that age—a current help provided for sluggish imaginations" (*M,*

168). The narrator then describes a spectacle in which a criminal, cast in the role of Marsyas, is flayed alive.

Criticizing novel readers is of course an enduring generic convention of the novel. Novelists routinely admonish the readers of their novels for reading novels. But I do not know of another example like this one, in which an equivalence is drawn between the experience of reading a novel and the experience of watching a man being flayed alive. One thing Pater is getting at here—and perhaps he *is* overstating his case just a bit—is the problematic nature of vicarious experience. Like novel readers, the Roman patrons of these bloody spectacles require stimulants of ever-increasing intensity to jump-start their "sluggish imaginations." That stimulus takes the form of an emotional investment in the fate of figures—slaves, criminals, fictional characters—whose personhood must be simultaneously granted and denied. (As Pater reminds us, slaves and criminals did not possess the status of persons under Roman law.) Like the novel reader's interest in the real-but-not-really figures in a book, the Roman spectators' interest in the performer-victims extends no further than their usefulness in providing an occasion for some intense emotions in the viewers—emotions that invariably include, as the narrator takes care to note, a "false sentiment of compassion" for their sufferings (*M*, 169). From the point of view of the sufferer, it makes little difference whether a spectator weeps generous tears or laughs with malicious delight. Pater again underlines the suspect self-indulgence, coupled with feelings best described as sadistic, that characterizes the pursuit of certain kinds of vicarious experience.[12] Such experience is not generally conducive to the cultivation of moral sentiment, as George Eliot would have it. Even in cases where "right feeling" is the result, that feeling is cultivated for its own sake and not from a desire to alleviate the sufferings of others. Most often it simply fosters the emotional sloppiness Pater finds so distasteful.

But just where does this leave us readers of Pater's novel, proud no doubt of our unsluggish imaginations, yet discomfited by the suggestion that the pleasures of novel-reading are hard to untangle from the interest of watching a "person"—Dorothea Brooke, Richard Feverel, Isabel Archer, Jude Fawley, but we can all choose our own favorites—being figuratively flayed alive for our benefit? At the very least, we may wonder how we are being asked to respond to the protagonist of *Marius the Epicurean*. Throughout the novel Marius's status as a "mere" representation is consistently underlined. Little effort is made to produce what Barthes calls "the glow of reality"[13] through the accumulation of telling details (of physical appearance, of habits of speech or behavior, of deportment and dress, of social setting) designed to produce an air of verisimilitude. Most notably, Marius is deprived of a voice, that most individuating of traits. Apart from his single question to Flavian, Marius is never "heard" in the novel.[14] Our access to his inner life is virtually unlimited, yet even here we are always aware of the mediating presence of the narrator, whose persistent use of free indirect style serves to distance us, slightly but decisively, from Marius himself.[15]

Such distancing is a familiar effect of free indirect style, but Pater employs it for unfamiliar ends. In his virtuosic *Jane Austen, or The Secret of Style,* D. A. Miller argues that "the significance of free indirect style . . . is not that it attentuates the stark opposition between character and narration, much less abandons it, but that it performs that opposition *at ostentatiously close quarters.*"[16] That is, narration "comes as near to a character's psychic and linguistic reality as it can get without collapsing into it."[17] Because free indirect style simultaneously "grants us . . . the experience of a character's inner life as she herself lives it, and an experience of the same inner life as she never could," our relation to fictional character takes "the paradoxical form of an impersonal intimacy."[18] Miller's compelling formulation allows us to gauge the distance separating Pater's conception of fictional character from that of a psychological realist such as Austen. To experience "a character's inner life as she herself lives it" we must first assent to the enabling fiction that "she herself" somehow enjoys an existence apart from the text in which we encounter her. We are persuaded to imagine a subjectivity too full, too "deep," to be entirely captured or conveyed by the novel we are reading. The illusion of a character's extratextual existence is basic to our experience of realist fiction. As Miller suggests, free indirect style contributes to that illusion by in a sense doubling it: the character is shadowed by a narrator whose own deep subjectivity is hinted at by the particular use she makes of and the particular tone she imparts to the free indirect style.

A reader's intimacy with character and narrator takes as its model the intimacy they enjoy with each other, thanks to the ostentatiously close quarters in which they operate. Miller argues that in Austen's novels such intimacy is impersonal because Austen's narrative voice, "free of all accents that might identify it with a socially accredited broker of power/knowledge in the world under question," is in fact the voice of "Style itself."[19] In Pater's case, free indirect style serves instead to highlight the nonpersonhood of protagonist and narrator alike. Our intimacy is impersonal precisely because there are no persons in view, just arrangements of words. To an unprecedented degree, Pater foregrounds the fact that his protagonist is equivalent to the sum total of what the narrator writes of him. Pater's insistence that Marius is not a person but a person-in-a-text radically alters our relation to him by dispelling the illusion of subjectivity that realist novels work so hard (and often so successfully) to create.[20] Because Marius is not "alive" in the sense we use when we commend realist novelists on their characters, he is not available for sympathetic identification on the part of readers.

To say that Marius is not alive is not, however, to say that he is a "flat" character in E. M. Forster's sense. He has depth, but it is a depth figured in historical rather than psychological terms. Interiority is displaced by anteriority. Pater is less concerned to present Marius as an autonomous individual than as a figure traversed by energies that originate outside and prior to him. He impersonates, so to speak, those energies rather than (as is conventionally the case) an imagined individual.[21] In this key respect Marius resembles other figures who appear in Pater's writings, early and late. While *Marius the Epicurean* is his only long work of fiction, the techniques used to portray Marius have analogues not only in the "Imaginary Portraits" Pater composed intermittently from the 1870s onward but also in the historical essays gathered in *The Renaissance* (1873, 1893), the work that made his reputation. Throughout his career Pater was engaged in tracing what, in his earliest extant essay, he called "the main current of the world's energy"[22] as it moves through history. The primary business of the critic, in Pater's view, is to reveal the dialectic between that energy and the various expressive forms it has taken. Pater's preferred method for disclosing the temporal movement of the world's energy is to bind it textually to a human life. Since this method is most clearly displayed in *The Renaissance*, it will help to turn to that work for a moment.

The Renaissance can be described as a collection of historical investigations organized under a series of proper names. Apart from the brief "Preface" and the equally brief and notorious "Conclusion," eight of the nine chapters in the book feature an individual's name in the title. These chapters do not take the form of biographical studies, however, and none presents a particular body of artistic or intellectual work in anything like a comprehensive way. Pater's goal instead is to identify what he calls the "special manifestation" of beauty characteristic of the Renaissance.[23] As Carolyn Williams notes, Pater's method is to foreground historical figures who serve to "punctuate the now-inaccessible complexity of past time with interpretable form. . . . Pater uses the form of the personal life to project a sense of unity in history."[24] The question the critic asks, Pater writes, "is always:—In whom did the stir, the genius, the sentiment of the period find itself?" (*R*, xxi).

The individual life gives form to the period, but in doing so that life necessarily loses its individuality. Williams points out that though "a focus on particularity is indispensible to his aesthetic agenda," Pater's "historicist attention ranges from historical particularity to general patterns of development."[25] Individual figures are quickly typified, absorbed into the abstract categories that make historical analysis possible. Pater leans heavily on the notion of human "type," which, as Williams reminds us, operates for him much like "species" does for biologists, as a general category used to ground arguments concerning diachronic change. At the same time, "type" retains for Pater its older theological meanings. The figures he identifies are typical not because they represent the common run of women and men of their day but precisely because they do not. They are instead emblems of the period's most vital energies, the place where "the stir, the genius" of the age becomes momentarily visible. Often they prefigure some cast of thought, disposition of character, or form of creativity that will be fully revealed only in the dispensation of a later age. Botticelli is significant for Pater in part because he prefigures Michaelangelo, Winckelmann because he prefigures Goethe (*R*, 48, 182). Indeed, drawing on yet another meaning of "type," Pater writes that because Winckelmann is a "type" he "*imprints* on the imagination of Goethe" the "completeness" characteristic of ancient Greek life (*R*, 182; emphasis added).

The essays in *The Renaissance* gesture toward the specificity of an individual's lived experiences only to put that specificity aside as irrelevant to the historian's larger purposes. Pater disparages as "antiquarianism" (a word he invariably pairs with "mere") an interest in the stray details of a particular life. His sketches of historical periods or of bodies of artistic work likewise rely on a method the very opposite of thick description. In each case—the life, the period, the work—Pater is primarily concerned to convey the essence or extract, to provide a distillation from which everything ephemeral has been allowed to evaporate.[26]

Pater frequently equates people with works of art, not in the facile way often found in fin de siècle writing but in order to underline his contention that both are, in a real sense, repositories of energy or "receptacles of so many powers or forces," as he puts it in the "Preface" to *The Renaissance* (xix).[27] What distinguishes the exceptional—that is, the typical—human being from the majority is what distinguishes the great work of art from the ordinary one. In both cases, the former is where "the greatest number of vital forces unite in their purest energy" (*R*, 188)—which, for Pater, is the same as saying that they are sites where a particular culture at a specific historical moment is discernible in concentrated form, though only from a vantage point later in time. In "The School of Giorgione," Pater defines the highest art as that which "presents us with . . . some brief and wholly concrete moment, into which, however, all the motives, and the interests and effects of a long history, have condensed themselves, and which seem to absorb past and future into an intense consciousness of the present" (*R*, 118). Such works "are like some consummate extract or quintessence of life" (*R*, 118).

It is likewise the fate and the privilege of the exceptional woman or man to be perceived in retrospect "to be like" the "consummate extract or quintessence" of some phase of human culture. That retrospective perception can occur only once the flesh and blood person has passed over into a representation, and the messy particularities of lived experience have been burned away to reveal the essential "form" of the "life." That form is not static, however. It continually changes as it takes into itself the ongoing and open-ended reception history of the figure in question. Inevitably, inaccuracies in the form of myth or legend or simply factual error will accrete around the biographies of influential figures, but for Pater such errors are often essential to the way those figures come to represent for later observers the "consummate extract" of an earlier phase of culture. Because myths or even persistent historical errors are often the surest index to the nature of an artist's or thinker's continuing influence, they are integral to the "life."

Thus the essay on Leonardo da Vinci opens by juxtaposing the painter's legend as conveyed by the "anecdotes which every one remembers" from Vasari's *Lives* with the modern historical researches of Carlo Amoretti, which "left hardly a date fixed, and not one of those anecdotes untouched" (*R*, 78). The questions of fact raised by Amoretti have since "become, one after another, subjects of special study, and mere antiquarianism has in this direction little more to do" (*R*, 78). What remains is for the critic to return to the artist's work "and try to reach through it a definition of the chief elements of Leonardo's genius" (*R*, 78). He is aided in this effort as much by the discredited myths and the archive of historical error as he is by the corrected record. The "*legend,* as corrected and enlarged by its critics, may now and then intervene to support the results of [his] analysis" (*R*, 78; emphasis in original). Pater's striking formulation—the legend is at once corrected *and enlarged* by the factual record—suggests that efforts to dispel potent myths and traditions ultimately serve to demonstrate just how vital they remain for anyone who seeks "the chief elements" of an artist's genius.

Equally striking is Pater's indifference to the fact that Leonardo's canon had shrunk substantially over the course of the nineteenth century. Just as historical research has dispelled many of the legends surrounding Leonardo's life, so too has a modern "technical criticism" of his paintings, by sifting "what in his reputed works is really his, from what is only half his, or the work of his pupils" (R, 78), significantly winnowed the canon of authentic works. As Jonah Siegel notes, Pater's response to this situation is not to lament the loss but to locate in it the chance "of a still greater intimacy" with the artist, achieved precisely through the study of those deattributed works long reputed to be his.[28] Siegel astutely sees Pater's essays on Leonardo and Giorgione (whose catalog had likewise been decimated) as complex responses to Romantic ideas concerning artistic originality. If genius is literally inimitable, then the products of a painter's workshop or of a school of his followers can be dismissed as merely derivative. Siegel argues that for Pater, by contrast, the "presence of the characteristics of an artist in spite of the absence of any physical work on his part becomes a manifestation of the powers of that artist to make others in his creative image."[29] Thus, writes Pater, "though the number of Leonardo's authentic works is very small indeed, there is a multitude of other men's pictures through which we undoubtedly see him, and come very near his genius" (R, 92).

Siegel focuses primarily on Pater's interest in the dynamics of pedagogy, through which Leonardo or Giorgione exercised a direct influence on pupils and followers.[30] But Pater is equally interested in the transmission of the Leonardoesque or the Giorgionesque across long stretches of time. In a remarkable paragraph at the midpoint of "The School of Giorgione," Pater reiterates his belief that "all is not done" once the facts have been distinguished from the legend, the authentic painting from the imitation, for "in what is connected with a great name, much that is not real is often very stimulating."

> For the aesthetic philosopher, therefore, over and above the real Giorgione and his authentic extant works, there remains the Giorgionesque also—an influence, a spirit or type in art, active in men so different as those to whom many of his supposed works are really assignable. A veritable school, in fact, grew together out of all those fascinating works rightly or wrongly attributed to him; out of many copies from, or variations on him,

by unknown or uncertain workmen, whose drawings and designs were, for various reasons, prized as his; out of the immediate impression he made upon his contemporaries, and with which he continued in men's minds; out of many traditions of subject and treatment, which really descend from him to our time, and by retracing which we fill out the original image. Giorgione thus becomes a sort of impersonation of Venice itself, its projected reflex or ideal, all that was intense or desirable in it crystallising about the memory of this wonderful young man. (*R*, 116–17)

The Giorgionesque is, paradoxically, "the *vrai vérité* about Giorgione" (*R*, 121). In Pater's account, Giorgione's authentic works are simply sites—prominent sites, to be sure, but there are others—where the "spirit or type in art" we recognize as the Giorgionesque makes itself known. Moreover, what we think of as "the real Giorgione," the flesh and blood man, is revealed to be essentially a back-formation. This figure is of relatively little significance to Pater, who is more interested in the way we "fill out the original image" of the artist by reascending the stream of time to touch the "many traditions of subject and treatment" that together make up the ongoing historical life of the Giorgionesque. That "original image" in turn becomes an "impersonation" not of Giorgione the man but of "Venice itself, its projected reflex or ideal." As, that is, the consummate extract or quintessence of cinquecento Venice, the (retrospective and always evolving) "original image" of Giorgione has the power to convey all that is "intense or desirable" in the culture of that place and time. From this perspective, Pater's essay can be seen as the latest filling out of that original image, a site where the Giorgionesque is made available once more.

If in *The Renaissance* Pater's main concern is to track the movement of the world's energy by assigning it a series of proper names, in his "Imaginary Portraits" he takes that strategy a step farther by detaching the name from any actual person. As the name suggests, these are prose portraits of imaginary figures; all but a few are set in the past. In his seminal 1965 study, U. C. Knoepflmacher points out that in terms of their technique the imaginary portraits "are almost indistinguishable from his presumably authentic portraits of real individuals."[31] Knoepflmacher's disapproval is muted but audible, and from one perspective perfectly justified. Pater's historical portraits fail to be "authentic" according to the norms of historical discourse, while his imaginary portraits fail to be "realistic" according to widely accepted criteria for the construction of fictional characters. That Pater employs the same techniques to portray real and fictional figures is, moreover, implicitly taken by Knoepflmacher as the sign of a literary failure.[32] In his view, Pater has either misapprehended the laws of genre or else has, regrettably, simply disregarded them. Yet we might instead take the continuity between the historical studies and the imaginary portraits as a reminder that Pater is in neither case concerned to produce the illusion of personhood. The portraits are not equivalent to fictional characters, which is to say that, like the "original image" of Giorgione, they are impersonations not of people but of complex cultural formations. As such, they represent forms of life and thought that reemerge under different names at different historical moments.

Marius the Epicurean is at once the most elaborate of Pater's imaginary portraits and his fullest exploration of their potential uses.[33] Marius himself is the impersonation of a cultural formation—post-Antonine Rome, poised between paganism and Christianity—at a moment of decisive transition. And, by a kind of temporal parallax, Pater continually shifts our vantage point so that we recognize in Marius the traces, atavistic or latent, of numerous cultural moments stretching from Periclean Athens to contemporary London. "Let the reader pardon me if here and there I seem to be passing from Marius to his modern representatives" (*M,* 181): by the time we reach this oft-quoted supplication, we have long since become accustomed to thinking of Marius in relation to both prior and subsequent avatars. In Pater's aestheticist version of the first law of thermodynamics, the energy to which Marius temporarily lends his name is never destroyed but is instead perpetually transformed.

In an 1868 review of William Morris's poetry, Pater writes that "to come face to face with the people of a past age . . . is as impossible as to become a little child, or enter again into the womb and be born."[34] The essays in *The Renaissance,* the imaginary portraits, and *Marius the Epicurean* elaborate this insight. We cannot come face to face with Giorgione or Leonardo; what we confront instead is the Giorgionesque or the Leonardoesque. The proper names that structure Pater's historical investigations are heuristic devices: shorthand symbols for the complex human energies that shape entire cultures or epochs as well as individual lives. We know a particular moment of the past only through the mediation of all the artifacts (visual, verbal, aural) that function as representations of it. Our engagements with those artifacts, Pater insists, can only be from the perspective of *now.* He relegates, this time to a "vain antiquarianism," the desire to achieve "anything in the way of an actual revival" of any aspect of the past. "We cannot conceive the age," he writes in his review of Morris's poetry; "we can conceive the element it has contributed to our culture."[35] Or, as he puts in his essay on Winckelmann, the "spiritual forces of the past, which have prompted and informed the culture of a succeeding age, live, indeed, within that culture, but with an absorbed, underground life" (*R*, 158).[36]

The image Pater most often invokes to figure the persistence of these "spiritual forces"—it recurs so frequently in his writing as to seem a kind of psychological reflex—is of an unearthed body, "still red with life in the grave" (*R*, 167). Liminal beings traverse his writings in the form of spirits, revenants, vampires, gods-in-exile, and the like, but none produce for Pater quite the frisson he finds in the idea of being at once dead *and* alive: a state of excess rather than of liminality. The dead-alive often emerge in Pater's texts by way of verbal constructions that themselves partake of excessiveness by seeming to be at once figurative and literal. Thus of Pico della Mirandola, Pater notes that "while his actual work has passed away, yet his own qualities are still active, and himself remains, as one alive in the grave" (*R*, 38). Common sense assures us that "as" in the final clause means "as if he were," but of course at the same time it also means "as." To be dead-alive is not to be resurrected but it is to be animate—and to animate—while remaining "absorbed, underground."[37]

The figures in Pater's imaginary portraits regularly take on the attributes—particularly the excess of meaning—that Pater assigns to the dead-alive. Over and again, we are confronted by tableaux in which dead organic matter is uncannily aligned with life. The corpse of Sebastian van Storck is found beside a sleeping child "swaddled warmly" in Sebastian's clothes.[38] Denys l'Auxerrois is dismembered by frenzied townsmen who insert "little shreds of his flesh . . . into their caps."[39] The unearthed bones of Duke Carl of Rosenmold become for a time a local tourist attraction.[40] The lifeless body of Emerald Uthwart, its lips still red, its flesh still firm with the "expression of health and life," is entombed under the fascinated gaze of an attending surgeon.[41] In each case (and there are others) there is not so much a confusion of categories—death/life—as an effort to activate both terms at once.

As we have seen, Marius himself is acutely aware of the ways in which life—his own and that of his time—is animated by the dead. In *Marius the Epicurean* Pater fully indulges his fascination with images of life and death entwined: not just through passing references to live burials (*M*, 192, 198) and a possibly miraculous resurrection (*M*, 277), and not just through Marius's approving sense of the Christian Mass as centering on the "veritable consecration, hopeful and animating, . . . of old dead and dark matter itself" (*M*, 249), or of the Christian practice of burial as arising from "some peculiar feeling of hope they entertained concerning the body" (*M*, 230), or of the fitness of the habit, shared by Roman and Etrurian and Christian communities alike, of situating the dwelling places of the dead in close proximity to the homes of the living (*M*, 45, 125, 229), but, more important, through Marius's perpetually renewed effort to commemorate the dead. For Marius, the act of commemoration ensures the continued vitality of his relation to a past—personal, familial, communal—that has formed him in ways he cannot fully know. "Dreaming now only of the dead before him" (*M*, 286), Marius returns at the end of the novel to his childhood home in order to tend to the family tomb. (We note the double work done by that "before": in front of, prior to.) Having performed the appropriate acts of ritual care, Marius feels a connection to his dead that seems tactile, even sensuous. "Dead, yet sentient and caressing hands seemed to reach out of the ground and to be clinging about him" (*M*, 288). Throughout *Marius the Epicurean* the familiar Gothic trope of the past returning uncannily to haunt the present is stripped of its Gothic affect. The hands that reach out of the grave are sentient and caressing, and Marius is comforted by their seeming touch. Earlier, moving among the funeral houses in the "old, mysterious, and visionary country of Etruria," he realizes that "the close consciousness of that vast population [of the dead] gave him no fear, but rather a sense of companionship" (*M*, 125).

It bears repeating that in Marius's view the dead have no existence outside his "close consciousness" of them. The ritual acts of commemoration he performs generate a sense of intimate connection, but it is an intimacy paradoxically linked to absence, to the awareness of distance and loss. In commemorating the dead, Marius replaces persons with ideas of persons, but they are ideas that have become in some occult way tactile, even sensuous. Marius is at once in possession of these ideas and possessed by them. They seem as personal as the movements of his own thought, yet Marius experiences them as if they came from elsewhere. Sensuous and impersonal, intimate and estranged, the absent dead animate Marius's consciousness through their presence there, just as he vitalizes them through ever-renewed acts of commemoration.

In *Plato and Platonism* (1893), Pater writes that Plato's distinctive gift as a thinker is his ability to carry "the discipline of sensuous love" into "the world of intellectual abstractions."[42] For him, Pater contends, ideas are experienced as sensations.[43] Indeed, "in the later development of his philosophy the highest sort of knowledge comes to seem like the knowledge of a person, . . . the peculiarities of personal relationship thus moulding his conception of the properly invisible world of ideas."[44] The philosopher is in a specialized sense a "lover": specialized because while "love must of necessity deal above all with visible persons" the philosopher deals above all with immaterial ideas.[45] Yet so impassioned is Plato's engagement with ideas that they become as if incarnate. It is "as if . . . the mind were veritably dealing with living people . . . who play upon us through the affinities, the repulsion and attraction of *persons* towards one another, all the magnetism, as we call it, of actual human friendship or love."[46] The "as if" is important, but so too is Pater's conviction that this simulacrum of actual human friendship and love nonetheless makes real claims upon us, just as it brings genuine benefits to us. Plato's genius as a writer, Pater continues, is most apparent in the simulacra of people he creates in his Dialogues. There he "gives names to the invisible acts, processes, creations, of the abstract mind, as masterly, as efficiently, as Adam himself to the visible living creations of old. As Plato speaks of them, we might say, those abstractions too become visible living creatures."[47]

Whether or not this is an accurate account of Plato's writings, it has obvious relevance to Pater's. Like the Plato he here describes, Pater endeavors to give names to the abstract processes and energies of human history and culture. He peoples his texts with incarnate abstractions, as it were, abstractions that have acted upon his mind with "the attraction and repulsion of persons." Like Plato too, Pater strives through his writing to create that same action in the minds of his readers. According to Pater, thanks to Plato's stylistic mastery, his writing "promotes in others" the "mental condition" that characterizes Plato himself.[48] In Pater's view, reproducing in another's mind one's own mental state is what artistic writing exists, first and foremost, to do. In Plato's case as in Pater's, that mental condition, in which ideas become sensuous and thoughts take on the "delightful colour and form" of individuals,[49] is suffused with a love that Pater at once aligns with and distinguishes from the love we might feel for "visible persons" in the world itself.

To read impersonally is, in Pater's view, to recognize the distinction between these two types of love. It is also to be always mindful of the fact that our relation even to the biographical figures we encounter in texts is necessarily mediated through language. As Andrew Miller points out, in his essays Pater frequently both writes about and strives to model the kind of responsiveness he hopes to evoke from his own readers. To take only one instance, Miller notes the delicate irony in describing, as Pater does, the relationship between Winckelmann and Goethe in terms of friendship, since the two men never met and Goethe's sole access to the older man was through his scholarly writings. By calling such a relationship a form of friendship, Miller writes, Pater "proposes one way for readers to understand [his] own relationship to the friendship he is describing, signalling his desire to join that friendship, through reading (and now writing), with these two people whom he himself never met, a friendship fed by the appreciation of physical directness but richly mediated through the abstractions of language."[50] Pater's essay in turn stands as an invitation to its readers to enter into (and ideally to continue) "this chained series of mediated relationships."[51]

For the reader—the person—who stands momentarily as the latest in that chained series, the preceding figures in the series are experienced not as persons but instead as the "forms of life" they have left behind. That phrase takes us back once more to *Marius the Epicurean*. At a key moment in his development, Marius realizes that "the products of the imagination must themselves be held to present the most perfect forms of life" and are therefore "the most appropriate objects of that impassioned contemplation" that is the highest form of consciousness (*M*, 118). Pater lifts the phrase "impassioned contemplation" from his own earlier essay on Wordsworth. In both places it signifies a disposition of engaged passivity in relation to the spectacle of human life and history and an impersonal love for the achievements of human minds and hands. This love is impersonal precisely because it is called forth not by persons but by the "perfect forms of life" they create. At its best, Pater writes, "poetry like Wordsworth's is a great nourisher and stimulant" of impassioned contemplation on the part of the receptive reader (*A*, 63). The receptive reader's relation to the poet himself is, again, intimate and impersonal. Intimate, because by way of his art Wordsworth promotes in others his own mental condition. Impersonal, because the Wordsworth we encounter through the poems is not equivalent to a flesh-and-blood person but, like the Giorgione of Pater's essay, an "original image" that has been filled out by the "many traditions of subject and treatment" that "descend from him to our time" (*A*, 62). Wordsworth's poetry is the inimitable product of a unique individual *and* a particular iteration of a sensibility that can be identified in "other poets who . . . [are] like him in ancient and more recent times" (*A*, 62).

Pater clearly wished *Marius the Epicurean* to be considered an exemplary product of the imagination and thus an appropriate object of impassioned contemplation. Through it, he hoped, readers would come into contact with the particular current of the world's energy at times called epicureanism, which for the duration of the novel is embodied in the figure named Marius. Yet, as Pater surely anticipated, the figure readers feel they encounter most intimately in *Marius the Epicurean* is Walter Pater. The tradition of reading *Marius* as thinly veiled autobiography begins early, with Mary Augusta Ward's 1885 review in *Macmillan's Magazine,* and continues strong through the present day. Ward attributes Pater's decision to displace his story onto that of Marius to a typically English aversion to "direct 'confessions,'" which led him to search for "some form of presentation more impersonal" than explicit autobiography.[52] More recent critics have dispensed with the argument from national character while continuing to claim that the novel indirectly expresses aspects of Pater's identity that he was unwilling or unable to acknowledge openly.[53] Such readings can be valuable, though they tend to ignore the extent to which our understanding of "Walter Pater" relies on notions, developed and elaborated by readers over the nearly century and a half since he began publishing, of the "Paterian." The Paterian is now the *vrai vérité* about Pater. Viewed from this perspective, the angle of an ever-moving now, the implied author we infer from the pages of *Marius the Epicurean* impersonates one or more aspects of that complex cultural formation, Late Victorian Britain. To an unusual degree, *Marius the Epicurean* is written with "us" in mind. That is, the novel is written in explicit awareness that with the passing of time its audience is ever more remote from the world that produced it. Remote but not dissevered: if readers of *Marius* can never come "face to face" with an earlier age, they can yet, Pater believes, conceive the element it has contributed to later ages.

The "Walter Pater" we find in the text of *Marius the Epicurean* is, like Marius, an aesthetic object made from words. All words come to us richly burdened with their own histories, as Pater, heir to the nineteenth century's philological traditions, often reminds us. In "Style," he points out that the language a writer works with "is no more a creation of his own than the sculptor's marble. Product of myriad various minds and contending tongues, compact of obscure and minute association, a language has its own abundant and recondite laws" (*A*, 12). The writer is engaged in a constant struggle—at once thrilling and hopeless—to find the arrangement of words that will transmit with utmost precision his sense of the world he moves in and of how that world in turn shapes his subjectivity. This struggle is a recurring topic in Pater's essays, and it is a prominent theme in *Marius* as well.[54] "Words were things," Marius realizes, but despite their thingness—a materiality as recalcitrant as marble—they become "valuable in exact proportion to the *transparency* with which [they] conveyed to others the apprehension . . . so vividly real within himself" (*M*, 122; emphasis added). What writing expresses is the genius of the writer and the genius of language together. For this reason, Pater claims, a writer cultivates a distinctive voice in order to write impersonally. The vividly real apprehension he seeks to convey is unique to himself, but the medium of conveyance is the common property of the culture. Artistic writing keeps us aware of both these truths simultaneously. "If the style be the man," Pater writes in "Style," "in all the colour and intensity of a veritable apprehension, it will be in a real sense 'impersonal'" (A, 37). Pater's own texts solicit a readerly response that is likewise impersonal. In our impassioned contemplation of the verbal artifact, we encounter not the "plenary substance" of the once-living individual named Walter Pater but instead the Paterian "phase or facet" that, dead-alive, continues to animate our present moment.

NOTES

1. Walter Pater, *Appreciations, with an Essay on Style* (1889; London: Macmillan, 1911), 12; hereafter abbreviated *A*.

2. The phrase "impersonal intimacy" appears in two illuminating recent books—D. A. Miller's *Jane Austen, or The Secret of Style* (Princeton: Princeton University Press, 2003) and Andrew H. Miller's *The Burdens of Perfection: On Ethics and Reading in Nineteenth-Century British Literature* (Ithaca: Cornell University Press, 2008)—whose concerns intersect in several places with those of this essay, especially in sections 3 and 5, which is where I take them up.

3. See, for example, Amanda Anderson, *The Powers of Distance: Cosmopolitanism and the Cultivation of Detachment* (Princeton: Princeton University Press, 2001); Jason Camlot, "The Victorian Critic as Naturalizing Agent," *English Literary History* 73, no. 2 (2006): 489–518; Bénédicte Coste, "'The Perfection of Nobody's Style': Impersonality and Emotion in Pater's 'Prosper Mérimée,'" *Impersonality and Emotion in Twentieth-Century British Literature*, ed. Christine Reynier and Jean-Michel Ganteau (Montpellier: Université Montpellier, 2005), 29–42; George Levine, "Two Ways Not To Be a Solipsist: Art and Science, Pater and Pearson," *Victorian Studies* 42, no. 1 (2000): 7–41; Carolyn Williams, "Walter Pater's Impressionism and the Form of Historical Revival," in *Knowing the Past: Victorian Literature and Culture*, ed. Suzy Anger (Ithaca: Cornell University Press, 2001), 77–99.

4. Stewart focuses on the interplay of two narrative strategies that Victorian novelists can be said to have perfected: direct address ("reader, I married him") and the staging of scenes of reading. In the first, the "real" reader is interpolated into the world of a novel and becomes, momentarily, a character in that world. In the second, the reader is enjoined to extrapolate out from the depicted scene of reading to her own situation. At such moments the reader's interpretation of action is reflected back at her by way of the action of interpretation being dramatized. Both these kinds of read-

erly conscription are evident throughout *Marius the Epicurean,* though this is not a book that Stewart takes up. Garrett Stewart, *Dear Reader: The Conscripted Reader in Nineteenth-Century British Fiction* (Baltimore: Johns Hopkins University Press, 1996).

5. Walter Pater, *Marius the Epicurean: His Sensations and Ideas* (1885; ed. Michael Levey [Harmondsworth: Penguin, 1985]), 100; hereafter abbreviated *M.*

6. Stewart draws on a distinction outlined by Roland Barthes in *S/Z* "between 'character' in the ordinary sense and 'figure' as the symbolic nexus that finds only occasional and partial incarnation" in a narrative's "persons" or "characters" (Stewart, *Dear Reader,* 16). As Stewart points out, in *S/Z* Barthes "is concerned with such pervasive symbolic figures, such organizing abstractions, as 'castration,' 'wealth,' 'the marriage of opposites,' 'the replicate body,' and so forth—as they are felt to surface in, by intersecting, the narrower determinations of given characters and their semic profiles" (Stewart, *Dear Reader,* 16). Stewart proposes that "reading" is a common Barthesian "figure" in nineteenth-century novels.

7. Adam Smith. *The Theory of Moral Sentiments* (1759; ed. D. D. Raphael and A. L. Macfie [Oxford: Clarendon Press, 1976]), 9.

8. Smith, *Theory of Moral Sentiments,* 10. Smith claims too that "we sympathize even with the dead," due in part to our worry that they "are in danger of being forgot by every body." Though "the tribute of our fellow-feeling" for the dead is from one perspective pointless, since "it can have no influence upon their happiness," the exercise of sympathy can still benefit the sympathizer by helping to sharpen her or his ethical sensibility (Smith, *Theory of Moral Sentiments,* 12–13). As I will be arguing in a moment, that last claim is one that Pater calls into question in *Marius the Epicurean.*

9. Adela Pinch, *Strange Fits of Passion: Epistemologies of Emotion, Austen to Hume* (Stanford: Stanford University Press, 1996), 29.

10. George Eliot, "The Natural History of German Life" (1856; in *Essays of George Eliot,* ed. Thomas Pinney [London: Routledge and Kegan Paul, 1963]), 263.

11. Henry James, "The Art of Fiction" (1884; in *Literary Criticism: Essays on Literature, American Writers, English Writers,* ed. Leon Edel and Mark Wilson [New York: Library of America, 1984]), 46.

12. See Hinton on the sadomasochism embedded in certain kinds of sympathetic engagement. Jaffe provides a compelling account of the relations between suffering and spectatorship in Victorian conceptions of sympathy. Jaffe notes that being able to indulge in feelings of sympathy and compassion is a sign of social privilege, a point also made, largely in an American context, by Berlant. Laura Hinton, *The Perverse Gaze of Sympathy: Sadomasochistic Sentiments from Clarissa to Rescue 911* (Albany: State University of New York Press, 1999); Audrey Jaffe, *Scenes of Sympathy: Identity and Representation in Victorian Fiction* (Ithaca: Cornell University Press, 2000); Lauren Berlant, "Introduction: Compassion (and Withholding)," in *Compassion: The Culture and Politics of an Emotion,* ed. Lauren Berlant (London: Routledge, 2004), 1–14.

13. Roland Barthes, *S/Z: An Essay,* trans. Richard Miller (1970; New York: Hill and Wang, 1974), 102.

14. A mere handful of paragraphs from the end of the novel, Marius, agitated, ponders the possibility of his own impending death. "Had there been any one to listen just then," the narrator tells us, "there would have come, from the very depth of his desolation, an eloquent utterance at last, on the irony of men's fates, on the singular accidents of life and death" (*M*, 291). Marius speaks, or perhaps just intends to, but there is no one to listen, not even a potentially interested reader.

15. As Carolyn Williams notes, "The narrative is closely focused in Marius's consciousness; yet all his 'sensations and ideas' are recounted at a distance in the third person, objectified through a mediating, critical perspective. Thus is subjectivity objectified at the same time that the objects of history are subjectified" ("Walter Pater's Impressionism," 93).

16. Miller, *Jane Austen*, 59; emphasis in original.

17. Miller, *Jane Austen*, 59.

18. Miller, *Jane Austen*, 60.

19. Miller, *Jane Austen*, 32, 2.

20. See Lynch for a compelling account of the material and aesthetic conditions that, beginning in the last decades of the eighteenth century, "worked to validate and naturalize a concept of [fictional] character as representational" and therefore as "'true' to our individualities" (Deidre Shauna Lynch, *The Economy of Character: Novels, Market Culture, and the Business of Inner Meaning* [Chicago: University of Chicago Press, 1998], 3). Pater, writing just past the zenith of the nineteenth-century realist tradition whose conditions of emergence Lynch so ably identifies, denaturalizes aspects of that tradition in *Marius,* allowing us to see again what the conventions of realist characterization had over time made more or less imperceptible to readers of Victorian fiction.

21. In his helpful essay on Dickensian sentimentality, Walsh argues that figures such as Little Nell in *The Old Curiosity Shop* were taken by contemporary readers to stand not for persons but for easily recognized communal values. Readers who wept at the death of Little Nell were responding "to the idea of innocence . . . rather than to the innocent girl to which that idea contributes" (Richard Walsh, "Why We Wept for Little Nell: Character and Emotional Involvement," *Narrative* 5 [October 1997]: 312). My argument has some obvious affinities with Walsh's. Pater's characters, though, are not readily assimilable to coherent or stable cultural values, and Pater of course uses those characters to move away from the conventions of the sentimental novel.

22. Walter Pater, "Diaphaneitè" (1864; in *Miscellaneous Studies: A Series of Essays* [London: Macmillan, 1910]), 247.

23. Walter Pater, *The Renaissance: Studies in Art and Poetry* (1873, 1893; ed. Donald Hill [Berkeley: University of California Press, 1980]), xix; hereafter abbreviated *R*.

24. Carolyn Williams, *Transfigured World: Walter Pater's Aesthetic Historicism* (Ithaca: Cornell University Press, 1989), 7.

25. Williams, *Transfigured World,* 7.

26. See Gallagher on Pater's conception of the critic as one who locates and extracts for the benefit of the rest of us what is essential in a particular body of artistic

work. Catherine Gallagher, "Formalism and Time," in *Reading for Form,* ed. Susan J. Wolfson and Marshall Brown (Seattle: University of Washington Press, 2006), 305–27.

27. "Pater depicted identity as a fantastically complex palimpsest of physical and cultural threads. Pater's typical hero is an almost incorporeal presence whose personality is covertly implied and whose physical existence seems to inhere in the 'texts' of his age, a living text as it were, woven from the aesthetic artifacts ... of the past" (Gerald Monsman, *Walter Pater's Art of Autobiography* [New Haven: Yale University Press, 1980], 24–25).

28. Jonah Siegel, " 'Schooling Leonardo': Collaboration, Desire, and the Challenge of Attribution in Pater," in *Walter Pater: Transparencies of Desire,* ed. Laurel Brake, Lesley Higgins, and Carolyn Williams (Greensboro: ELT Press, 2002), 134.

29. Siegel, " 'Schooling Leonardo,' " 140.

30. See Siegel, " 'Schooling Leonardo,' " especially 144–45. For extended treatments of pedagogy in relation to *Marius,* see Matthew Kaiser, "Marius at Oxford: Paterian Pedagogy and the Ethics of Seduction," in *Walter Pater: Transparencies of Desire,* ed. Laurel Brake, Lesley Higgins, and Carolyn Williams (Greensboro: ELT Press, 2002), 189–201; Matthew Potolsky, "Fear of Falling: Walter Pater's *Marius the Epicurean* as a Dangerous Influence," *English Literary History* 65, no. 3 (1998): 701–29.

31. U. C. Knoepflmacher, *Religious Humanism and the Victorian Novel: George Eliot, Walter Pater, and Samuel Butler* (Princeton: Princeton University Press, 1965), 165.

32. Matters are further complicated by the fact that the first of the four pieces collected in *Imaginary Portraits* is a fictionalized portrait of the (real) painter Jean-Antoine Watteau.

33. *Marius the Epicurean* was to be the first of a triptych. Not long after its publication, Pater informed an American correspondent that he was planning two further volumes "of a similar character; dealing with the same problems, under altered historical conditions" (*Letters of Walter Pater,* ed. Lawrence Evans [Oxford: Clarendon, 1970], 65). In the event, he completed only a portion of the second narrative panel, *Gaston de Latour,* whose hero is "a sort of Marius in France, in the 16th Century" (Pater, *Letters,* 126). The final installment, never begun, was to be set in late eighteenth-century England. The idea of tracing the fortunes of the same "character" in three different historical moments is in keeping with Pater's interest in the way forms of thought and being persist through time.

34. Walter Pater, "Poems by William Morris," *Westminster Review* 90 (October 1868): 306.

35. Pater, "Poems by William Morris," 307.

36. "The demarcation between what is now and what was is persistently foreshortened [in *The Renaissance*], partly by linguistic devices—the use of the verbal imperfect and present rather than the perfect—partly by a panoply of intertextual references which generate an exchange between past and present . . . but mainly by implying an affinity between the perceiving consciousness of each of the Renaissance personae and that of the author" (J. B. Bullen, "The Historiography of *Studies in the History of the Renaissance,*" in *Pater in the 1990s,* ed. Laurel Brake and Ian Small [Greensboro: ELT Press, 1991], 159).

37. On the topos of the unearthed body in Pater's writing, see Jeffrey Wallen, "Alive in the Grave: Walter Pater's *Renaissance*," *English Literary History* 66, no. 4 (1999): 1033–51.

38. Walter Pater, "Sebastian van Storck," *Imaginary Portraits* (1887; London: Macmillan, 1910), 114.

39. Walter Pater, "Denys L'Auxerrois," *Imaginary Portraits* (1887; London: Macmillan, 1910), 76.

40. Walter Pater, "Duke Carl of Rosenmold," *Imaginary Portraits* (1887; London: Macmillan, 1910), 119.

41. Walter Pater, "Emerald Uthwart" (1892; *Miscellaneous Studies: A Series of Essays* [London: Macmillan, 1910]), 245.

42. Walter Pater, *Plato and Platonism: A Series of Lectures* (1893; London: Macmillan, 1910), 140.

43. Marius courts "vivid sensations, and such intellectual apprehensions, as, in strength and directness and their immediately realized values at the bar of an actual experience, are most like sensations" (*M*, 116).

44. Pater, *Plato and Platonism*, 134.

45. Pater, *Plato and Platonism*, 134.

46. Pater, *Plato and Platonism*, 140; emphasis in original.

47. Pater, *Plato and Platonism*, 141.

48. Pater, *Plato and Platonism*, 140.

49. Pater, *Plato and Platonism*, 140.

50. Miller, *Burdens of Perfection*, 17.

51. Miller, *Burdens of Perfection*, 18.

52. Mary Augusta Ward, Review of *Marius the Epicurean* (1885; rpt. in *Walter Pater: The Critical Heritage*, ed. R. M. Seiler [London: Routledge and Kegan Paul, 1980]), 130–31.

53. For informative treatments of autobiographical elements in *Marius*, see Heather K. Love, "Forced Exile: Walter Pater's Queer Modernism," in *Bad Modernisms*, ed. Douglas Mao and Rebecca L. Walkowitz (Durham: Duke University Press, 2006), 19–43; Monsman, *Walter Pater's Art of Autobiography*; Ira B. Nadel, "Autobiography as Fiction: The Example of Pater's *Marius*," *English Literature in Transition* 27, no. 1 (1984): 34–40; and Michael Ryan, "Narcissus Autobiographer: *Marius the Epicurean*," *English Literary History* 43, no. 2 (1976): 184–208. To varying degrees, all these critics see their task primarily in terms of finding the "authentic" Pater disguised in the novel. Adams offers a useful corrective to this approach in his subtle reading of the erotics of secrecy and masking in *Marius*. Adams quotes Henry James's evaluation of Pater: "He is the mask without the face" (James Eli Adams, *Dandies and Desert Saints: Styles of Victorian Masculinity* [Ithaca: Cornell University Press, 1995], 184).

54. On Pater's relation and response to nineteenth-century philology and the history of languages, see Linda Dowling, *Language and Decadence in the Victorian Fin de Siècle* (Princeton: Princeton University Press, 1986); Camlot, "Victorian Critic as Naturalizing Agent."

Reading and Re-reading

WILDE, NEWMAN, AND THE
FICTION OF BELIEF

RACHEL ABLOW

What is the difference between real belief and fictional belief? What is the difference, in other words, between a belief we hold to be true and a belief we adopt for the sake, say, of reading a novel? According to Elaine Scarry, ordinarily the distinction between the real and the fictional is self-evident: "Though there may be moments when we forget their inventedness," she writes, "poems, films, paintings, sonatas are all framed by their fictionality: their made-upness surrounds them and remains available to us on an ongoing basis."[1] Recently Jeff Nunokawa has suggested that Oscar Wilde would have agreed. For Wilde, Nunokawa argues, what is wonderful about art is the way it shields us from "the sordid perils of existence."[2] Hence, although Wilde inverts Scarry's implicit hierarchy of the real over the fictional, the basic commitment to the opposition between the two registers remains intact. In making these claims, both Nunokawa and Scarry focus primarily on readers' emotional responses to representations that readers know have no immediate real-life corollary.

In this essay I argue that when we shift our focus to the question of belief, a different picture emerges. In "The Portrait of Mr. W.H." (1889) and elsewhere, rather than valuing fictional beliefs for their opposition to or immunity from the real, Wilde suggests that the beliefs we adopt in reading fiction represent only an extreme version of the beliefs we ordinarily regard as our own. He argues for the difficulty of holding beliefs *except* as fictions, in other words, as ideas that might or might not be true, and, even more important, that might or might not be our own. Further, he implicitly claims to base this argument on an (admittedly idiosyncratic) reading of the work of John Henry Cardinal Newman. Leader of the Oxford movement, famous convert to Catholicism, vociferous antiliberal and author of *An Essay in Aid of a Grammar of Assent* (1870) among many other works, Newman is usually regarded as seeking to defend the utter reliability and knowability of belief.[3] Yet in "The Portrait," Wilde suggests an alternative understanding of Newman: as committed to belief's status as a kind of fiction, insofar as it is brought to life by means of our attachment to an aesthetically pleasing and erotically desirable other.

Despite recent efforts to claim Wilde as an important theorist of aesthetics,[4] politics,[5] sexuality,[6] and language,[7] the writer's interest in issues of belief has largely gone unremarked.[8] His concern with religion in general and with Newman in particular have been especially devalued. Even someone like Ellis Hanson, who criticizes recent critics' "eager[ness] to trivialize [Wilde's] religious beliefs," is principally interested in the writer's "profound attraction to Catholicism as a work of art," rather than in his thoughts about belief, per se.[9] Here, I argue that Wilde's reading of Newman suggests the writer's serious participation in an ongoing debate with which he is rarely identified, regarding the sources, nature, and consequences of belief. His account additionally calls attention to a suggestion in Newman's work that we believe our beliefs to be true not *just* because of what it feels like to hold them—a common reading of his work—but also because of what it feels like to love *someone else* who holds them.[10] Finally, Wilde's reading of Newman has the potential to provide us with a different way of thinking abut the relation between belief and the experience of reading fiction. Rather than providing a way to understand and therefore respect other people's beliefs, as some critics have argued,[11] fiction's usefulness lies in the way it encourages readers to experience beliefs *as if* they were their own—a state that ultimately comes to seem indistinguishable from believing it "for real."[12]

Certitude

Newman's *Essay* is too complicated for me to summarize in detail here. Briefly, in it, the Cardinal seeks to describe the different ways in which people arrive at and hold beliefs. Thus, he provides a list of different modes of holding and apprehending propositions. He describes the differences between various forms of assent: notional and real; simple and complex. He discusses the character of certitude as opposed to ordinary assent. He debates the role and limits of inference, or the process of coming to logical conclusions on the basis of evidence. And he defines what he calls the illative sense: the "power of judging and concluding" with which we are born that he claims determines both what we know and how we know it.[13] His purpose is not, he insists, to change minds on particular subjects or even to advocate specific modes of belief over others. Instead, insofar as he has a goal, it is simply to demonstrate that "Certitude is a natural and normal state of mind, and not (as is sometimes objected) one of its extravagances or infirmities" (E, 172). However modest this goal may seem, it has proven to be the most controversial aspect of the work, for by "certitude" Newman designates a belief that is, in fact, true, and that we can know to be true because of what it feels like to hold it.

> [Certitude] is accompanied, as a state of mind, by a specific feeling, proper to it, and discriminating it from other states, intellectual and moral. . . . When a man says he is certain, he means he is conscious to himself of having this specific feeling. It is a feeling of satisfaction and self-gratulation, of intellectual security, arising out of a sense of success, attainment, possession, finality, as regards the matter which has been in question. (E, 168)

Mistakes happen, of course; not everything we believe is true. We even, occasionally, think we have achieved certitude when in fact we have only achieved conviction—a belief of which we do not feel certain and hence that may or may not be true. But such cases are highly unusual, Newman insists. By and large, when we feel certain we do so because what we believe is in fact, true.[14]

The problems posed by this claim have been pointed out repeatedly. As J. A. Froude writes bluntly, "No one can seriously maintain that a consciousness of certitude is an evidence of facts on which I can rely."[15] Yet that is precisely what Newman appears to claim—and he does so by making the consciousness of certitude in matters of faith seem identical to one's consciousness of certitude in everything else. As Jonathan Loesberg explains, by grounding truth in feeling, Newman "argues, effectively, that our apprehensions of and assent to propositions about the empirical world are not qualitatively different from our apprehensions of and assents to propositions of any other discourse about any other level of reality."[16] He thus attempts to place "trust in one's own judgment, one's own consciousness, in the seductive light of the sole alternative to the complete skepticism involved in mistrusting our senses."[17] If we trust our ability to know that the sun is shining or that we are in pain, we must also trust our ability to know the existence of God.

In "The Portrait of Mr. W.H." Wilde offers several thought experiments in the problems posed by the idea of certitude, and the nature of the illative sense that supposedly leads us to it. Like Newman, Wilde embraces the idea of the illative sense as what determines "those first elements of thought which in all reasoning are assumptions, the principles, tastes, and opinions, very often of a personal character, which are half the battle in the inference with which the reasoning is to terminate" (E, 282). Unlike Newman, however, Wilde emphasizes the resemblance of the illative sense to both aesthetic taste and erotic desire—and hence the ways in which it can vicariate as easily as it can personalize knowledge.[18] He thus emphasizes the way the illative sense comes to resemble something like the feeling of falling in love. The plot of "The Portrait" revolves around three characters' changing relationships to a belief about the identity of the mysterious Mr. W.H. to whom Shakespeare's sonnets are dedicated. The content of this belief remains stable: that Mr. W.H. was the addressee of many of the sonnets, and that he was a beautiful young actor named Willie Hughes. Like Newman's belief in God, this theory cannot be proven empirically; despite the characters' repeated attempts to discover some material proof of Willie Hughes's existence, none is forthcoming.[19] As a result, each character believes the theory on different grounds at different moments and holds it in different ways: as an aesthetic preference; as an erotic desire; and as the product of inference—but also, always, as a kind of fiction.

The originator of the theory, Cyril Graham, dies before the story begins: the narrative opens with his old school friend, Erskine, telling his history to the narrator who remains unnamed throughout. According to Erskine, Cyril originally derived the theory "purely from the Sonnets themselves": on the basis of internal evidence that he claimed reveals the name, position, and profession of Mr. W.H.[20] However, he ultimately came to believe that it "depend[s] for its acceptance not so much on demonstrable proof [or] formal evidence, but on a kind of spiritual and artistic sense, by which alone [Cyril] claimed could the true meaning of the poems be discerned" ("P," 41). Like Newman's illative sense, this "spiritual and artistic sense" enables a form of assent that its possessor experiences as unconditional: that is, offered without condition or reservation. As "apprehension is a concomitant, so inference is ordinarily the antecedent of assent," Newman explains, "but neither apprehension nor inference interferes with the unconditional character of the assent, viewed in itself. . . . Assent is in its nature absolute and unconditional" (*E*, 135). Assents may originate in evidence or reason, but once taken on as assents, they exist independently of those potentially limiting grounds.

As we have already seen, this notion of assent fails to explain how one can be sure that what one feels is certitude rather than simply conviction, or an assent that fails to rise to the level of certitude: Newman fails to explain how we can be sure that our beliefs are, in fact, true. But this is not the principal problem that Wilde complains of. By choosing as relatively trivial a belief as the object of his characters' credulity—rather than the existence of God, for example—he makes the truth-value of the theory seem unimportant. What he does regard as a problem, however, is the privacy and hence apparent incommunicability of the illative sense. Cyril's knowledge of the truth of the Willie Hughes theory may have all the force of truth for him, but because it rests on feelings rather than reason, he is powerless to convey it to anyone else. According to Newman, the personal nature of certitude casts no doubt on its validity: "Light is a quality of matter, as truth is of Christianity; but light is not recognized by the blind, and there are those who do not recognize truth, from the fault, not of truth, but of themselves" (*E*, 319). Nevertheless, it does create problems for converting others. Thus, despite Cyril's assurances that he knows his belief is true, Erskine persists in his demand for "independent evidence" ("P," 43) of Willie Hughes's existence before helping his friend publish the theory. "If this could be once established," Erskine explains, "there could be no possible doubt about his identity with Mr W.H.; but otherwise the theory would fall to the ground" ("P," 43).

Cyril is "a good deal annoyed at what he called [the] philistine tone of mind" that makes Erskine incapable of intuiting the truth. Nevertheless, he dutifully pores over the "registers of City churches, the Alleyn MSS, at Dulwich, the Record Office, the books of Lord Chamberlain" in a vain attempt to find evidence of the actor's existence ("P," 43). And then when these efforts fail, he turns to forgery: after several weeks of futile labor, Cyril claims to have discovered "by the merest chance" a portrait of a beautiful young man "with his hand resting on the dedicatory page of the Sonnets . . . on the corner of [which] could be faintly seen the name of the young man himself . . . 'Master Will Hews'" ("P," 44). Erskine is temporarily persuaded by this apparent evidence and resumes preparations to publish the theory—only then to discover that Cyril commissioned the painting himself. From Erskine's perspective, the fact that Cyril invents evidence constitutes a tacit concession that Willie Hughes never existed. "'You never even believed in [the theory] yourself,'" he tells Cyril. "'If you had, you would not have committed a forgery to prove it'" ("P," 46). From Cyril's perspective, by contrast, since evidence can only ever demonstrate something he already knows to be true, its only value is as a kind of pedagogical tool. As a result, it does not matter whether it is real or fake: "the forgery of the picture had been done simply as a concession to [Erskine]," Cyril insists, "and did not in the slightest degree invalidate the truth of the theory" ("P," 46).

In this forged evidence, I think we can see a satirical reference to Charles Kingsley's famous charge that "Truth, for its own sake, had never been a virtue with the Roman clergy. Father Newman informs us that it need not, and on the whole ought not to be; that cunning is the weapon which heaven has given to the Saints wherewith to withstand the brute male force of the wicked world which marries and is given in marriage."[21] Newman denied the allegation, writing his *Apologia Pro Vita Sua* (1864) in part to refute them.[22] However, like the Newman of Kingsley's imagination, Cyril uses whatever stratagems he has at his disposal to bring his friend to the one true faith. And then, when his deception is revealed, he proceeds to bear out the Cardinal's assertion that there are certain assents that we hold with such "keenness and energy" that we would not hesitate to lay down our lives in defense of them— and he kills himself (*E*, 35). In his suicide note, he claims that "in order to show [Erskine] how firm and flawless his faith in the whole thing was, he was going to offer his life as a sacrifice to the secret of the Sonnets" ("P," 46). According to Newman, such self-sacrifice *should* carry the weight of persuasion.

> Many a man will live and die upon a dogma: no man will be a martyr for a conclusion. A conclusion is but an opinion; it is not a thing which *is*, but which we are "*quite sure about;*" and it has often been observed, that we never say we are sure and certain without implying that we doubt. To say that a thing *must* be, is to admit that it *may not* be. No one, I say, will die for his own calculations: he dies for realities. (*E*, 89)

"Newman . . . seems to believe that no-one could be a martyr for anything less than a vision of the reality of absolute truth," Jan-Melissa Schramm explains.[23] Martyrdom for him is the ultimate test, a wholly reliable means of showing another not just that one believes, but that what one believes is true. The problem is that from the perspective of the skeptical Erskine, such a claim is as open to question as any of the other "evidence" Cyril has offered. As Erskine tells the narrator, "'a thing is not necessarily true because a man dies for it'" ("P," 47). The narrator is even more cynical: "No man dies for what he knows to be true. Men die for what they want to be true, for what some terror in their hearts tells them is not true" ("P," 100).[24] According to them, all Cyril's death ultimately tells us is that he sought to promote his belief, not that it had any purchase on the world—or even that he fully believed it himself.[25]

The Problems and Pleasures of Inference

While certitude's privacy poses obstacles to the conversion of others, inference, or rational deduction on the basis of evidence or accepted principles, seems as if it should solve this problem quite neatly. As Newman admits, the highly personal nature of the illative sense means that "even when we agree together, it is not perhaps that we learn one from another, or fall under any law of agreement, but that our separate idiosyncrasies happen to concur" (E, 291–92). Inference or reason, by contrast, is defined by the fact we all have equal access to its terms and procedures. For Newman inference is limited most importantly by the fact that there are certain things that cannot be inferred—such as the existence of God. But he also complains of its tendency to lead us into philosophical questions that impede our reaching conclusions. Inference, Newman complains, requires that "every prompting of the intellect be ignored, every *momentum* of argument be disowned, which is unprovided with an equivalent wording, as its ticket for sharing in the common search after truth" (E, 211–12). It demands that "the authority of nature, common-sense, experience, genius, go for nothing" (E, 212). In order to demonstrate this problem, he offers the example of recent debates over the authoritative version of a line from Shakespeare's *Henry V.* Inference is helpless, Newman claims, when confronted with one version of the line from 1623 that makes no sense, a second version from 1632 that makes sense but has no obvious claim to authenticity, and a third version that makes sense, is aesthetically pleasing, and has become the popular standard, but was invented by the eighteenth-century editor, Theobald.

> Thus it appears, in order to do justice to the question before us, we have to betake ourselves to the consideration of myths, pious frauds, and other grave matters, which introduce us into a *sylva,* dense and intricate, of first

principles and elementary phenomena, belonging to the domains of archaeology and theology. Nor is this all; when such views of the duty of garbling a classic are propounded, they open upon us a long vista of sceptical interrogations which go far to disparage the claims upon us, the genius, the very existence, of the great poet to whose honour these views are intended to minister. For perhaps, after all, Shakespeare is really but a collection of many Theobalds, who have each of them a right to his own share of him. (*E*, 220–21)

In order to resolve the problem of the corrupted line by inference, one must entertain all kinds of absurdities and reconfirm "first principles" that most of us resolved, more or less unconsciously, a long time ago. Such a case, Newman concludes, demonstrates "how little syllogisms have to do with the formation of opinion; how little depends upon the inferential proofs, and how much upon those pre-existing beliefs and views, in which men either already agree with each other or hopelessly differ, before they begin to dispute" (*E*, 221–22). Even in an instance like this one that seems as if it should be decidable on the basis of evidence, we ultimately rely on the illative sense, or what Newman describes as premises that are "hidden deep in our nature, or, it may be, in our personal peculiarities" (*E*, 222).[26]

While Newman objects to the *sylva* into which inference can lead us, perhaps unsurprisingly for Wilde those "distractions" are a source of intense pleasure—as he demonstrates by means of his second adherent to the Willie Hughes theory, the narrator. Erskine tells the narrator the sad story of Cyril's suicide without believing the Willie Hughes theory and with no intention of promoting it. Nevertheless, the narrator is instantly persuaded. "'It is the only perfect key to Shakespeare's Sonnets that has ever been made,'" he insists. "'It is complete in every detail'" ("P," 47). Against all Erskine's objections, therefore, he sets out to prove it. At this point Wilde's story shifts gears and turns into a scholarly essay, providing close readings of the sonnets, a meditation on the strengths and weaknesses of the theater as an art form, a history of romantic friendships from the Greeks through to the nineteenth century, an account of the changing position of boy actors on the Elizabethan stage, and the probable histories of the three principal actors in the sonnets: Shakespeare, Willie Hughes, and the Dark Lady. Even in the comparatively abbreviated form that was published during Wilde's lifetime, the essay portion of the story was so extensive that several of its first readers assumed it was the real point of the text and asked why Wilde bothered to frame his theory with a narrative at all.[27] The version published after his death offers even more historical information to support and explain the theory.

A number of critics have called attention to the way this essay mocks scholarly pedantry.[28] In the only paragraph he footnotes, for example, Wilde offers nine largely useless references to Shakespeare's sonnets—an explosion of references that, on the page, is quite funny. Yet despite the mockery, Wilde doesn't entirely dismiss the value of scholarship. Instead, as he explains in his defense of period-appropriate costume design in "The Truth of Masks" (1891), although "archaeology" may be uninteresting in itself, it is nevertheless necessary for great art. "Perfect accuracy of detail, for the sake of perfect illusion, is necessary for us. [The details] must be subordinate always to the general motive of the play. But subordination in art does not mean disregard of truth; it means conversion of fact into effect, and assigning to each detail its proper relative value."[29] Wilde is careful to keep archaeology in its place, claiming that "archaeology is only really delightful when transfused into some form of art."[30] But he still insists on its importance to the effect of the whole. As a result of archaeology, he explains, the stage is made the arena for "the return of art to life": "The ancient world wakes from its sleep, and history moves as a pageant before our eyes, without obliging us to have recourse to a dictionary or an encyclopaedia for the perfection of our enjoyment" ("P," 289, 290).

The problem with inference for Wilde, then, is not that it leads us astray, as Newman claims. Instead, his concern is that inference has so little power to retain our interest. "After two months [of research] had elapsed," the narrator tells us,

> I determined to make a strong appeal to Erskine to do justice to the memory of Cyril Graham, and to give to the world his marvellous interpretation of the Sonnets—the only interpretation that thoroughly explained the problem. . . . I went over the whole ground, and covered sheets of paper with passionate reiteration of the arguments and proofs that my study had suggested to me. ("P," 93–94)

Such certainty would seem to be the point of his weeks of labor. And yet, as soon as he posts his letter, the narrator loses all interest: "No sooner, in fact, had I sent [the letter] off than a curious reaction came over me. It seemed to me that I had given away my capacity for belief in the Willie Hughes theory of the Sonnets, that something had gone out of me, as it were, and that I was perfectly indifferent to the whole subject" ("P," 94).[31] Once he has persuaded himself, it seems, there is no longer any reason to care about the theory one way or another. As Wilde complains in "A Few Maxims for the Instruction of the Over-Educated," "The English are always degrading truths into facts. When a truth becomes a fact it loses all its intellectual value."[32] It isn't just that the narrator no longer believes the theory; it is that he no longer has any stake in it.

Newman, too, recognized and feared the way beliefs can be eviscerated, objecting to assents "made upon habit and without reflection; as when a man calls himself a Tory or a Liberal, as having been brought up as such; or again, when he adopts as a matter of course the literary or other fashions of the day" (*E*, 53). Assents like these are "so feeble and superficial, as to be little more than assertions" (*E*, 52). The problem for him, then, as for Wilde, is how to keep belief alive. And for both writers, the answer comes in the form of love.[33]

"To Do Philosophy with Love"

At a certain point in the nested essay describing the product of the narrator's research, the essay shifts into a more lyrical vein.[34] After dozens of pages describing relatively abstruse debates, we suddenly get this.

> We sit at the play with the woman we love, or listen to the music in some Oxford garden, or stroll with our friend through the cool galleries of the Pope's house at Rome, and suddenly we become aware that we have passions of which we have never dreamed, thoughts that make us afraid, pleasures whose secret has been denied to us, sorrows that have been hidden from our tears. The actor is unconscious of our presence: the musician is thinking of the subtlety of the fugue, of the tone of his instrument; the marble gods that smile so curiously at us are made of insensate stone. But they have given form and substance to what was within us; they have enabled us to realize our personality; and a sense of perilous joy, or some touch or thrill of pain, or that strange self-pity that man so often feels for himself, comes over us and leaves us different. . . .
>
> As from opal dawns to sunsets of withered rose I read and re-read [the Sonnets] in garden or chamber, it seemed to me that I was deciphering the story of a life that had once been mine, unrolling the record of a romance that, without my knowing it, had coloured the very texture of my nature, had dyed it with strange and subtle dyes. Art, as so often happens, had taken the place of personal experience. I felt as if I had been initiated into

the secret of that passionate friendship, that love of beauty and beauty of love, of which Marsilio Ficino tells us, and of which the Sonnets, in their noblest and purest significance, may be held to be the perfect expression. ("P," 91–92)

"Reading and re-reading" may not help the narrator determine the identity of Mr. W.H., but it gives him something far more valuable: insight into a kind of relationship, here termed "passionate friendship," that is both beautiful and ennobling. Interestingly, the status of that understanding or experience remains ambiguous: even as Wilde seems to suggest that the experiences art "reminds" us of were already ours—"we become aware that we have passions of which we have never dreamed"; the actor and musician give "form and substance to what was within us"—not only must those "passions" be brought to our attention by some stimulus from without, large portions of the narrator's experience are explicitly *not* originally his.[35] The identity of the original possessor of "a life that had once been mine" in the second paragraph remains unspecified, but it is clearly not the narrator. At the same time that art seems to make us aware of who we "really" are, therefore, it also makes us experience another's experience as if it was really truly our own.

The connection between "passionate friendship" (the content of what the narrator learns) and "reading and re-reading" (the means by which he comes to experience it) takes place in several different registers.[36] As a number of critics have pointed out, erotic desire motivates all of the characters' attempts to understand the Sonnets.[37] Cyril's investment in the Willie Hughes theory seems to stem at least in part from his identification with another object of an older and greater man's desire.[38] Meanwhile, Erskine's initial willingness to be persuaded by Cyril is inextricably connected to his attachment to the young friend he describes as "the most splendid creature I ever saw" ("P," 36). And finally, the narrator's initial interest in the Willie Hughes theory grows out of his "strange fascination" with the "wonderful portrait" that Erskine shows him ("P," 35). It is also implicitly motivated by his love for Erskine—as well, possibly, as his interest in Cyril, the beautiful boy Erskine knew at school.

In addition to *motivating* reading and re-reading, at moments "passionate friendship" comes to seem very nearly indistinguishable from that practice. As Wilde explains, writers like Shakespeare were inspired, at least in part, by the example provided by Plato. And for Plato, at least in Wilde's account, the intellectual and the erotic are very nearly the same thing.

> In its [the *Symposium*'s] subtle suggestions of sex in soul, in the curious analogies it draws between intellectual enthusiasm and the physical passion of love, in its dream of the incarnation of the Idea in a beautiful and living form, and of a real spiritual conception with a travail and a bringing to birth, there was something that fascinated the poets and scholars of the sixteenth century. ("P," 65)

Christopher Craft points out in the context of *Dorian Gray* that even though he claims to summarize Plato in a passage like this one, Wilde consistently mischaracterizes in order to reject "the deracinated sublimatory motive driving thought and desire throughout the Platonic schedule."[39] For Plato, love of the Idea ultimately replaces love of the beautiful boy. In the passage cited above, by contrast, Wilde insists not on the substitution of physical passion by intellectual enthusiasm, but on the "analogies" between them. In Renaissance versions of Platonic love, Wilde claims, "There was a kind of mystic transference of the expressions of the physical sphere to a sphere that was spiritual, that was removed from gross bodily appetite, and in which the soul was Lord. Love had, indeed, entered the olive garden of the new Academe, but he wore the same flame-coloured raiment, and had the same words of passion on his lips" ("P," 66). Love of the Idea here in some sense *is* love of the friend. The two are mutually constituting and mutually sustaining. The narrator's initiation into the secret of passionate friendship is thus not just the *product* of reading and re-reading; it comes to seem analogous to it, imbricated in it, and perhaps even indistinguishable from it. We know because we love, and we love because we read of things that are at best only ambiguously true. Belief, experience, love, and reading all come to seem, if not the same, then profoundly interdependent.

Further, in attaching Shakespeare's love to an actor, Wilde insists on the extent to which love itself is ideally already in the realm of the fictional. Recent critics have tended to focus on the significance of a gay writer discussing the object choice of the bard as a way to establish a lineage of gay writing, as a way to normalize homosexuality, and as a daring flirtation with self-revelation.[40] When the story was first published, however, it was by no means shocking to suggest that the sonnets were addressed to a young man.[41] The sonnets themselves are very explicit about the sex of their principal addressee, and despite the efforts of some contemporary commentators to claim that the beloved was an abstraction,[42] a woman,[43] Shakespeare himself,[44] or even Queen Elizabeth,[45] most did accept the obvious—even if some also agreed

with Henry Hallam that "notwithstanding the frequent beauty of these sonnets . . . it is impossible not to wish that Shakespeare had never written
them."[46] So the key issue in the story is not *just* the gender of Mr. W.H. Nor is
it his name: as the narrator himself asserts, "To have discovered the true name
of Mr W.H. was comparatively nothing" ("P," 50). Instead, what all the characters identify as crucial about the theory is that Mr. W.H. was an actor: "to
have discovered his profession was a revolution in criticism," the narrator
concludes ("P," 50).

Throughout Wilde's work, actors are consistently identified with imper-
manence and self-transformation. As Dorian Gray explains to Lord Henry,
"'Ordinary women never appeal to one's imagination. . . . One knows their
minds as easily as one knows their bonnets. . . . But an actress! How different
an actress is!'"[47] Thus what is appealing about Sibyl Vane is that she is "never"
herself: "'One evening she is Rosalind, and the next evening she is Imogen. I
have seen her die in the gloom of an Italian tomb, sucking the poison from
her lover's lips. I have watched her wandering through the forest of Arden,
disguised as a pretty boy in hose and doublet and a dainty cap'" (and so on,
and so on).[48] In "The Portrait" the principal possessor of this mysterious—
and mysteriously attractive—power, of course, is Willie Hughes. "'How is it,'
says Shakespeare to Willie Hughes, 'that you have so many personalities?' and
then he goes on to point out that his beauty is such that it seems to realize
every form and phase of fancy, to embody each dream of the creative imagination" ("P," 50). Like Sibyl Vane, then, Willie Hughes is less a person than a
character whose attractiveness appears to lie at least in part in the fact that he
is never exactly himself. Even love, it seems, is ideally directed at someone or
something that is not entirely or exactly real.

Reading and Re-reading Newman

All this might seem very far from Newman: in insisting on the role of "passionate friendship" in the production of belief, Wilde appears to strike out on
his own. Yet, despite Newman's repeated insistence that belief comes from
within, he repeatedly celebrates the power of beliefs that are developed in relation to some attractive and lovable other.[49] In his novel *Loss and Gain: The
Story of a Convert,* for example, the hero Charles is inspired to convert to Roman Catholicism, at least in part as a result of an encounter with his friend
Willis, who has already converted.

[Willis said,] "May God give you that gift of faith, as He has given me! ..."
He drew Charles to him and kissed his cheek, and was gone before Charles
had time to say a word.

Yet Charles could not have spoken had he had ever so much opportunity. . . . It seemed as if the kiss of his friend had conveyed into his own
soul the enthusiasm which his words had betokened. He felt himself possessed, he knew not how, by a high superhuman power. . . . He perceived
that he had found, what indeed he had never sought, because he had never
known what it was, but what he had ever wanted,—a soul sympathetic
with his own.[50]

Here, the debates the hero has been mulling over in private—regarding the
meaning of the sacraments, the nature of the authority of the Church, the relation between the Church of England and Roman Catholicism—are suddenly, magically, brought to life. As in Wilde's "passionate friendship," love of
the man comes to seem inextricably linked to love of a belief in the idea.
Shortly after the conclusion of this scene, Charles travels to Rome and com-
pletes his conversion.

As Andrew Miller explains, Newman repeatedly stages moments like this
one in which "Reason is relinquished for an internalized intimacy, the epistemological for the social. Truth, Newman writes, 'has been upheld in the world
not as a system, not by books, not by argument, nor by temporal power, but
by the personal influence of such men . . . who are at once the teachers and
patterns of it.'"[51] The passage Miller cites comes from Newman's sermon
"Personal Influence, the Means of Propagating the Truth," in which he defines
the great teacher *not* in terms of his ability to tell his followers how to act:
"Moral character in itself, whether good or bad, as exhibited in thought and
conduct, surely cannot be duly represented in words."[52] Instead, the teacher's
"influence" derives from his ability to inspire his pupils with "the natural
beauty and majesty of virtue," the "novel[ty] and scarc[ity]" of his "holiness
and truth" that inspire "curiosity and awe" in his spectators—combined with
the fact that "the object of [men's] contemplation is beyond their reach."[53] As
a result of these attributes, the teacher "will become the object of feelings different in kind from those which mere intellectual excellence excites"[54] and so
able to "be an instrument in changing (as Scripture speaks) the heart, and
modeling all men after one exemplar; making them like himself, or rather like
One above himself, who is the beginning of a new creation."[55]

Admittedly, while Newman's ideal object of love is an Apostle who brings his lover to the one true faith, Wilde's is the actor who is incapable of ever being fully himself—or even, it seems, of being a conduit for a single authoritative message. (Willie Hughes was notoriously unfaithful, after all, and acted in several writers' plays.) And yet when juxtaposed in this way, Wilde's form of loving belief comes to seem like only an exaggerated version of Newman's. In both cases, by virtue of being vicariated through a beloved, the belief in question comes to seem both intensely and not exactly one's own. In both cases, in other words, the believer believes because he loves—and as Wilde insists, when we love we join ourselves to the beloved in a way that ultimately looks like nothing so much as what we do when we "enter into" or read a fiction.

I do not wish to erase the differences between the two writers—even if I could. After all, while Newman's goal is certitude, Wilde's is what William Cohen has described as "indeterminacy," as is demonstrated most clearly at the end of the story.[56] After mailing the letter describing his research to Erskine—and subsequently losing his faith in the Willie Hughes theory—the narrator rushes to his friend's to prevent him from reading it. But he arrives too late: Erskine has already been fully persuaded, even though he admits the theory will probably never be proven. The two men quarrel, then part, and the narrator doesn't hear from his friend again until he receives a letter informing him of Erskine's intention to kill himself "for Willie Hughes' sake: . . . and for the sake of Cyril Graham, whom I drove to his death by my shallow skepticism and ignorant lack of faith" ("P," 98). When the narrator arrives at Erskine's house, he finds that his friend has already died, but from consumption, not suicide—and that Erskine was fully aware that he was about to die of natural causes when he wrote the suicide note. "Why had Erskine written me that extraordinary letter?" the narrator demands. "Why when standing at the very gate of death had he turned back to tell me what was not true?" ("P," 100). Failing to come to any satisfying answer, at the end of the story the narrator hangs the forged portrait on the wall and admits that he still sometimes thinks "there is really a great deal to be said for the Willie Hughes theory of Shakespeare's Sonnets" ("P," 101). This is a conclusion that is no conclusion at all; it is simply a way to keep us in a state of suspense. It thus could not be further from the firm faith with which Newman concludes *Loss and Gain*. Upon converting, we are told, "there was more than the happiness of childhood in [Charles's] heart; he seemed to feel a rock under his feet; it was the *soliditas*

Cathedrae Petri. He went on kneeling, as if he were already in heaven, with the throne of God before him, and angels around; and as if to move were to lose his privilege."[57] This is anything but "fictional belief," it seems; it is simply certitude, pure and simple. And yet, even at this moment, belief is triangulated in a way that serves to ambiguate it. Immediately after the ceremony, Willis— now Father Aloysius—and Charles are reunited.

> "Oh," said Charles, "what shall I say?—the face of God! As I knelt I seemed to wish to say this, and this only, with the Patriarch, 'Now let me die, since I have seen Thy Face.'"
>
> "You, dear Reding," said Father Aloysius, "have keen fresh feelings; mine are blunted by familiarity."
>
> "No, Willis," he made answer, "you have taken the better part betimes, while I have loitered. Too late have I known Thee, O Thou ancient Truth; too late have I found Thee, First and only Fair."[58]

When Charles references "Thee, O Thou ancient Truth," we have to assume he is referring to the Roman Catholic church, but the syntax is confusing: he could just as easily be referring to Willis himself. And in this context of Wilde's critique it is hard not to see this as a moment of what Wilde describes as fictionalization—a moment, in other words, in which a belief is brought to life and so also ambiguated and vicariated by means of a beautiful and compelling other. And for Wilde, at least, such fictionalization is only a version— and perhaps even a less intense one, at that—of what happens when we read and re-read: in love, as in fiction, we become the possessor of a "life that had once been" our own.

In *Reading for the Plot,* Peter Brooks describes "narrative desire" in terms of a structurally impossible desire for origins and hence for certainty, closure, and ultimately death.[59] Here I am arguing for a different form of narrative desire—one that is oriented less toward the hallucinated plenitude of an origin we wish for but can never achieve than toward the ambiguous alterity of the beloved. Where Brooks sees the form of desire generated by fiction in terms of the desire to know one's true identity, in other words, both Wilde and Newman offer it as a way to imagine who we are not: who we love; who we might believe in. Beliefs possessed by means of this desire may be only ambiguously our own, but for that very reason they are passionately, vibrantly, alive.

NOTES

1. Elaine Scarry, *The Body in Pain: The Making and Unmaking of the World* (Oxford: Oxford University Press, 1985), 314. For Scarry, the power to perceive the difference between real and fictional experience has enormous ethical weight, for it guarantees that reading Amnesty International reports or enjoying a performance of *King Lear* is something other than sick voyeurism.

2. Jeff Nunokawa, *The Tame Passions of Wilde: The Styles of Manageable Desire* (Princeton: Princeton University Press, 2003), 35.

3. See, for example, J. M. Cameron's discussion of how for Newman, "Revelation ... is of an object that is given, known in us by an impression which is self-authenticating in the way the impressions of normal sense perception authenticate the reality of the objects to which they correspond" ("Newman and the Empiricist Tradition," in *The Rediscovery of Newman: An Oxford Symposium*, ed. John Coulson and A. M. Allchin [London: Sheed and Ward, 1967], 81–82).

4. See, for example, Bruce Bashford, "Oscar Wilde, His Criticism and His Critics," *English Literature in Transition, 1880–1920* 20, no. 4 (1977): 181–87; Peter Allen Dale, "Oscar Wilde: Crime and the 'Glorious Shapes of Art,'" *Victorian Newsletter* 88 (Fall 1995): 1–5; Lawrence Danson, "Wilde as Critic and Theorist," in *The Cambridge Companion to Oscar Wilde*, ed. Peter Raby (Cambridge: Cambridge University Press, 1997), 80–95; Patrice Hannon, "Aesthetic Criticism, Useless Art: Wilde, Zola, and 'The Portrait of Mr. W.H.'" in *Critical Essays on Oscar Wilde*, ed. Regenia Gagnier (New York: G. K. Hall, 1991), 186–201.

5. This tradition can be traced back at least to Raymond Williams, *Culture and Society, 1780–1950* (New York: Columbia University Press, 1958). More recent examples include Regenia Gagnier, "A Critique of Practical Aesthetics," in *Aesthetics and Ideology*, ed. George Levine (New Brunswick: Rutgers University Press, 1994), 264–82; Amanda Anderson, *The Powers of Distance: Cosmopolitanism and the Cultivation of Detachment* (Princeton: Princeton University Press, 2001); David Wayne Thomas, *Cultivating Victorians: Liberal Culture and the Aesthetic* (Philadelphia: University of Pennsylvania Press, 2004); Leela Gandhi, *Affective Communities: Anticolonial Thought, Fin-de-Siècle Radicalism, and the Politics of Friendship* (Durham: Duke University Press, 2006).

6. See, for example, Linda Dowling, *Language and Decadence in the Victorian Fin de Siècle* (Princeton: Princeton University Press, 1986); Eve Kosofsky Sedgwick, *The Epistemology of the Closet* (Berkeley: University of California Press, 1990); William A. Cohen, *Sex Scandal: The Private Parts of Victorian Fiction* (Durham: Duke University Press, 1996).

7. See, for example, Cohen, *Sex Scandal;* Joel Fineman, *Shakespeare's Perjured Eye: The Invention of Poetic Subjectivity in the Sonnets* (Berkeley: University of California Press, 1986).

8. Critics who have been interested in Wilde's epistemology include Wendell V.

Harris, "Arnold, Pater, Wilde, and the Object as in Themselves They See It," *Studies in English Literature, 1500–1900* 11, no. 4 (Autumn 1971): 733–47; Eva Thienpont, "'To Play Gracefully with Ideas': Oscar Wilde's Personal Platonism in Poetics," *The Wildean* 20 (January 2002): 37–48; William Shuter, "Pater, Wilde, Douglas and the Impact of 'Greats,'" *English Literature in Transition, 1880–1920* 46, no. 3 (2003): 250–78; Herbert Sussman, "Criticism as Art: Form in Oscar Wilde's Critical Writings," *Studies in Philology* 70, no. 2 (1973): 108–22. Philip E. Smith II and Michael S. Helfand have done important work in placing Wilde's work in the context of contemporary debates about evolution and Hegelian materialism. They have focused more on his interest in social development and theories of truth than on the vexing problem of how we know what we know, why we believe what we do, and the conditions and consequences of changing one's mind. Philip E. Smith II and Michael S. Helfand, ed. and commentary, *Oscar Wilde's Oxford Notebooks: A Portrait of Mind in the Making* (New York: Oxford University Press, 1989); Philip E. Smith II and Michael S. Helfand, "Anarchy and Culture: The Evolutionary Turn of Cultural Criticism in the Works of Oscar Wilde," *Texas Studies in Literature and Language* 20, no. 2 (Summer 1978): 199–215.

9. Ellis Hanson, *Decadence and Catholicism* (Cambridge: Harvard University Press, 1997), 231, 233. In making this claim, Hanson is participating in a tradition that dates back at least to Wilde's friend Vincent O'Sullivan, who claimed, "He knew little about theology, and the theological mind he abhorred. All he had retained out of Newman was the passage about the snapdragon under the walls of Trinity" (qtd. in George Woodcock, *Oscar Wilde: The Double Image* [Montreal: Black Rose Books, 1989], 69). At the opposite end of the spectrum is someone like Jan B. Gordon who points out the similarities between Newman's *Apologia* and Wilde's *De Profundis*. Gordon is primarily interested in the formal resonances, however, rather than any connections between their philosophies of belief ("Wilde and Newman: The Confessional Mode," *Renascence: Essays on Value in Literature* 22, no. 4 [Summer 1970]: 183–91). On the history of Wilde's interest in Newman, see Richard Ellmann, *Oscar Wilde* (New York: Knopf, 1988).

10. See Oliver S. Buckton for a discussion of the question of Newman's homosexuality. *Secret Selves: Confession and Same-Sex Desire in Victorian Autobiography* (Chapel Hill: University of North Carolina Press, 1998).

11. See, for example, Martha C. Nussbaum, *Love's Knowledge: Essays on Philosophy and Literature* (New York: Oxford University Press, 1990).

12. My thanks to Audrey Jaffe for this formulation. I make a different but related argument in "Oscar Wilde's Fictions of Belief," *Novel* 42, no. 2 (Summer, 2009): 175–82.

13. John Henry Cardinal Newman, *An Essay in Aid of a Grammar of Assent*, 1870; Intro. Nicholas Lash (Notre Dame: University of Notre Dame Press, 1979), 276; hereafter abbreviated *E*.

14. See *E*, 181–208, for a discussion of the "Indefectibility of Certitude." Also see Jonathan Loesberg's discussion of certitude in *Fictions of Consciousness: Mill, Newman, and the Reading of Victorian Prose* (New Brunswick: Rutgers University Press, 1986), chap. 6.

15. J. A. Froude, *Short Studies on Great Subjects,* 2nd series (New York: Charles Scribner's Sons, 1905), 106. Froude continues: "He may say that we may be convinced of what is false, but only certain of what is true. But this is nothing to the purpose, so long as we have no criterion to distinguish one from the other as an internal impression" (*Short Studies,* 106). Also see Hugo Meynell, "Newman's Vindication of Faith in the Grammar of Assent" in *Newman After a Hundred Years,* ed. Ian Ker and Alan G. Hill (Oxford: Clarendon, 1990), 255–59; and Martin J. Svaglic, "John Henry Newman: The Victorian Experience" in *The Victorian Experience: The Prose Writers,* ed. Richard A. Levine (Athens: Ohio University Press, 1982), 47–82.

16. Loesberg, *Fictions of Consciousness,* 116. Also see Meynell's discussion of the continuity Newman wants to stress "between the kind of reasoning suitable in religious matters and that which applies to science and to ordinary life" ("Newman's Vindication of Faith," 250). Also see Nicholas Lash, "Introduction," John Henry Cardinal Newman, *An Essay in Aid of a Grammar of Assent* (Notre Dame: University of Notre Dame Press, 1979), 1–21; and Robert Pattison, *The Great Dissent: John Henry Newman and the Liberal Heresy* (New York: Oxford University Press, 1991).

17. Loesberg, *Fictions of Consciousness,* 117. Other commentators who have pointed out the problems created by appearing to ground truth in feeling in this way include David A. Pailin, *The Way to Faith: An Examination of Newman's* Grammar of Assent *as a Response to the Search for Certainty in Faith* (London: Epworth Press, 1969), and Thomas Vargish, *Newman: The Contemplation of Mind* (Oxford: Clarendon, 1970).

18. In *The Epistemology of the Closet,* Eve Sedgwick describes Wilde's "sentimentality" as a way to vicariate desire at a moment when homosexuality was being defined in terms of the love of the same. In this essay I discuss a similar conflation or confusion of identification and desire, but rather than the tragic detour desire must take in a homophobic social order, in "The Portrait of Mr. W.H.," I argue, vicariation is couched as the means by which all belief is brought to life. Sedgwick, *The Epistemology of the Closet,* chap. 3.

19. Hanson notes how Wilde casts belief in the Willie Hughes theory in religious terms (*Decadence and Catholicism*).

20. Oscar Wilde, "The Portrait of Mr. W.H." (1889; rpt. in *The Soul of Man under Socialism and Selected Critical Prose,* ed. Linda Dowling [London: Penguin, 2001]), 41; hereafter abbreviated "P."

21. John Henry Cardinal Newman, *Apologia Pro Vita Sua* (1864; rpt. New York: W. W. Norton, 1968), 2.

22. For a thorough discussion of this debate, see Newman, *Apologia Pro Vita Sua,* "Note G: Lying and Equivocation" (259–69).

23. Jan-Melissa Schramm, *Testimony and Advocacy in Victorian Law, Literature, and Theology* (Cambridge: Cambridge University Press, 2000), 162.

24. In a letter from 1885 to H. C. Marillier, Wilde claimed similarly, "I think I would more readily die for what I do not believe in than for what I hold to be true" (rpt. in Merlin Holland and Rupert Hart-Davis, *The Complete Letters of Oscar Wilde* [London: Fourth Estate, 2000], 272).

25. According to Sussman, "within the terms of aestheticism," Cyril's death serves as a "vindication by showing his theory as the form given to his own intense feeling" ("Criticism as Art," 116). As Cohen points out, Wilde's insistence that suicide is a tragic form of skepticism suggests otherwise (*Sex Scandal,* 204).

26. As Robert Pattison explains, Newman's goal here is to reject the liberal premise "that reason alone validated belief" on the grounds that such a claim "ignored the role of the illative sense in shaping a view of life" (*The Great Dissent: John Henry Newman and the Liberal Heresy* [New York: Oxford University Press, 1991], 152).

27. See, for example, "Books and Magazines," *Sunday Times* (June 30, 1889): 2. Critics have debated which version of this essay should be regarded as authoritative: the shorter version that was published in *Blackwood's Edinburgh Magazine* in July 1889 or the expanded version that Wilde attempted and failed to publish during his lifetime. See, for example, Lawrence Danson, *Wilde's Intentions: The Artist in His Criticism* (Oxford: Clarendon Press, 1997). I have chosen to use the longer version since it enables me to make my case in a slightly stronger form. For a detailed discussion of the history of the text, see Horst Schroeder, *Oscar Wilde, The Portrait of Mr. W.H. — Its Composition, Publication and Reception* (Braunschweig: Technische Universität Carolo-Wilhelmina zu Braunschweig, 1984).

28. See, for example, Norbert Kohl, *Oscar Wilde: The Works of a Conformist Rebel* (Cambridge: Cambridge University Press, 1989).

29. Oscar Wilde, "The Truth of Masks" (1891; rpt. in *The Soul of Man under Socialism and Selected Critical Prose,* ed. Linda Dowling [London: Penguin, 2001]), 297.

30. Wilde, "Truth of Masks," 290.

31. Both Cohen and Paul K. Saint-Amour claim that the narrator's ability to give away his belief suggests the problem with regarding belief as a kind of object. For Cohen, this objectification represents a fall from the "indeterminacy" that Wilde privileged in both his life and his philosophy of interpretation—a fall that results from a hermeneutics that turns literature into nothing more than a puzzle to be solved. In Saint-Amour's account, the fact that the narrator loses his belief only to have his friend Erskine pick it up turns the story into a parable of intellectual property: "So long as ideas, expressions, or beliefs can be owned as private property, they will circulate like private property. . . . By contrast, ideas and beliefs untrammeled by intellectual property forms might be the matrix of community" (*The Copywrights: Intellectual Property and the Literary Imagination* [Ithaca: Cornell University Press, 2003], 110). For both critics, then, object-hood is the source of the problem. Yet on many occasions Wilde praises those who regard beliefs as things insofar as it makes them available to certain forms of play. See, for example, the description in *Dorian Gray* of how Lord Henry "played with the idea, and grew willful; tossed it into the air and transformed it; let it escape and recaptured it; made it iridescent with fancy, and winged it with paradox" (Oscar Wilde, *The Picture of Dorian Gray* [1891; ed. Joseph Bristow (Oxford: Oxford University Press, 2006)], 38).

32. Oscar Wilde, "A Few Maxims for the Instruction of the Over-Educated"

(1894); rpt. in *Complete Works of Oscar Wilde,* Intro. Merlin Holland (Glasgow: HarperCollins, 2003), 1242.

33. It is worth noting the contrast between this solution and that offered by someone like John Stuart Mill. While in *On Liberty,* Mill insists on the importance of disputation as a way to make believers aware of and invested in their own beliefs, Wilde and Newman call attention to the role of love. John Stuart Mill, *On Liberty* (1859; London: Penguin, 1985), chap. 2. Also see William James, "The Will to Believe," on the distinction between living and dead beliefs (1897; rpt. in *The Will to Believe and Other Essays in Popular Philosophy; and Human Immortality: Two Supposed Objections to the Doctrine* [New York: Dover, 1956], 3).

34. The heading is a phrase Wilde repeats several times in the notebooks he kept at Oxford. It also appears in "The Portrait": "I had never seen my friend, but he had been with me for many years, and it was to his influence that I had owed my passion for Greek thought and art, and indeed all my sympathy with the Hellenic spirit. [To do philosophy with love.] How that phrase had stirred me in my Oxford days! I did not understand then why it was so. But I knew now" ("P," 92–93).

35. As Rei Terada explains, "Pity separates the empirical from the conceptual, the unrepeatable from the expressible, and animality from humanity" (*Feeling in Theory: Emotion after the "Death of the Subject"* [Cambridge: Harvard University Press, 2001], 35). "'Without a certain nonidentification,' pity loses its grip" (34). Hence, "that strange self-pity that man so often feels for himself" (this is Wilde again) places even our "sense of perilous joy" or "some touch or thrill of pain" at something of a distance (91).

36. I disagree here with Danson's claim that "Wilde tried to speak about sexual desire by withholding the language of his own speaking—always deferring the revelation the language promises, because that revelation, being *in* language, would necessarily falsify his truth" (*Wilde's Intentions,* 106). Despite his apparent defense of indeterminacy here, Danson still seems to hold up the sexual as the ultimate referent here, whereas in my account the point is the very impossibility of disaggregating the sexual from the epistemological.

37. See, for example, Cohen, *Sex Scandal;* Kevin Kopelson, "Wilde, Barthes, and the Orgasmics of Truth," *Genders* 7 (March 1990): 22–31; Richard Halpern, *Shakespeare's Perfume: Sodomy and Sublimity in the Sonnets, Wilde, Freud, and Lacan* (Philadelphia: University of Pennsylvania Press, 2002); Stephen Arata, *Fictions of Loss in the Victorian Fin de Siècle* (Cambridge: Cambridge University Press, 1996); Hanson, *Decadence and Catholicism.*

38. As Joseph Bristow writes (characteristically drily), "The 'Portrait,' to say the least, provides an exemplary instance of transference" (*Effeminate England: Homoerotic Writing After 1885* [New York: Columbia University Press, 1995], 44).

39. Christopher Craft, "Come See About Me; Enchantment of the Double in *The Picture of Dorian Gray,*" *Representations* 91 (Summer 2005): 117. Also see Danson's discussion of how "the description of the translation itself and of its effects is marked by the numinous words—strange, curious, subtle; colour, influence, passion—that also

describe the 'poisonous' yellow book that Lord Henry Wotton gives Dorian Gray" (*Wilde's Intentions,* 115). Finally, see Linda Dowling, *Hellenism and Homosexuality in Victorian Oxford* (Ithaca: Cornell University Press, 1994).

40. See R. B. Kershner Jr., "Artist, Critic, and Performer: Wilde and Joyce on Shakespeare," *Texas Studies in Literature and Language* 20, no. 2 (Summer 1978): 216–29; Joseph Bristow, "Wilde, *Dorian Gray,* and Gross Indecency," in *Sexual Sameness: Textual Differences in Lesbian and Gay Writing,* ed. Joseph Bristow (London: Routledge, 1992), 44–63; Danson, *Wilde's Intentions.*

41. Arata discusses this issue at some length in *Fictions of Loss.*

42. See for example Edward Dowden, *The Sonnets of William Shakspere* (London: Kegan Paul, Trench, 1881), introduction.

43. See Samuel Taylor Coleridge, "Shakespere's Sonnets," *Table Talk and Omniana* (London: George Bell, 1903), 220–23.

44. See Dowden, *The Sonnets of William Shakspere,* 7.

45. See James Boaden, "To What Person the Sonnets of Shakespeare were Actually Addressed," *Gentleman's Magazine,* n.s., 102, no. 25 (September 1832): 217–19.

46. Henry Hallam, *Introduction to the Literature of Europe in the Fifteenth, Sixteenth, and Seventeenth Centuries,* vol. 3 (London: John Murray, 1872), 264.

47. Wilde, *Picture of Dorian Gray,* 46.

48. Wilde, *Picture of Dorian Gray,* 45.

49. As George Levine points out, he also acknowledged the role of the will in belief (*The Boundaries of Fiction: Carlyle, Macaulay, Newman* [Princeton: Princeton University Press, 1968]), chap. 3. Also see David DeLaura, *Hebrew and Hellene in Victorian England: Newman, Arnold, and Pater* (Austin: University of Texas Press, 1969), chap. 23.

50. John Henry Cardinal Newman, *Loss and Gain: The Story of a Convert* (1848; Teddington: Echo Library, 2008), part II, chap. 20.

51. Andrew H. Miller, *The Burdens of Perfection: On Ethics and Reading in Nineteenth-Century British Literature* (Ithaca: Cornell University Press, 2008), 155.

52. John Henry Cardinal Newman, "Personal Influence, the Means of Propagating Truth" (1832); rpt. in *Fifteen Sermons Preached before the University of Oxford between A.D. 1826 and 1843* (Notre Dame: University of Notre Dame, 1997), 85.

53. Newman, "Personal Influence," 92–93.

54. Newman, "Personal Influence," 95.

55. Newman, "Personal Influence," 86–87.

56. Cohen, *Sex Scandal,* chap. 6. Also see Kopelson, "Wilde, Barthes, and the Orgasmics of Truth."

57. Newman, *Loss and Gain,* part III, chap. 11.

58. Newman, *Loss and Gain,* part III, chap. 11.

59. Peter Brooks, *Reading for the Plot: Design and Intention in Narrative* (Cambridge: Harvard University Press, 1984).

Reading Feeling and the "Transferred Life"

THE MILL ON THE FLOSS

GARRETT STEWART

No commas in my title. There is a series implicit there (reading, feeling, and its intersubjective results), but any such distinguishable sequence is swept up in a more intense textual transfusion by George Eliot's *The Mill on the Floss* (1860). Reading and feeling separately contribute, yes, to their own version of what Eliot calls the "transferred life" of human sympathy and identification. But to show this, to prove it on the pulse of her narrative, she stages a scene not just of reading feeling but (in both grammatical senses) of feeling read: the textually transcribed decipherment of desire offered up, from within plot, as gift to a heroine desperately needing to have that desire read rightly by another.

Supposedly transcending such textual interchange, a different motive holds sway a decade and a half later in Eliot's *Daniel Deronda* (1876). In my study of affect's rhetorical circuitry in nineteenth-century British fiction, I wanted to show, in a chapter called "Mordecai's Consumption," how the tubercular visionary scribe by that name in *Deronda*, surrendering to oblivion the actual words of his proto-Zionist writings, dies into, as well as in the arms of, the eponymous hero. He does so in order to embody in part, or better to disembody, a deflected fable of literary consumption itself.[1] His message survives its medium by giving up on any textual materiality of "transmission" to become an idea incorporate in another. With the not only vicarious but vampiric overtones of the dying writer's power play in this case, Mordecai's transfer of his life to a surrogate consciousness anticipates the late-Victorian "gothic of reading" taken up in the subsequent and last chapter of *Dear Reader*. At the same time, it plays out in an unnerving key the daydream of a writer's abstracted vision living on—in the spirit if not the letter—through the passive receptacle of a participant reader (Daniel, our stand-in). This is the reader for whom the ultimate power of writing, including ruminative prose fiction, would be internalized and remotivating rather than citational. Imagined in Eliot's tacit parable, then, is a literate but ultimately ethical community in which a text's unifying force of idea will always reverberate in excess of its own specific wording.

This is the novelist's fantasy. Call it her fiction. Certainly her metafiction—where the *feeling of reading*, objective and subjective genitive alike, is so keen and immersive that it maintains itself in reflection long after the text has been set aside. It thus provides its own textual agency in that characteristic Victorian strand of moral perfectionism unmistakable in Eliot's prose ambition. Compared to *Daniel Deronda*, though, there is something less disingenuous at the climax of *The Mill on the Floss*, where it is writing per se that must candidly be made to carry the burden of whatever text-sponsored perfectionism a novel can end by imagining, and this in the form, always for Eliot, of widened fellow-feeling. Writing: with all its rhetorical hooks, bonds, connectivities—not some vague ether of racial uplift into which the permeating word of faith has been released. Writing in its most personal form: a letter addressed from one character to another, hero to heroine, and through her to us. There are reasons in the earlier novel for this vesting of faith in the intersubjectivity of a palpably exchanged text. In contrast to the later transpersonal aura of *Daniel Deronda*, in *The Mill on the Floss* the threat of skepticism (in a philosophical problematic central to the work of Stanley Cavell, to which we will be returning) is more everyday than doctrinal, secular rather than religious. Under its shadow, where belief in others must survive—is in fact all that can survive—a dethroned faith in the metaphysical One, whether God or His chosen people, a private act of writing in itself can generate a modest utopian valence (whatever the devastations of plot itself). This is the gesture that would later be inflated for the dreamed social consolidation at the close of *Daniel Deronda*.

If Georges Poulet is even half right about the phenomenology of literary cognition when he proposes that in reading "I am the subject"—the subject, not the object—"of thoughts other than my own," then Eliot's last novel would contrive the symbolic bypass of such textual mediation altogether.[2] Where reading is ordinarily a kind of thought-transference conveyed by expressive language, *Daniel Deronda* carries the dynamic of inspiration to the point of an almost literal metempsychosis. Where did this idea come from in Eliot's work? By what route did an ethics of affect and cognitive osmosis associated with the specific rhetorical force of potent writing evolve into the uncanny dimensions of Mordecai's death wish for a transauthorial identity prolonged by verbal divestment? With this question brought to focus in the rearview mirror of Eliot's last novel, we can look back past the more straightforward communitarianism of reading in *Middlemarch* (1871–72)—with its envisioned salutary reception, on the closing page, of the Dorothea "whose story we know," a story whose generative aftershocks we may embed in our own thoughts or even reembody in action—to an earlier and more grievous narrative affect sketched out at two levels of enactment in *The Mill*. For Maggie Tulliver's story makes for a novel in which the vicarious emotive investment in character—what Freudian psychoanalysis would come as if in unconscious echo of Eliot to categorize as "transference"—bears directly on the genre determinations of prose fiction as not only understood but explicated by Eliot in the novel's own pages. In the process, the texture of Maggie's story invites a reading of fictional prose as such, as worded plotting, that I call narratography.[3]

Asking where Mordecai's fantasy comes from—his dream of spiritual delegation without textual transmission—is a way of asking, therefore, how deep it goes in Eliot's conception of fictional power. At the origin of reading's metaphysical tropology in Eliot, well short of its spectral invasiveness in the word-cleansed purity of Mordecai's posthumous introjection by Daniel, what we will find is that Eliot's "gift of transferred life" (7,3:503) in *The Mill* locates the identificatory self-transcendence of what Paul Ricoeur would call *Oneself as Another*.[4] But this function, in comparison with *Daniel Deronda*, is so little mystified in Eliot's early novel—so little fantasized to lie beyond either the grave or the emotive capacities of written language—that it is conveyed instead by an epistolary act of textual confession. This is a letter designed, in reception, to retrace and crystallize our own relation as readers both to the letter writer himself as character, whose frustrated passion we live through as if from within, and to the heroine (his and ours) whose trauma he renarrates in prose so that she might see at last, and we in turn might revisit, the way her own anguished life is "transferred" to meaning in the eye of the Other: if only the meaning of literary affect itself, a function dispossessive and self-forgetting. As more perversely yet in *Daniel Deronda*, literary force becomes in this way a model for living sympathy rather than for textual continuance or literary immortality.

Narrative Vantage: Plot's "Unmapped River"

With its opening and entirely open frame, *The Mill on the Floss* turns nostalgic autobiography (the unnamed narrator's hazy brief retrospect) into a veritable figure for identification more generally. But this is only before it dissolves the whole inaugural apparatus into a mere allegory of dreamlike invention. No sooner implanted than dismantled, this initial framing device dissipates on the spot into the historical tense of a fictional chronicle, with no return to the locus of narration from the social sphere of plot. The sympathetic vibrations established between the unnamed autobiographical narrator and the emergent heroine in these first pages must, from there on, be delegated as pathos—within the provincial ethos of plot—to an alternately bookish and scribal character, that reader and metanarrative letter-writer, known in both aspects as Philip Wakem, whose expressive intuition is installed as the reader's own further literary tuition.

After the launching pages, that is, a personified narrator with a Wordsworthian measure to her phrase, recognizable as Eliot herself at her most pastoralist, gives way to a depersonified narrative discourse. Only much later in the story do we return not just to the perspective but to the prose itself—at first unconscious, then written out—of a participant witness as figured reader, articulating the plot in his own invested words of response. And it is only after this—in Maggie's rush toward death, to which only omniscience is privy—that Philip Wakem's epistolary narrative *to* Maggie is supplanted in the last pages by Eliot's resumed version of the story to us. The late rhetorical maneuver is definitive in its inversion of interpretive focus. Redoubling identification, we take up the heroine's own newly vacated position as reader of her own story in Philip's letter, a reading under the force of its sympathetic comprehension. In its dizzying ingenuity, this gesture of Philip's writing falls so little short of spectacular exaggeration that it makes a spectacle of our own riveted investment in Maggie's tale.

But not until we have the narrator's own famous intervention about Maggie's missed chances as well as flawed energies. "'Character,' says Novalis, in one of his questionable aphorisms—" and we hang on the word in suspended quotation long enough to start clustering our own associations around it; this, until they are syntactically dispelled with the exhaustive romantic equation that "character is destiny" (6,6:401). Inaugurating the vest-pocket narratology to follow, the passing narratographic irony of this grammatical hovering is clear. Despite emphatic repetition in such an oratorical aside, character (like the noun itself) can in no sense stand alone. Enter Eliot as theorist of the novel, in her wittiest sparring posture. "But not the whole of destiny." If there had been no murder in the family, even Hamlet might have "got through life with a reputation of sanity, nothwithstanding many soliloquies, and some moody sarcasms . . . " (6,6:402).

In the paragraph from *The Mill on the Floss* immediately following Eliot's own loaded disquisition on Novalis, Eliot writes of her heroine, soon to drown, that her as yet "hidden" end, her "destiny," must wait, no less, "to reveal itself like the course of an unmapped river" (6,6:402). Prophecy is perversely seeded in cliché. What will emerge depends in part on what comes to Maggie, of course, as to anyone. So far, the writing is trying to finesse what plot cannot directly address, reminding us ominously that "we only know that the river is full and rapid, and that for all rivers there is the same final home" (6,6:402). Across the headlong assonance of "that . . . rapid . . . that" within the intractable prophetic arc of "know . . . home," prose makes its further alliterative mark along the fricative syllabification of "rivers full . . . rivers . . . final." In this way, in narratographic response to Eliot's own narratological trope, a rhetoric of temporality can be found locally floated upon a stylistics of the interval.

That's at the alphabetic stratum alone. Within the broader logic of the trope, the charted "course" of the river is also its felt coursing. Both "full and rapid," its weighted vector is dynamized as a medium. The point is obvious, the rhetoric ingrown and almost flagrant: even given the fullness of who Maggie is, we must still wait to see what she does—and what is done to her in the defeat of her overflowing desires, where what wells up in her is often so brimful that she can be submerged and choked off by it. In the work of plot, being and becoming must be linked to happening, outcome to contingency, character to circumstance. Yet by troping her life as a course of unknown duration despite its certain end, contingency is overdetermined by dramatic irony, figuration shriveled to mere prefiguration. We can sum it up this way: accident drenches—and finally drowns—the heroine in the very symbol of her own being. This is Eliot's ultimate formal gamble, her move to assuage the gap, and synthesize the rift, between character and incident. Such is the design upon us of plot all told, its narratological conversion of the pitiful to the epiphanic. Carried along by this plot, narratography nonetheless resists its naturalization by stalling momentarily over the subsidiary tropes that would secure it, tropes that even penetrate, as we will find, to the phonetic fissures of syntax itself as the medial residuum of the signifier. Never more strikingly solicited in Victorian fiction than by the phonetic eddying and backwash of *The Mill on the Floss,* narratography stays vigilant to just this sliding byplay of the novel's mediating prose—and especially to those passages, associated with Philip Wakem's distanced intimacy with the heroine, that read our own reading back to us. And do so just before releasing narrative—now preordained in its response—back to the heavily stylized apocalypse of private annihilation. Put another way, character in fiction is inflected by, among other things, *verbal* circumstance.

From Omniscience to Empathy: Framing and Its Avatars

The telos of Eliot's plot is the turn from reflective grief to the totality of elegiac form—and this as mediated by the associative logic of figuration. Moreover, this transition from lived misery to formal mastery is brokered by, and embodied in, one character above all in *The Mill on the Floss.* This is the heroine's disappointed lover Philip, subtly intelligent, humpbacked, doting: that sensitive and deformed surrogate—as he will become—for the reader's own exclusion from Maggie's world. Phrased otherwise, the only thing that can make good on the heroine's wasting fate is the good it can be imagined to do us—and, furthermore, can already be imaged as doing by proxy from within the text. This restorative force transpires across Philip's own elevation, even before Maggie's actual death, from mourning to the state of meaning. Hence the exemplary value, the almost parabolic role, of Philip's hard-won selfless affect as he lives through (in both sense) Maggie's suffering and survives to tell of it—and of its potent hold on him.

More to the point, however, he does so not as her doom's residual legatee and narrator. He tells Maggie's story back to the heroine *herself.* This happens in the letter that struggles to justify her grief as it were to herself, on the very way to her death by drowning. Without benefit of our omniscient narrator, Philip writes to her what he knows must have happened in the suspected elopement with Stephen. He thus gives her the chance to read of her ordeal, rather than merely endure it, to read of it briefly under a sympathetic spiri-

tual analysis, compressed, distilled, and totalized by a comprehensive understanding and forgiveness. He offers this grace of form, in fact, in the explicit
terms of a returned "gift." With the heroine almost too numbed by misstep
and ill luck even to think straight, Philip takes up the reflective function and
helps not just to objectify her own life for recognition—but to render it sub-
jectively again, as if from the inside. In a sense, Philip has thus taken over
from the nameless narrator of the prologue, who passed the baton to omniscience early on. Now it is left to a character's own written prose to formulate
the meaning of the story on the very eve of closure. By Philip's ultimate term
for an unshaken faith in Maggie, as we'll see, he finds a cure for skepticism in
that quintessentially novelistic ratio of being to meaning that he calls "belief."
Trying like the reader to extricate plot's spiritual gist from its sad contingen-
cies, Philip's language thus positions us for the one remaining turn of plot:
the sudden death by unmapped floodwaters in a stream so symbolic that one
sinks in it as in time itself, recovering in the process the long-lost currents of
childhood.

Until Philip's letter, there have been two faces to his empathy: depending
on whether his sensitivities are facing forward or back. In contrast to his gen-
erosity of interpretation at the end, there is the shock of prefiguration. Philip
seems almost to script the fatality in advance. It's one thing for the novelist after Austen to claim unimpeded access to the inner lives of others through the
indirect discourse of characterization. But projecting that access, that intersubjective attunement—that form of self-effacement, yet ultimately that
form of power—back into plot is likely to happen only at the risk of the uncanny, of the clairvoyant or the telepathic. Fending against this, Eliot's impulse is to *personify* sympathetic apprehension as an indwelling grace. Thus
does she compensate the disabled Philip Wakem, who adores Maggie, with so
thorough an empathy for her heroine that he is with Maggie even in her
coasting toward another man, living in and through her passion and ethical
panic, both to Philip's pain and to his spiritual exaltation.

All this he will spell out in that final letter to her—well after we have seen
its emotional force in action upon him in his role as a speculative plotter of
her future: an action that amounts at one crucial point to a dream vision like
that of the narrator's own in the pastoral proem. But more than this is ac-
complished when Philip's desire dips into its unconscious fears. To take the
psychoanalytic measure—and scan the narrative horizons at the same time—
of his premonitory nightmare, we must first return to the opening of the
novel to mark how mimesis dreams its way into its own *setting* before coming

fully awake to plot. In a Wordsworthian gambit of tranquil restoration almost narcoleptically figured, what the narrator evokes by present description ("I remember . . . I remember") is her having long ago paused on a stone bridge—a quasi-natural extension of the land—at exactly the moment when a little girl stops at water's edge, facing a swollen "stream" that "half drowns" the bank under a sky whose "clouds are threatening." It is a case of narratology by stylistic premonition in a novel that will end in that girl's storm-tossed descent beneath the same waters, engulfed by the overflow of passion's own tidal swell. The parallel between present remembrance and past avatar seems to conjure the girl as a younger self, but a self who will never have survived, we are to find, into such nostalgic reflection.

As this brief descriptive proem quickly fades to a plot of monolithic disappointment, what narratography, even so far, can add to the fleeting dual perspective of such an opening is to calibrate the slack in grammatical ligature that abets a curious semiconscious parallel between reflective scene-setting and triggered plot. Suggested in this way, through the merest noddingoff of prose itself (into lyric diffusion), is the passage's forced strain toward continuity across the years. For the narrator turns from her position on the bridge to the girl who has been standing "on the same spot"—not on the bridge, we quickly correct ourselves, but on her own standing-ground—"the same spot at the water's edge since I paused on the bridge." This minuscule adverbial ambiguity projects its own dreamlike equivalent of temporal suspension into the tacit conflation of identities. The meditative arrest of the two human figures—youth herself being a rhetorical figure for consciousness in another time and condition—is thus emblematically coterminous so far. But plot must immediately begin separating the motivated trajectory of the young girl from her deceptive teleological incarnation (given the impending tragedy) as a potential narrating voice. Whatever empathetic unity of understanding has been implicitly vested in advance in the discourse of this nameless autobiographic decoy, the voice of this persona must now be stripped from the doings of the emergent heroine, who is sent fresh into event to pursue the seemingly unmarked but in fact thoroughly inscribed course of her own decline.

Just as the narrator's arms are starting to grow numb from leaning on the cold stone, the girl goes (is in fact sent by narration) inside from the river bank, back to family life—back to those social constraints, whatever their fireside temptations at this imagined moment, that are always to be interrupting her satisfaction in the outdoor world she so freely and fixedly loves.

All is now rational: "It is time [she] went in, I think." The Wordsworthian fall is upon her. From here out, countless dead metaphors of natural impulse for the onrush and drain of emotion, for tidal sweeps of feeling, begin circulating through the text. In just this regard, we are reminded that Georg Lukács sees in romantic disillusionment a compound alienation from two natures at once: impersonal, often insentient nature, strictly speaking, and the "second nature" of society, equally given to the individual life yet entirely constructed by culture, even while deceptively naturalized in its humanist bulwarks.[5] Alienation from the landscape is therefore, in the novels Lukács studies, a back-formation from social estrangement. This fits perfectly—up to a point—the case of Maggie Tulliver. Nature's fullness only becomes lethal to her because of the killing effect of a repressive society's "second nature." But it isn't that simple. Because Maggie is herself presented as naturalness personified—and not least in her frustrations, repeatedly described as bursting the seams of propriety, swamping her own judgment, drowning her will in the undertow of native and ungovernable impulse. Playing a double game, figuration aspires to a dialectic all its own, whose strain tells upon the registers of narratographic reading at every other turn.

From the point at which heroine and plot together detach from the "metaformal" voice of the inaugural narrative discourse, second nature begins encroaching poisonously onto first, especially in its pastoral rather than fluvial aspects—weeding out the very roots of its own would-be emotional tenacity. Returning to the imagined scene and final domestic trope of the elegiac opening, we see that the door is closed behind the heroine's fullest prospects once and forever by plot itself, for which the launching narratorial daydream is both metaphor and also matrix. "Ah, my arms are really benumbed," adds the bestirred narrator, for "I have been pressing my elbows on the arms of my chair and dreaming." Architecture fades away to architectonic emblem: the proverbial bridge to the past. Yet it is a structure too frail in this case to sustain its engineering across the long arc of plot. As an autobiographic gesture of romantic nostalgia, this whole retrospective (and, in light of the coming fatality, paradoxical) apparatus vanishes now into thin air. Summoning back the scene of her own youth, it would seem, and displacing it onto Maggie's, has been the necessary first—and credibly unconscious (dreamlike)—move on the narrator's part in initiating her tale, which then takes on a life, and death, of its own. It will need, or tolerate, no return whatsoever to this vaporous scene of inception—with its passing narratology of fateful forecast and its fleeting narratography of phantom coterminous habitation ("on the same spot"). There is to be room from here out only for Maggie's own person, not for her virtual future avatar, in the selfsame Wordsworthian "spot of time" along the ultimately lethal Floss. As plot opens out to a wider social scene, the narrator withdraws to a choric rather than a personified function in order to micromanage—at the level of diction and syntax—both the coming premonitions and their figuratively redemptive dead end.

The Fall into Plot

The least shadow of a narrative persona has thus been thrown over plot in the mode of authorial comment but never again stationed, located, or personified in any similar fashion. Dreaming one's way into Maggie's story is a function eventually delegated not to an authorial persona but to a substitute for the reader in our by now cumulative investment in Maggie's fate. Having developed her brief dream scene as prologue, Eliot then goes so far as to yield up her very seat in the easy chair of reflective invention to her most obvious functionary within plot. When Philip, many chapters later, "threw himself, with a sense of fatigue, into" his own version of the "arm-chair" at the opening (6,8:427), he is in his "painting room" rather than some generalized and idiomatic *drawing room*.[6] This is a specific site of representational labor in which he finds himself "looking *round* absently at the views of water and rock that were ranged *around*" (emphasis added)—with that almost narcotic repetition stationed to precede the moment when "he fell into a doze" (6,8:427). Apart from prose echoes, one vector is undeniable. Down into his chair he throws himself, and further to sleep he falls, complete with its subsequent dream of a further plummet for his beloved Maggie—and, as it turns out, its now hallucinated further "view" of both "water and rock" as if they were retinal afterimages from his own drawings. By such means has the initial domestic "absence" been redoubled. Not just absentmindedly staring at the images of absent things, he absents himself further into their nightmare reconfiguration.

The very materials of his mimetic art—of Eliot's too, of course—are thus ominously recombined in a fantasized vision of a torrent and its threat of rocky impact. No benign Wordsworthian "sounding cataract" ("Tintern Abbey," line 76) of externalized "passion" (line 92) here, in the "pathetic" fallacy of "an appetite; a feeling and a love" (line 90). Instead, a "hungrier" desire in Maggie, gone unelevated and unsublimated, is projected as catastrophe. For it is in this ensuing dream that Philip "fancied Maggie was slipping down a glistening, green, slimy channel of a waterfall, till he was awakened by what seemed a sudden, awful crash" (6,8:427). The door opens—and his mind with it, again, to consciousness: the recognition that his father, Mr. Wakem, has come to wake him—with even this tacit wording spun into the vortex of dream association. How immediately, though, has the dream been left behind? Are we meant to sense in exit from its vision the same abrupt transition that plunged us from drawings of rock and water to an oneiric waterfall? In other words, is the noise of the "seeming" crash perhaps enclosed by the far rim of Philip's sleep—as the nightmarish thud of Maggie's implacable fate—as well as offering the dream's point of foreclosure in the real? If we suspect this in retrospect—suspect that Philip is awakened *by* rather than *before* a violent truncation within a clairvoyant fantasy—then it is no doubt in part because of the internal telos of Eliot's own grammar in this scenario of nightmare, with all its syllabic obtrusions. For after the thickened ligature of "glistening green," caught up as it is in the slimy lubricated rush of this erotic fantasy gone fatal, lexical compression is released to a more encompassing irony. Across a partial anagrammatic topple from "waterfall" to "awful"—in the skid of reading itself—we hear again those staged accidents of lexical cadence that offer narratography's most ingrained clue to the pace of the inevitable.

And that's only the first phase of Eliot's coordinated, spooky effect. For the most uncanny aspect of this so far strictly figurative violence in Eliot's plot is that, just three pages after Philip's dream, Maggie has a comparable hallucination of her own in one of her heady waking encounters with Stephen. The fleeting moment brings into dazed focus her own fears of "slipping." In fact, this highly charged erotic sensation makes explicit the sexual submission— the veritable fall—that Philip's unconsciously punning "waterfall" dream has literalized. With Maggie smitten by the immediate thrill, and thrall, of Stephen Guest's touch, what prose gives us again—transferred from the keenness of its jealous anticipation—amounts to the recurrent nightmare omen behind the glamorous dream-come-true of erotic fascination. For when Maggie takes Stephen's arm in an unguarded moment, her reach for support results in just the opposite. In the ensuing momentary swoon, she loosens her grip on herself, so that she was "feeling all the while as if she were sliding downwards in a nightmare" (6,8:447). Adverbial wording itself graphs the relay from Philip's anxious premonition to this waking analogue for it. This is not a dreamlike fall exactly, but a drop "downwards" both "in" and implicitly "into" a nightmare. And one not entirely her own. In effect, Maggie—even while awake at least in body—is having Philip's own worst armchair dream of her sinking integrity, her drowning of moral will in betraying her cousin Lucy's trust by the flirtation with Stephen.

The almost telepathic bond forged here between the heroine and her transferential alter ego in Philip sets the figurative template for the metaphorics of watery annihilation to come. This imagery continues implicit, for instance, in Maggie's summary fears about the "submergence" of "personality" in "the will of another" (6,13:467). Thus the further challenge to Eliot's metaphors. Rescued to some degree for "personality" rather than lodging merely a natural analogue for its pitiless social circumstance, her heroine's watery end requires, as noted, not just a diluvial accident but a figurative immersion in the superfluity of her own passionate nature: an epitome and a fulfillment rather than a surrender. This Philip also comes to recognize as soon as Maggie has gone astray—and drifted downriver—in her boating excursion with Stephen. Having foreseen her watery plummet as a nightmare landscape, Philip now images to himself the actual scene of her last-minute resistance along a waking waterway. People have started talking left and right about the shocking elopement of Maggie and Stephen, but only Philip can really picture the event from the inside, taking on the role of its ideal reader even without access to a written text. In this way, and for a second time, his foresight into Maggie's spiritual crisis is timed to precede and inflect the actual scene of Eliot's narration when plot actually catches up with the boating couple.

Story "Wrought Out"

Here, then, is the way Philip's fantasy cuts through rumor to spiritual and erotic probability. "His imagination wrought out the whole story" (6,13:462), the passage begins, with the undertone of the overwrought: hinting at exactly that pitch of envy and projection to which Philip's powers are wound up. He has "wrought" rather than just "worked" it out, implying further the shaping imagination of a narrator rather than just of a paranoid suitor. So, too, with the choice of "story" rather than "situation" or "affair," where indirect discourse not only seems to ventriloquize Philip's worst-case scenario but, at the same time, appears to be exposing—by a decided metanarrative turn—the busy labors of the novelist as plot engineer. In the process, as if resonating with the emotional crossed-wires involved in Maggie's dilemma, Eliot's indirect discourse comes to muddy the clipped grammar of Philip's own clairvoyance: "Stephen was madly in love with her; he must have told her so; she had rejected him, and was hurrying away. But would he give her up, knowing—Philip felt the fact with heart-crushing despair—that she was made half helpless by her feeling toward him?" (6,13:462). These last two clauses are not easy to read. An extra effort of attention must be made to keep the stinging pronouns (for his rival) clear of his own governing noun. Those potentially ambiguous "he's" and "him" mark the very strain of Philip's exclusion from the scene he despairingly conjures. And yet there is a truth, too, in the grammatical waver, since, beyond her sexual yearning, part of Maggie's helplessness, the *other* half, is indeed her sentiment toward Philip. In the end, feeling is a force divided against itself, as traced here along the inner rim of its own designation. It is for the sake of others that she cannot act for her own sake, on her own erotic account; it is her love that keeps her from her desire. Narratography registers the cleaving, in both senses, of her own sentiments through the sounding board of an excluded lover who has become not only her ideal reader but her temporary narrator.

No sooner has Philip "wrought out" the scene of Maggie's temptation than Eliot herself resumes the narrative challenge, solo, just a couple of pages further on. As she will do again after Philip's subsequent letter, in her return to plot at flood tide. Even earlier, though, with passion putting caution at risk, plot must again attempt the hopeless task of equilibrating character with circumstance. Reading of Maggie alone on the river with Stephen, one can almost taste the temptations of her craving nature as prose gives us—gives rather than simply depicts—the synesthetic blending of sense in a "*delicious* rhythmic dip of the oars" (6,6:464; emphasis added on the appetitive—in answer, finally, to her long-starved "hungry nature"). In fact, the alliterating *d* picks up on the elided phonetics just before in the personified "young, unwearied day"—rather than "young, unweary day"—as if spelling out alphabetically, and even under local negation, the eventual drag of passivity that comes to the weary when hope is worn down. Holding this back for a self-enacted prose interval, the lightly iambic thrum of "delicious rhythmic dip" offers a protective lulling that also keeps at bay those words between the lovers that would, in the sudden reflex—or reflux—of conscience, become a fatal "*inlet* to thought" (6,6:464; emphasis added).

In silence, they luxuriate in that "grave untiring *gaze*" of reciprocated desire (6,6:464) whose phrasing recruits the phonetics of prolongation and ligature in a last clutch at happiness. As the reader's own gaze is made voyeuristically privy to this scene of erotic indulgence, narratography goes further in all but eavesdropping on the enunciation itself. For with "untiring gaze," writing's quiet velar and glottal snare is smoothly mutual and binding, rather than viscous and thickening—as, by contrast, in Philip's "glistening green" waterfall. Yet no less treacherous. For in the further syllabic eddying of this seductive fixation, such a blinkering "gaze" envelops the oblivious couple, only a few lines later, in an "enchanted haze" that is also, by the lapsarian slackening of ethical vigilance (and the drifting dental sound of *d*), a spiritual "d(h)aze" as well, rapidly disenchanted. With the short-lived couple carried along, so to say, by a force bigger than both of them in this accidental elopement, narratology would of course mark a defining fork in life's river of no return—and in the heroine's cloven subjectivity as well, torn as she is between kinds rather than degrees of love. At tighter scale, narratography charts the medial riptide of this suspended indulgence.

Dearest Reader: The Returned "Gift" of Belief

Earlier, Philip saw Maggie's erotic deadlock all too clearly in prospect, and narrated it for us. Now, he phrases it back to its heroine herself, with new understanding, transmitting in a last letter his devoted overview of her own story. Having once "wrought out" the "whole story" as surrogate narrator, he now writes it out. In the process, Philip speaks not just of his moral faith in Maggie's spiritual wrestling. He also speaks up for the poetic license of Eliot's gathering tragedy—and its deeper if improbable verisimilitude. First off in the letter, in a language of aesthetic credence as much as ethical trust: "I believe in you" (7,3:520). He always has, and it has bestowed on him—this fully suspended disbelief—an ability to live in and through another's sensibility. He calls it the "gift of transferred life" (7,3:503): a gift that is not only bestowed but innate. Like a reader's sympathy, investment is a deftness of empathy as well as a debt owed to the heroine for her vividness. Not a borrowed or a vicarious life: a "transferred" one, in all the lateral exchange of energy this implies, the giving and the taking part. In Philip's bookish and aesthetically buttressed remove from social contact, that "new life into which I entered" in knowing Maggie configures the reader's own emotional access in its more erotically disinterested vein. Like the reader, Philip has seen the peace of approaching the other "not with selfish wishes—but with a devotion that excludes such wishes" (7,3:504)—excludes even when it cannot preclude, marginalizes and transmutes, or in a word sublimates, them. The violence of her ongoing sacrifice remains. What is new here is the explicit yield of the ordeal: the "gift" that keeps on giving.

A recent account of reading's ethical valence in Victorian letters gives us further terms for this, even though *Daniel Deronda* rather than *The Mill on the Floss* is the critic's chosen example from Eliot. In *The Burdens of Perfection,* Andrew H. Miller follows Stanley Cavell's arguments for an overcoming of philosophical skepticism (by "acknowledgment") in seeing Victorian moral psychology and literary rhetoric alike as modeling an *intimacy not taken personally*.[7] As befits Miller's paradigm of Victorian epistemological relations reread as social relations, but inverting the trope of wedded otherness that he sees the Victorians sharing with Cavell, Philip's written-out understanding of Maggie's spirit transpires at a reader's rather than a lover's distance. His heroically disinterested knowledge of her ordeal—turned upon her now as a prose mirror—is a returned "gift" *to* her for all he has felt *through* her, vicariously, in separation, across her years of avid yearning and travail: what we've seen him specify as "the gift of transferred life." It is a yield recognized just in time, right before her violent death. Philip's longstanding impalpable reach into Maggie's motives and emotions is thus an emblem of our own novelistic experience even before he spells it out *in writing,* for her and all to read. In the key of unreciprocated passion, his is indeed an immediacy of feeling he learns to value without taking it personally, whether as desire or its frustration.[8] Philip's selfless adoration of Maggie is the price he pays for knowing her as he might a Nobody, a fictional heroine.[9]

The "gift of transferred life" is, then, a characterological access to the Other conveyed to begin with through the verbal nuances and intuitions of a prose wrought up by feeling. No need of a return to that opening frame narrator when we have Philip's interpolated letter to sum things up: to achieve a paradoxical distance from within. The ethic of Victorian plotting is delivered straight into our hands as well as Maggie's, by letterpress in our case rather than postmarked envelope. And by Philip's heart-wrung prose, we are primed for what remains of Eliot's—out of his ken, and awaiting only his mourning presence in the aftermath. As we know, though, this drive toward closure has been sedulously "mapped" and anticipated—and called out by stylistic flagging of all sorts. Such local foreshadowing, associated of course with the broader narratological foreshortening of the mapped river trope, has been variously manifested at the level of phonemic and syllabic junctures, fluctuating lexical figures, syntactic latches and loosenings, even some awkward snagged ganglia of alphabetic sequence. In the process, a general rhetoric of temporality has in this case been monolithically narrowed to both a grammar and a metaphorics of omen.

Sounded in Prose: "The Depths in Life"

At approximately the midpoint of the novel, for instance, the narrator steps in (or aside) with an editorial interjection: "No wonder, when there is this contrast between the outward and the inward, that painful collisions come *of it*" (3,5:235; emphasis added on the phonetic collision within the antecedence of an abstract singular). Disaster issues, that is, from this missed fit between desire and world, entirely counterindicated by the prose that evinces it. Prefigured here, as well by this seemingly dead metaphor is the "awful crash" that ends Philip's equally predictive dream scenario, only to be fulfilled in turn by the colliding crush of wooden machinery that drowns brother and sister in the end.[10] Here a fateful binary is backed by the anticipatory metaphor of head-on violence that will be realized in just these terms when Maggie's boat converges with the massive flotsam and jetsam of her outward world. Apart from such direct premonition, and among the many figurations of this divide between "the outward and the inward," has been the particularly evocative run of prose leading up to this authorial "No wonder," which amounts to a foreseeing—or forehearing—in its own right of the heroine's eventual vulnerability to Stephen's unctuous singing voice. For at that point we find Maggie "with a*n ear* straining after dreamy music that died away and would not come near to her" (3,5:235). Framed by the muting of "ear" into the final "her," as if in the reduced volume of an echoing keynote, as well as by the "anti-pun" on "straining" in relation to "dreamy music," is a yet more striking effect.[11] This occurs by local phonemic anticipation when the negated "near" in the musical liaison of "an ear" slips out from under script as the ultimate metaphonemic pun on life's unheard melodies—even while Eliot might seem, at least to her critics, to be overexerting her own rhetoric in such passages with a strained romantic euphony.

Her heroine, in any case, has later closed her eyes to her abstract musical "studies"—and gone deaf to their sounded temptations—after the final separation from Stephen. By then only the friction of prose itself (and again its fricative alliteration) can sound the phonetic intervals necessary for even an ironized harmonic pattern. For it is now "as *if every* sensi*tive fib/ re* in h*er were* too enti*rely* preoccupied by pain *ev/er* to *vib*rate again to anoth*er in*fluence" (7,2:492). The novel's cumulative motif of seductive aurality is recognized at this point only under negation, from within the throes of a phonetically evoked exclusion of all that will never again "come near" her mind's ear. In that same later passage of blocked future "influence," also phonically conveyed but not troped as such, all the losses and anxieties of Maggie's life "beat on her poor heart"—not the inner beat of vitality but the outer barrage of circumstantial destiny. One result is that "hard" is sounded as the immediate echo of "heart"—"in a har*d*, *d*riving, ceaseless *storm*" (7,2:492), with a further, half-anagrammatic specification of that atmospheric metaphor in the tenor of "mingled love, re*mors*e, and pity." Not merely "hard-driving," as idiom might have it, the adjectival assault is more emphatically beaten out as "hard, driving," and thus all the more likely to be heard as well—cross-lexically—as implying the riving of desire that torments Maggie with the frustrating half measures and counterpulls of her failed allegiances and emotional defeats. The force that drives is the force that rives. And the river is its final emblematic site.

In the swelling rhetoric of spiritual inundation and drowning, just before floodwaters begin literally to rise, we find Maggie trying to convince Lucy that Stephen loves her still: "Forgive him—he will be happy then . . . " (7.4:510). The next paragraph catches hold in a stagger of lexical recoil that reads like the squeezing out—and to death—of a single phonetic cluster, with even the emergent "were wrung forth" finding its own later echo in the strenuousness of her desperation: "These words were wrung forth from Maggie's deepest soul, with an effort like the convulsed clutch of a drowning man" (7,4:510), where the routine male gendering of the simile scarcely mitigates the premonition. No Victorian novel could come any closer to giving its plot away—if it hadn't done so more quietly and cumulatively beforehand—with a single melodramatic simile. Maggie's grasping panic in the reach for something beyond her, her stifled effort to keep breathing amid the airless foreclosures of her hopes: such figures sum her life on the way to their own melodramatic reenactment in death.

In a similar vein, a single turn of phrase in *The Mill on the Floss*, one of the earlier appearances of the aquatic subtext in Eliot's premonitory rhetoric— and one of the purest models for the emblematic nature of flow in the book—comes deflected from the heroine's story onto the decline of her father. For Tulliver is overcome at one moment by a "flood of emotion" that "hemmed in all power of speech" (5,6:352). Here, exposed almost as a family trait, is that inner rush so familiar in Maggie's frustrated life: that impulse that proves a counterforce to expressivity. Idiomatic and inconsequential in

some other novel, perhaps, the cliché "flood of emotion" shows its true linguistic colors—in this weighted context—as a "genitive metaphor," where the
impact of the preposition is equative rather than hierarchical: designating not
so much the emotion that floods (the content of an inertial force) as the emotion that is itself a flood (the form of its own medium). Extrapolated to the
larger story that survives the father's death, and to the allegorical floodwaters
that close it, the grammar of rhetoric elicits in this case a narratography of
ventless impulse and pregnant silence. Moreover, to vary Eliot's famous remark in *Middlemarch,* these (little) things are a parable. Prepositions delimit
entire cognitive horizons.

Consider in this sense the forced chiasm just before the double drowning
of heroine and her brother. Trapped between vague horizon and threatening
immediacy, vastness and devastation, horizontal amplitude and sheer con-
verging bulk, brother and sister have been swept beyond all help or control.
At this impasse, converted to a hammering phrasal antinomy around the
swivel of chiasmus, "the wide area of watery desolation was spread out in
dreadful clearness around them—in dreadful clearness floated onwards the
hurrying, threatening masses" (7,5:521).[12] Captured by inversion in a vanishing temporal and spatial latitude, formless and undelimited, the focal point
of perception is itself threatened. The effect is a pure melodrama of perspective, vacuuming out the standard breathing-room of such syntactic symmetry, sharpening it to a point of ominous collision. Within the leveled clarity of
the flooded scene, spread round in a sweeping 360-degree shot of undeter-
mined extension, lies the clear and present emergency of the river's continuing, its still approaching, violence. The symmetry of form, we may say, is un-
done by the watery scene's own disruptive force: a force staged in action
across the stalled (and vulnerable) flow of its own syntactic trope of poised
reversal. In an unusually stark and discrepant phrasal lamination, we see here
the imposition of form upon content.

At the level of such plotting, the flood has brought Maggie round to Tom's
temporary rescue—if not him round to her quite yet. But the whole point is
that this too must come. Her last words are her call to steer the boat toward
Lucy. Almost by parable, she would sacrifice herself yet again to save her
cousin—as she has already done in giving up Stephen. Tom's last words follow, responding by sudden instinct to the objective correlative of their renewed sibling effort in just that "fatal fellowship" now confronting them: the
barreling forward of linked debris, "huge fragments" in a mocking union of

joined force. Tom's words depend on their tacit grammatical antecedent in the idea of death itself, whose concrete signifier is always premature, always in advance of the abstract signified to which it points: "'It is coming, Maggie!' Tom said, in a deep hoarse voice, loosing the oars, and clasping her" (7,5:521). Even in the cessation of rowing for this clenched human subject, potential loss is softened to release, to "loosing," with the instrumental sense of a "clasping" seemingly displaced from the vocabulary of an oarlock into the somatic moment of embrace. Just before this, the spatial dead metaphor of "deep hoarse voice," that everyday idiom of tonality, marks the lowered pitch of his awe and acceptance, with its own sonic ripple seeming to pass from "hoarse" to "oars" along a phonetic field of force that sets the whole brief moment reverberating with the impact of its negative sublimity. The purified incestuous *Liebestod* is fully prepared.

In the recuperative thrust of drowning alleviation, distant memories of happiness return now in a dubious vision of childhood joy. Thus is the clasp, transferred from oar to Maggie, to be further transferred, just a few sentences later, from present terror to past delight. For, in the instant of death, brother and sister are not seen but said, posited, in the final proof of transcendental omniscience, to be "living through again in one supreme moment the days when they had *clasped* their little hands in love, and roamed the daisied fields together" (7,5:521; emphasis added). Time is the force that brings remission only when it closes to zero—and detonates a spatially compressed moment outside of duration altogether. Death is time's way of marking the complete submergence of past events into a vanishing instant of present reflection.

This is surely the rhetorical engineering of narrative time in its most ironic (and entirely stylized) form: telescoping temporal force into pure end-stopped fantasy—and its instantaneous effacement. Elapsed duration is metamorphosed into captured essence, and with understanding at last; with interpretation, however involuntary. For all of a sudden, facing his sister as potential rescuer, "the full meaning of what had happened rushed upon his mind" (7,54:520)—and did so with such an "overpowering force" that the phrase "had happened" seems to condense all of the plot into one conjugated loss. A broad-gauged narratological irony finds itself powered here—and graphed in predication—by the force of tense's own approximation of time's layered weight. Tom realizes, that is, not just the immediate accidents of the tides in bringing Maggie and her boat to him. He sees the bigger picture at last. He comes to recognize the yet more pluperfect tense and tension of the moment, realizes what "had happened" ever since their early days together, in the long intransigence of his grudging life and the wonder of her still offered and unembittered love.

Even for the unimaginative Tom Tulliver, temporality has its redemptive if at the same time decimating rhetoric. For him, in line with the reader at last, time is irradiated with irony only in the moment of pending death. For the banished sister comes back to the rescue when it is, twice over, too late: too late to be floated out of harm's way, too late (or almost, except by trope) to re-live the spoiled years. In that horizontal influx of awareness for Tom, that "rush" or surge of recognition, that onset of final "force," there is also, in its "overpowering" grace, a "new revelation to his spirit": a vertical descent into "the depths in life, that had lain beyond his vision." Here may be the most subtly charged dead metaphor in all of this novel's overworked aquatic the-saurus. For these "depths" upon which Tom is momentarily suspended in recognition, and that will shortly bring him under, are not only metonymi-cally linked to the present river of no return, itself allegorical to begin with, but metaphoric for the full volume of life's spiritual inscrutability and its in-eluctable power.

Swept away by feeling at last, as the text all but explicitly has it in a voicing of its own repressed matrix, Tom utters the heroine's name in the retroactive form of her nickname, "the old childish 'Magsie!'" And in Maggie's elation at this recognized recognition, his very acknowledgment works further to con-vert a flood tide's "depth," as all but unmarked idiom, into the equally muted figuration of tonalities low (rather than high) on the aural scale—or in other words somatically deep in the chest of transferred feeling. For "Maggie could make no answer but a long deep sob." She doesn't weep. She has time only for a single convulsion of tragic ec-stasis, its stairstepped descent of monosylla-bles followed by the scalar uplift of incremental alphabetic "intervals." This is because the depth of her inward sob, not only its spiritual transport but also its formal transformation, comes from its taking shape—once released from watery chaos—as a "long deep sob of" dialectical resolution: "that mysterious wondrous happiness that is one with pain." Sprung from the triadic phrasing of the "long deep sob" is the metrically as well as emotionally cadenced run of phonemic recursion that makes mystery, wonder, and happiness seem preter-naturally symmetrical and continuous—as if a single multisyllabled force gives them form ("mysterious wondrous happiness") by cresting through them in series; or as if the medium they shared were other than just linguis-tic. By a more disruptive league of alliteration and anagramming, a similar sublexical force may be seen to release the essentialized place of "pain" in the very articulation of the phonetically softened "happiness." Beyond this, the abiding Romantic paradox of aching joys and stinging sublimity—that quintessential form of pleasure whose content is sadness, or vice versa—is captured reciprocally when the phantom participle of victory ("won" from ruin) is itself wrested effortlessly from this ambiguous phonetic node. Eliot achieves at this turn a spectral form of expression whose legible content is instead the adjectival continuum (at "one" with ruin) between Maggie's lethargic misery and her cathartic bliss.

Won in Defeat

What we also find in this climactic passage from *The Mill on the Floss* goes further yet to the heart of our topic. In that very phrasing of victory rescued from sacrifice, the rhetoric of plotted duration appears by way of an ironic vanishing point transformed on the spot into the singular doubleness of "won" as "one." In the lexical dialectics of this inscription, abjection is subsumed to transcendence. Here we may remember our earlier sense of wording in its generative flux—or say its narratographic force, on the very cusp of form—operating so as to dynamize an inert categorical binary. Such is the zone of sheer lexical potential when mapped as the neutral quadrant of the semiotic square: the double negation, in this case, of both the subjective and the objective alike, epiphany and effacement, in their lexical underside as the intuitive and inchoate, the latent, the formative. In this case, over against (over and above) the fluctuant undecidable "w/on/e" in an ethical as well as linguistic field of the neither/nor—where personal triumph and human expungement confront each other as nonbinding alternatives, yet where victory would seem at odds with obliteration—we intuit the opposite (indeed "upper") quadrant of resolved antithesis, the both/and of lyric resonance. Performed by Eliot's prose in this obviated deadlock, then, is a paradox you can die with at last, if not live with: the achieved (or enforced) oneness of dialectical negation, transfiguring narrative violence to spiritual sign. But—even at that—still only fluid, insurgent, uncertain. In this way alone can fictional prose hope to find, from within the form of plot, its no longer dispersive but now unifying (though still radically differential) force. That's Eliot's effort anyway, the work of her prose, if only half intentional. Narratographic reading is meant to respond to just such exertions, to accept their transference from the linguistic unconscious of plot.

One recalls an important paragraph on the combined accident and inevitability of death, the distinction it "dismantles" between "fate and freedom," in Terry Eagleton's *Sweet Violence:* a discussion sprung, in fact, from an allusion to the tragic ambitions of *The Mill on the Floss* along with *Samson Agonistes*—and phrased almost as if Eagleton had Eliot's critique of Novalis in mind.[13] Eagleton is contemplating at this turn the very eros of thanatos: "Like the desire with which it is so closely affiliated" (and in Eliot's case by sibling filiation), death itself "is a link between the alien and the intimate,"[14] personal and impersonal alike. The fitness of death to self is the one "sweetness" of its violence in such aspirant tragedy: turning contingency inward to meaning—a meaning carried precisely by the least turn of phrase. Narratographically tracked across the articulated form of storytelling in Eliot's case, the opposites of pity and terror, pleasure and pain, are not sublimated together under a stable synthesis. They vie for ascendancy within the same taut folds of text. Paradox works itself out in prose, the extent of whose narratographic impact only reading can tell.

Reading, but of a certain kind: reading the plot for its prose, or via that prose at least. Not reading through it, in the other sense, to the structures that subtend it and require no specific phrasal manifestation. Like consciousness in the world—very like it, and sometimes in transferential enactment of the mind's own dynamic of repression and return—reading proceeds by realizing, in fits and starts, the conditioning potential of its own medium. In engaging *The Mill on the Floss* in this way, one is struck in the end by the narrative rejection, on the heroine's behalf, of all possibility except in death. Granted, alternatives to this would have been modest enough, however infinitely preferable. Female heroism of a certain grandeur can never come again in its fabled forms. So Eliot's next novel, *Middlemarch,* closes by admitting. No new Theresas or Antigones, in church or theater history, because in both understandings of the term at once, social and literary, "the medium" as such, the milieu and its means, "in which their ardent deeds took shape is for ever gone."[15] Eliot thus acknowledges a world entirely postepic in both its social setting and its mimetic imaginary: absent the pertinent "media" in either sense. Into this vacuum, the novel asserts its own mediation as the carrying force of Victorian cultural ideas. But Maggie has not been caught up in, or rescued for, such possibility. She can't be said, in her truncated youth—as we hear about the "insignificant" people alluded to at the end of *Middlemarch*— to have "lived faithfully a hidden life."[16] In such phrasing, vitality stands forth as the self-definitional object of subjectivity's own duration. A humanist keynote thereby modulates on inspection into a synthetic interval pried open by the reciprocities of grammar itself, all within the syntactic subcode of the so-called cognate object. To live a life, rather than any other mode of existence that might be predicated for such a life: that is Eliot's abiding prosaic gesture, reaching in a new (low) key the supposed Greek harmony between being and essence that is Lukács's point of departure into postepic fiction.

Life vividly lived, rather than in any other way instantiated or incarnated or endured: this is the life force accessed by novelistic form per se in *Middlemarch*, enclosed, self-defining, retroactively essentialized, however much beset and violated along the way. Instead, Maggie dies her life. Her ordeal is over at last in the seventh book, ambiguously titled "The Final Rescue." Always ahead of us in the past tense of plot, Philip is there before us to read that elapsing life into a shape neither coterminous with any words of Maggie's nor with Eliot's either, but nonetheless, unlike the fantasy of transcended writing in *Daniel Deronda,* inseparable to some degree from the prose of its "transferred life." Without which no residual affect could be induced. As dubious as are the tyrannies of plot in this one novel, it is not difficult to draw the implied analogy out into the open. Maggie reads Philip, on the topic of herself—and almost as her own outered subject—the way we are conscripted into reading the rest of the novel from that turning point and tutor scene forward: crediting her destitution, even identifying with it, through the evocative cast of prose, waiting for its devastations to be shaded with meaning and thereby offered up to significance as the final and only rescue.

Feeling Read

In any sense of a perfectionist imperative orchestrating the plot dynamics of Victorian texts, it may be said that few characters have suffered more from "the burdens of perfection" (plural), in their gross denial of anything like it to her, than Maggie Tulliver. Singular as well as plural, the onus of perfection is often the sheer weight of its absence as a monolithic vector of possibility. This is to say that, in her gradual defeat by circumstance, Maggie internalizes, in utopianist disappointment, the world's crushing indifference to her hopes. In alluding again to Andrew Miller's thesis, we can at this point usefully return not only to a leading impetus for it in the philosophical writing of Stanley Cavell but, further back, to the sponsoring place of Emersonian thought in Cavell's own sense of the skeptical problematic in its tension with any perfectionist telos.[17] In Miller's terms, epistemological anxiety, as represented in

Victorian texts, struggles for resolution, if not final satisfaction, in the sphere of the social: the shared zone of intersubjective commitment. Plot, we may say, is a name for the harrowing phases of this struggle and their final reward or, alternately, for the gradual failure of such self-realization. Reading is the feeling out, by taking in, of either fate.

Our reading of Philip's letter over Maggie's shoulder—where he sums up her spiritual deadlock, for and to her, in terms we too well recognize as the novel's own—has, therefore, an oblique philosophic pedigree. It amounts to a translation into Victorian narrative format of a crucial theory of reading in American Transcendentalism, where, in the launching paragraph of Emerson's "Self-Reliance," reading is understood to be, in layman's terms, the recognition of one's own best self—or, in Emerson's terms, the return of one's "rejected" thoughts in the "alienated majesty" of a writer's finer words. That "rejection" (of one's foregone intuitions) seems part of Philip's message to his long-suffering friend: You *once* believed in yourself, Maggie—believed instinctively in what you might do in life—so that still, even now, from the midst of your desolation, I trust that, in reading of what you've *done for me,* you might recognize and thus recover a "rejected" and better thought of yourself, for yourself, projected through the eyes of the other.

Eliot would have been as quick as Emerson in subscribing to a sense that powerful writing can become, if only *in reception,* a model of full being. That explains the roundabout way in which, to call back my opening comparison, the prophetic aspirations of Mordecai in Eliot's later and last novel, absent his actual writing, require that his author contrive for him to live on in the other by way of extratextual interpretation and its residual impact. This transpires in the form not of Daniel Deronda reading him, but of our reading *Daniel Deronda.* The work of a major novel is never over till it's over. Not unrelated is Eliot's earlier and more modest activation of this novelistic strategy in the *writing out* of Maggie Tulliver's life, where reality's fullness can only be modeled by prose's formal shape. But in that earlier case, Eliot embeds an actual nexus of thinly disguised reading acts to prove it. Rather than leaving it to the novel itself, all told, to maintain the intersubjectivity of its vision, Eliot puts the reader in Philip's place, appreciating the heroine's story from start to foreshadowed finish—with our surrogate first working up the worst-case scenario in his mind, then working out its further understanding on paper— and then in turn puts Maggie in our place, reading her story through to its present crisis from the vantage of its spiritual beneficiary.

Eliot's double structural regress shows how the vaunt of Emersonian intersubjectivity can be novelized in the name not of a mirroring "self-reliance"
but in the service of something more like everyday self-acceptance. Still, given
Eliot's metafictional twist on this act of writing, it is well to remember its par-
allels in the question-begging circularity and potential short-circuit of Emersonian alienated recognition. These complications grow apparent in Cavell's
gloss on "Self-Reliance," where perfectionism is deferred to the voice of the
other as its tacit fulfillment. In his highly reflexive reading of a single Emersonian dictum, Cavell understands the famous "But do your work, and I shall
know you" to be singling out, in particular, the work of reading per se, here
and now. "Your work, what is yours to do, is exemplified, when you are confronted with Emerson's words, by reading those words . . . subjecting yourself
to them as the writer has by undertaking to enact his existence in saying
them."[18] Subjection, undertaking: the gothic of reading in a transcendental
key. It is important to note how this is more than seeing your "rejected"
thoughts majestically alienated and refreshed by the self-reliant bravery of
another's greater rhetoric, the once ejected now redeemed as projected. It is
more than the recuperative Emersonian gesture of "Let's face it: deep down
you know what I mean." Closer to the phenomenology of reading at large in
Georges Poulet (where "I am the subject," again, "of thoughts other than my
own"), it amounts to a linguistic and hence a cognitive inhabitation. The result, in Cavell's phrasing once more, is that "you undertake to enact my existence" in the very processing of my words. You know what I mean by this
writing because in saying it to yourself you are the only one now present who
can, and I knew you'd do so, mean it for me.

"I believe in you." Skepticism of other minds, the barrier in Cavell to any
sublimation of epistemological doubt in social relations, has seldom been
more decisively inverted than by Philip's textual initiative. I put my faith in
you: a "gift" outright and repaid at once. If this is the charter of a certain
utopian streak in Victorian sentimentalism, as brought to a head in Philip's
letter, it is also the very license of verisimilitude in the realist novel. Eliot's
metafictional sleight of hand—in one of the most tear-jerking moments in all
Victorian fiction, where rhetorical affect is itself thematized as redemptive—
is hard to resist in its ingenuity and its dramatic charge alike. Say hard to be
skeptical about. Not impossible: that's the point; but offering a carefully
paced and coached exercise in the overcoming of resistance by emotional investment. To paraphrase Cavell's Emerson in Eliot's terms, as they emerge

precisely from Philip's letter to Maggie: See here, you're great; your idealism may have failed you but it has sustained me. And now, by your work of recognizing yourself in my image of you, I shall know I've known you rightly.

So it goes, the shuttle of identification *put into writing*. It is in this way that, by imaging back to the heroine, in "wrought" words of his own, an image of a "rejected" rather than her now abjected self, Philip has done for Eliot's character as much as the author herself could ever hope to do: making sure in words that the heroine is credible enough to inspire belief—and self-belief into the bargain. More than cold comfort, this "feeling read" rightly is Maggie's only way of having been loved, as woman as well as fictional character. So that at the close of Eliot's melodrama it is our credence, not just Philip's, that is recruited for solace—if not for ultimate amelioration. Fiction is a trial of skepticism yet again, or say the laboratory of its *pharmakon*—testing the poison of doubt and its cures at once—and thus in the end a therapy for disbelief.

NOTES

1. Garrett Stewart, *Dear Reader: The Conscripted Audience in Nineteenth Century British Fiction* (Baltimore: Johns Hopkins University Press, 1996), 301–28, where Mordecai's dream of fraternal incorporation as a "willing marriage which melts soul into soul" (308) can not only be taken as a figurative version, freed from both sexual and racial difference at once, of that companionate bond under scrutiny in Rachel Ablow, *Marriage of Minds: Reading Sympathy in the Victorian Marriage Plot* (Stanford: Stanford University Press, 2007), but where, varying the terms of Ablow's subtitle, this whole network of exchanged feeling in Eliot's last novel becomes a reading, an interpretation, of reading's own sympathy. Conversely, the reading scene to which the present essay returns in *The Mill on the Floss*—Maggie Tulliver coming to interpret herself through the vicarious emotive penetration of Philip Wakem's letter—officiates by internalized prose over an unimpeded (or in Shakespeare's terms unimpedimented) marriage of tested and true minds otherwise unavailable to the discontents of flesh in that novel.

2. Georges Poulet, "Phenomenology of Reading," *New Literary History* 1 (October 1969): 56.

3. A fuller methodological account of this approach, as distinct from traditional narratology, appears in my *Novel Violence: A Narratography of Victorian Fiction* (Chicago: University of Chicago Press, 2009). The present essay expands on a section of that book's chapter on George Eliot.

4. All parenthetical citations from Eliot's novel refer to book, chapter, and page in George Eliot, *The Mill on the Floss*, ed. Gordon S. Haight (New York: Oxford Univer-

sity Press, 1996). See also Paul Ricoeur, *Oneself as Another,* trans. Kathleen Blamey (Chicago: University of Chicago Press, 1992).

5. Georg Lukács, *Theory of the Novel* (Cambridge: MIT Press, 1971), 63–64.

6. Without mentioning Philip's role at all in this regard, Neil Hertz, in *George Eliot's Pulse* (Stanford: Stanford University Press, 2003), sees Mr. Tulliver instead as taking up the opening narratorial position when found "resting his elbows on the arm-chair . . . striving after vanishing images like a man struggling against a doze" (66). Hertz links the debt-ridden man to Eliot's own sense of writing as "the acquittal of a debt" (63). My emphasis on Philip's doubling of the narratorial "doze" falls instead on the projective identifications of the unconscious as a trope for reading more than for writing.

7. See Andrew H. Miller, *The Burdens of Perfection: On Ethics and Reading in Nineteenth-Century British Literature* (Ithaca: Cornell University Press, 2009).

8. Although this particular Eliot novel goes undiscussed by Miller (n. 7 above), its logic of empathy as sublimation—extended implicitly from character to reader, and cleansed as far as possible (at least so its rhetoric would have it) of both voyeurism and fetishism—bears out one extreme version of what Miller quotes as motto from Browning's "Fra Lippo Lippi," that "Art was given for that . . . lending our minds out" (lines 304–6). The psychoaesthetic act is not just figured by Browning here as a lending of these minds—or a bestowing of them in words—but as a lending of them *out,* as "at interest": an idiom tinged with usury in this supposedly disinterested bargain, signaling (as in Eliot's extended example) the accrued emotional interest of narrative investment and its ethical and affective rather than sexual returns.

9. I allude here to that licensed incorporation without trespass that sets the proprieties of fictional investment and identification off from the materialism of property rights in Catherine Gallagher, *Nobody's Story: The Vanishing Acts of Women Writers in the Marketplace, 1670–1820* (Oxford: Clarendon Press, 1994).

10. Though not linking it to the founding metaphor of "collisions," Jules Law notes the anticipation of mechanical fatality on the river in this oneiric "crash." See "Water Rights and the 'Crossing of Breeds': Chiastic Exchange in *The Mill on the Floss,*" in Linda M. Shires, ed., *Rewriting the Victorians; Theory, History, and the Poetics of Gender* (New York: Routledge, 1992), 64, where such structural symmetries are related in a loose sense to the rhetorical figure of chiasmus (see n. 12 below).

11. On Christopher Ricks's concept of the "anti-pun," see *Reading Voices: Literature and the Phonotext* (Berkeley: University of California Press, 1990), 47–48, where I separately mention such other soundplay in *The Mill on the Floss* as "strains of music affect me strangely" (212).

12. Here, unmentioned in his essay, is a local syntactic instance of that governing figural logic of chiasmus that Jules Law (n. 10) sees articulating the punishing symmetries of Eliot's novel even when not given actual grammatical manifestation by it. This is a reading not explicitly traced back to de Man but paralleling "The Rhetoric of Temporality" (*Blindness and Insight* [Minneapolis: University of Minnesota Press, 1983], 187–229) in its general thrust, given Law's emphasis on plotted structures of fate

and reprisal as covert rhetorical figurations. In any case, Law's close attention to the river and its drowning motif as scene and structuring metaphor both, including its place in Philip's anxiety dream (n. 10 again), rightly gives no quarter to Leavis's baffling dismissal (52: "the flooded river has no symbolic or metaphorical value").

13. See Terry Eagleton, *Sweet Violence: The Idea of the Tragic* (Oxford: Blackwell, 2003), 121.

14. Eagleton, *Sweet Violence*, 121.

15. George Eliot, *Middlemarch*, ed. Bert G. Hornback (New York: Norton, 1977), Norton Critical Edition, "Finale," 577.

16. Much of the "moral psychology" at issue in the cued reception of Victorian fiction, as discussed by Andrew H. Miller (above, n. 7), can be seen coming to a head in this passage. Miller makes a compelling case for the optative mood of literary form as predicating a certain trajectory in Victorian perfectionist thought as well as in the reader's relation to fictional characters: delimiting the alternate universe of the might-have-been, sometimes looming as a telos of the still socially possible. What Lukács saw as the lethal "should-be" that "kills life" in the literature of romantic irony thus finds its obverse valence in the incrementalism of Victorian psychology and social theory. This seems confirmed, even within the evoked gradualism of historical betterment in the last paragraph of *Middlemarch*, by the double-negative form of the might-have-been lodged in the clausal insistence "that things are not so ill with you and me as they might have been" if it were not for those "insignificant" people "living" in good faith their "life." Things might have been worse; and under such continuing influences, things might eventually be bettered. Reading about the "Dorothea whose story we know"—or in other words coming to know Dorothea through reading—seems a good part of the epistemological turned social operation (a major emphasis of Miller's argument) at stake in this tacitly metatextual passage, where narrative process itself conduces to social progression. In light of Victorian "perfectionism," for a fuller narratographic reading of the close of *Middlemarch*, including the double-vectored phrase "growing good" and its Tennysonian overtones, and capping a more extensively theorized account of subvocalization in Eliot's prose in that novel and especially *The Mill on the Floss*, see my "Phonemanography: Romantic to Victorian," in the "Soundings of Things Done," special issue of the *Romantic Circles Praxis Series* (April 2008), ed. Susan J. Wolfson, www.rc.umd.edu/praxis/sounds/index.html.

17. Stanley Cavell, "Being Odd, Getting Even (Descartes, Emerson, Poe)," *In Quest of the Ordinary: Lines of Skepticism and Romanticism* (Chicago: University of Chicago Press, 1988), 105–29.

18. Cavell, "Being Odd," 118.

Contributors

RACHEL ABLOW is Associate Professor of English at the University at Buffalo, SUNY. She is the author of *The Marriage of Minds: Reading Sympathy in the Victorian Marriage Plot* (2007) and the editor of a special issue of *Victorian Studies* on "Victorian Emotion" (2009). She is currently working on a study of belief, conversion, and persuasion in Victorian literature.

STEPHEN ARATA is Associate Professor of English at the University of Virginia. He is the author of *Fictions of Loss in the Victorian Fin de Siècle* (1996) and a general co-editor of Edinburgh University Press's *New Edinburgh Edition of the Collected Works of Robert Louis Stevenson* (forthcoming).

NICHOLAS DAMES is Theodore Kahan Associate Professor in the Humanities at Columbia University. He is the author of *Amnesiac Selves: Nostalgia, Forgetting, and British Fiction, 1810–1870* (2001) and *The Physiology of the Novel: Reading, Neural Science, and the Form of Victorian Fiction* (2007). He is currently working on a history of the chapter, from manuscript bibles to the modern novel.

KATE FLINT is Professor of English at Rutgers University. She is the author of *The Transatlantic Indian, 1776–1930* (2008), *The Victorians and the Visual Imagination* (2000), *The Woman Reader, 1837–1914* (1993), and *Dickens* (1985). She is General Editor of the Victorian volume of the *New Cambridge History of English Literature* (forthcoming 2010) and is currently working on "Flash! Photography, Writing, and Surprising Illumination."

JOHN PLOTZ is Professor of English at Brandeis University. He is the author of *The Crowd: British Literature and Public Politics* (2000) and *Portable Property: Vic-*

torian Culture on the Move (2008). His current project is tentatively titled "Semi-Detached: Virtual Worlds and Everyday Life."

LEAH PRICE is Professor of English at Harvard University. She is the author of *The Anthology and the Rise of the Novel* (2000) and co-editor of *Literary Secretaries/Secretarial Culture* (2005) as well as of a special issue of *PMLA* (2006). *Reader's Block: The Uses of Books in Victorian Britain* is forthcoming from Princeton University Press. She writes on old and new media for the *New York Times Book Review,* the *London Review of Books,* and the *Boston Globe.*

CATHERINE ROBSON is Associate Professor of English at New York University, and a member of the faculty of the University of California Dickens Project. She is the co-editor of the Victorian period volume of *The Norton Anthology of English Literature* and author of *Men in Wonderland: The Lost Girlhood of the Victorian Gentleman* (2001) and *Heart Beats: Everyday Life and the Memorized Poem* (forthcoming).

GARRETT STEWART, the James O. Freedman Professor of Letters at the University of Iowa, has published on poetics, painting, and film as well as the novel. His most recent books on Victorian literature are *Dear Reader: The Conscripted Audience of Nineteenth-Century British Fiction* (1996) and *Novel Violence: A Narratography of Victorian Fiction* (2009).

HERBERT F. TUCKER is John C. Coleman Professor of English Literature at the University of Virginia, where he also serves as associate editor of *New Literary History* and co-editor for the series in Victorian Literature and Culture at the University of Virginia Press. He is also the editor of several books including *Victorian Literature, 1830–1900* (2001) and *A Companion to Victorian Literature and Culture* (1999). His online scansion tutorial *For Better for Verse* is now freely available at http://prosody.lib.virginia.edu/.

Index